D1044848

The Politics of
School Reform
1870–1940

The Politics of

LA
216
.P46
1985

Paul E. Peterson

School Reform

1870–1940

WITHDRAWN

The University of Chicago Press
Chicago & London

353976   Tennessee Tech. Library
Cookeville, Tenn.

PAUL E. PETERSON is director of the Governmental Studies Program at the Brookings Institution. He is the coauthor of *Race and Authority in Urban Politics* and the author of *School Politics, Chicago Style,* which received the Gladys M. Kammerer Award of the American Political Science Association, and of *City Limits,* which received the Woodrow Wilson Award of the American Political Science Association. All are published by the University of Chicago Press.

THE UNIVERSITY OF CHICAGO PRESS, CHICAGO 60637
THE UNIVERSITY OF CHICAGO PRESS, LTD., LONDON

© 1985 by The University of Chicago
All rights reserved. Published 1985
Printed in the United States of America

94 93 92 91 90 89 88 87 86 85   54321

Chapter 1 is a revised version of Paul E. Peterson, "Urban Politics and Changing Schools: A Competitive View," in *Schools and Cities: Consensus and Conflict in American Educational History,* ed. Diane Ravitch and Ronald Goodenow, pp. 223–48 (New York: Holmes and Meier, 1983); portions of chapter 5 will appear in revised form in *Schooling for All: Race, Class, and the Decline of the Democratic Ideal* by Ira Katznelson and Margaret Weir, to be published by Basic Books, Inc.; chapter 6 is a revised version of David Plank and Paul E. Peterson, "Does Urban Reform Imply Class Conflict? The Case of Atlanta's Schools," *History of Education Quarterly* 23 (Summer 1983): 151–73; and chapter 7 is a revised version of Rick Ginsberg, Paul E. Peterson, and Carol D. Peterson, "Rethinking Early Twentieth Century School Reform: The 1917 Illinois Compromise," *Issues in Education* 1, nos. 2–3 (1984): 107–32.

LIBRARY OF CONGRESS CATALOGING IN PUBLICATION DATA
Peterson, Paul E.
    The politics of school reform, 1870–1940.

    Bibliography: p.
    Includes index.
    1. Education—United States—History. 2. Politics and education—United States—History. 3. Education, Urban—United States—History. 4. Education—Social aspects—United States—History. I. Title.
LA216.P46   1985   370'.973   85-1042
ISBN 0-226-66294-2
ISBN 0-226-66295-0 (pbk.)

Contents

To David, Sarah, and John

Acknowledgments

This project spanned four years and a continent. Help and support were given by many more people than can be recognized in this brief acknowledgment. Some are mentioned in notes and in the appendix to chapter 4, but there is little doubt I have overlooked many others whose help has been invaluable, if not crucial.

Of the vast amount of material collected by the study, only a portion could be used in this book, and I bear the responsibility for determining what was to be included and for the analysis and interpretation of the data in each chapter. But even though the contributors whose names are given below cannot be held responsible for the overall thrust and tone of the book as a whole, their work on specific chapters has been of the utmost importance. In some cases the individual is appropriately listed as the principal author of the chapter. The distribution of responsibility is as follows:

Chapter 2, Carol Peterson and Margaret Weir
Chapter 3, Carol Peterson
Chapter 4, James Christiansen, principal author, and Carol Peterson
Chapter 5, Margaret Weir, principal author, John Echeverri-Gent and Marcia Turner-Jones
Chapter 6, David Plank, principal author
Chapter 7, Rick Ginsberg, principal author, and Carol Peterson
Chapter 8, Carol Peterson, principal author
Chapter 9, John Echeverri-Gent, David Plank, Carol Peterson, and Margaret Weir.

The study owes a substantial debt to Ira Katznelson, who was joint principal investigator. We received helpful commentary on various portions of the manuscript from Charles Bidwell, William Boyd, Elizabeth Hansot, Douglas Mitchell, Diane Ravitch, and David Tyack. Gail MacCall, who was the project officer for the study at the National Institute of Education, made many useful suggestions.

Research assistance was provided by John Bowman, John Clark, Kathleen Gille, Susan Sherman Karpluss, Bernard Knoth, Sandra Prolman, and Kenneth Wong. In addition to her contributions to individual chapters, Carol Peterson edited the entire manuscript. Word processing and other staff assistance was provided by Annette Barrett, Carol Forster, and Adele Pardee at the University of Chicago and by Julie Bailes, Pamela Harris, Janet Hathaway, Diane Hodges, and Robert Londis at the Brookings Institution. A more helpful and cooperative group of assistants would be hard to find.

Part One

Forming Public Schools

1 The Pluralist Politics of Public Schools

Immediately after the Civil War, urban school systems were still fragmentary structures scattered in ramshackle buildings under the loose direction of part-time school boards. Atlanta's system was not founded until the 1870s, Chicago's was nearly destroyed by the great fire, and as late as 1906 the San Francisco earthquake dealt the city's schools a severe blow from which it took them several years to recover. But physical threats to survival were the least of the problems schools faced. Public schooling still had to assert its dominance over a variety of competitors—private academies serving the middle classes, denominational schools teaching immigrants, and vocational schools training workers for the new industrial empire.

By 1925 schools had formed a partially autonomous system of political power. They now provided education to the vast majority of the community, teaching the children of both the middle and the working classes, training both the native-born and the immigrant, and socializing both the preschooler and the young adult. Their responsibilities extended to secondary education, vocational education, community schools, kindergartens, continuing education classes, and adult evening schools. The rivals to public schools were retreating from the educational scene, and it would be decades before they would enjoy a small revival.

The management of schools reflected the prestige the system had secured. By the 1920s, full-time professional administrators with impressive credentials exercised great influence over school policy. Part-time lay boards, which had once hired teachers and supervised daily activities, played an almost advisory role. School budgets were no longer quite so dependent on decisions taken at city hall, and even the siting and building of new schools became strictly a prerogative of the school system itself.

This partial separation of schools from the rest of city politics was achieved only because schools, as public institutions, were accepted as a fundamental part of the social order. Viewed from an organizational perspective, schools managed to transform themselves from mere organizations into institutions whose legitimacy was beyond doubt. What had once been problematic became certain. What had changed and fluctuated became stable and permanent. Indeed, public schools became as sacrosanct to society as children had long been to their parents.

An earlier generation of historians, working under the influence of Ellwood Cubberly, characterized the history of schooling as a valiant effort of schoolmen to overcome the forces of darkness. In our more pessimistic age, historians no longer treat the school leader as a hero, but they are scarcely less inclined to see schools as the product of some single force at work in society or some limited group of individuals exercising inordinate influence.[1] Reformers are no longer treated as the Lord's messengers to mankind, but their capacity to influence institutions and societies is perceived as hardly less superhuman. The pronouncements of businessmen are given far-reaching significance, and the momentary triumphs of reformers are said to have long-range consequences. Few recall the observation of Tammany Hall's philosopher-politician George Washington Plunkitt, who knew that reformers were only "mornin' glories—looked lovely in the mornin' and withered up in a short time, while the regular machines went on flourishin' forever, like fine old oaks."[2]

Reformers, businessmen, and social elites all had a part to play in the development of urban education, but to exaggerate the role of any one as the single factor explaining the development of urban schools drastically oversimplifies the processes of social change. School policies were developed in the course of conflict and competition among groups, leaders, and organizations. Diverse participants focused on those specific objectives in which they had the greatest stake. Although some related their specific demands to larger views of the good society, their demands were met by counterclaims with alternative visions.

The evidence for this argument is necessarily circumscribed. First, observations are limited to Atlanta, Chicago, and San Francisco. Although these cities are in three different regions of the United States and varied substantially in their socioeconomic development, generalizations to the United States as a whole can be made only at some risk. This risk, it must be said, is somewhat less than that taken by a good deal of recent historiography, which has assumed that experiences in a small town in Massachusetts, or in the city of New York, are prototypical. Second, our analysis is limited because we are concentrating on the role of working-class groups and organizations. Although we do not ignore the activities of business groups, reform leaders, teacher organizations, and other influential participants in school politics, we view their involvement primarily in light of their impact upon working-class concerns.

STATUS, CLASS, POLITICS, AND THE NINETEENTH-CENTURY SCHOOL

The terms of political competition in nineteenth-century America were set by a threefold system of stratification—class, status, and political power.

First, individuals varied in their access to the marketplace. Variations in earning power and accumulated wealth produced a class structure that yielded distinctions among gentlemen, merchants, artisans, unskilled laborers, domestic servants, and contract laborers. As the processes of production became more industrialized, as machine power replaced labor power, and as units of production became larger, the class structure underwent significant changes, some of which had implications for urban schooling. But even in the more primitive economy of the post–Civil War period, class differences affected educational opportunities.

Second, Americans varied in their social status, the honor accorded them somewhat independent of their market standing. Because Americans had only a pale imitation of a European aristocracy, variations in status did not have the exactitude such distinctions had in Europe. Yet the differences in cultural heritage associated with and revealed through varying religions, languages, nationalities, and races were the primary criteria for estimating the social worth of others. In the case of blacks, Orientals, and native Americans, cultural distinctions were taken so seriously that status became castelike. Although cultural distinctions were less rigorously drawn among those of European descent, Protestants distrusted Catholics, Yankees were suspicious of those who could not speak English, and northern Europeans shunned their more swarthy neighbors from the southern and eastern parts of the continent. Nativist movements arose and passed; members of Catholic religious organizations, it was alleged, were sworn to commit the most diabolical acts; and recent immigrants were said to carry vicious diseases.

Class and status distinctions overlapped, of course. Since recent European immigrants and racial minorities shared the lowest rungs of the occupational ladder, their impecuniosity reinforced racial and ethnic prejudices. Yet class and status position were not one and the same. Even economically successful immigrants did not find ready acceptance outside their cultural group, and expressions of prejudices focused on the language, religion, and cultural style of the foreigners and minorities, not on their poverty per se.

In a society where ascriptive criteria determined a person's place, sex differences also had great social significance. Most women were expected to maintain their households, to derive their social worthiness from the status of their husbands, and to avoid active engagement in political life. Although suffragists were beginning to challenge this definition of women's place, few accepted their claim that sex was an unreasonable basis for differentiation. Along with race, religion, language, and nationality, sex was a primary basis for evaluating the social place of others.

Political power formed a third dimension of stratification in nineteenth-century America. Those who had special access to the power of the state were able to use its coercive authority for their own ends. In many times and places, political power reinforced and sustained class and status differences. But as a consequence of the democratizing wave that had swept eastward across the Appalachians during the Jacksonian period, political relations were as egalitarian in the United States as anywhere in the world. Most white males in the 1840s voted, and of those eligible to vote, rates of participation in the election of 1844 were as high as those in 1984.[3] Even the Civil War did not provide elites with an opportunity to close polling places or to reduce the size of the electorate; throughout the nineteenth century, national elections remained closely contested and aroused the involvement of an overwhelming proportion of the electorate. Where every vote counted, even the outcast had to be mobilized. Not only the Irish and the Germans, but also the Scandanavians, Italians, and Poles were urged to vote. Naturalization occurred all the more quickly because judges and politicians needed these new Americans as partisans on election day.

These relatively egalitarian political relationships had important economic and social consequences. Indeed, were it not for widespread citizen involvement in politics, it is likely that the status differences in a culturally pluralistic society would have led to systematic repression of minorities. The significance of politics for other sectors of social life becomes fully apparent when one considers the deviant cases where politics did not soften status distinctions and repression was severe. When the post-Reconstruction South denied blacks their voting rights, it ensured that social barriers would not be breached for decades. And few groups were treated with such shameless discrimination as the voteless Orientals, whom Californians unceasingly tried to remove from their shores. Not only was the absence of political rights itself a mark of the blacks' and Orientals' pariah status, but it also denied these groups the means to redress their grievances.

Class, status, and political distinctions thus defined the stratification system of industrializing America. In many cases they overlapped and reinforced one another, and where this occurred the structure of educational institutions was itself noticeably inegalitarian. At the same time change in social relations depended upon the partial separation of the economic, the social, and the political. Because these systems of stratification were not perfectly coordinated, groups could use their resources in one sector to advance themselves in another. Changes were not so dramatic that at any point one can say social relationships were transformed. But looking back on nineteenth-century institutions a century later, the cumulative impact of specific changes can be more fully appreciated.

Status Conflicts in the Late Nineteenth Century

The connection between school politics and ethnic pluralism in nineteenth-century America has been widely appreciated. The controversies surrounding religion, race, ethnicity, and immigration have been noted both by Cubberly and by his latter-day critics.[4] But while earlier scholars believed that schools softened status distinctions, recent writers have argued that status politics expressed itself in the form of cultural imperialism. Anglo-Saxon reformers used the awesome power available to them to stamp out foreign cultural patterns. Their homogenizing mechanisms included kindergartens, continuing education programs, community schools, and, more generally, compulsory education.

Although some reformers probably had a high assessment of the value of their own culture, status politics was more competitive and complex than this view acknowledges. For centuries, education had been primarily a means of affirming one's character as a gentleman, not a way of enhancing one's employment opportunities. In nineteenth-century America, educators still had not forgotten that their historical mission was to transmit the learning of the past to a new generation. For some, "learning" meant knowledge of classical wisdom; for others it meant the received wisdom contained in the Bible. For still others it meant the scientific and literary classics of modern European culture. But whether defined in religious or secular terms, education was necessary for participation in the circle of the elect.

Education was a way of declaring one's social worth. In a society where breeding did not by itself ensure social standing, education assumed special importance. When family background meant little, the one thing that distinguished the *gentle* man from the mere businessman or merchant was the respectability that education, learning, and cultivated taste could provide. Education was therefore prized not so much for the economic benefits it afforded as for its capacity to confer dignity and honor upon the individual.

If education was a way of confirming an individual's worthiness, it was no less a medium for validating the status of social groups. Providing education was a means of distributing social honor among the nationalities, races, sexes, and other groups that made up nineteenth-century society. As a consequence, school conflicts in the post–Civil War period were conflicts over the criteria by which the status-conferring functions of schooling would be distributed. What language was to be the medium of instruction? What, if any, religious practices were to be allowed in school? What access to public schooling was to be provided to social outcasts? From which groups were teachers to be selected?

The competition for the honor that education could confer was accentuated by the great emphasis the most "honored" social group placed on literacy and education. The Anglo-Saxon Protestants who adhered to one or another variant of the Calvinist tradition had their own religious reasons for insisting that education be provided. Because the fundamentals of reading and writing were important for achieving a direct encounter with God's Holy Word, education became a missionary activity. Both in Europe and in the United States, these Calvinists assumed the leadership in extending primary education to the mass population.[5] In the United States, for example, common schooling expanded most rapidly in Massachusetts and other New England states, where the Puritan heritage was the most vigorous. The spread of primary education, moreover, was linked to the migration of these "Yankees" into the Old Northwest Territory and across the northernmost tier of the United States.[6]

The prestige of Yankee culture in nineteenth-century America was unquestioned. If even today the Boston area remains a major cultural and intellectual center, one can only begin to envision its stature in American society at the time when that small area not only contained the major universities, the profound religious thinkers, and the leaders of so many of the country's moral crusades, but also included great centers of manufacturing and major locales for finance and commerce. Throughout the United States local communities aspired to the economic and social position that Massachusetts and its sister states enjoyed. Indeed, Horace Mann became America's chief midcentury educational spokesman not only because he provided intellectual coherence to a statewide educational program, but also because actions taken by leaders from this state were generally given nationwide attention.

As the Calvinists from the Northeast were propagating their culture through schooling, other groups began to emulate them. Groups strove to close the gap between themselves and the white Anglo-Saxon Protestants by obtaining comparable educational opportunities for their children. Schooling was not imposed on religious and racial minorities; instead, education was a prize to be won by each social group in order for that group's culture to be affirmed, legitimated, and perpetuated.

A group's success in obtaining schooling for its children was a function of its place in the society's stratification system. Compared with other "minorities," women were treated generously from the beginning, in part because Calvinism saw literacy as necessary for their salvation too. However, secondary education for the women of Atlanta and San Francisco was initially provided only in segregated institutions that had limited access to the higher educational system. Secondary-school sex integration, with the concomitant opportunity for women to pursue college training, came only after suffragists had become an organized political force. Germans were also a relatively favored minority, whose children were able to obtain education in the language of their forebears. In fact, efforts to remove instruction in the German language from schools in Illinois, including Chicago, were singularly unsuccessful until World War I. Germans had special capacities for achieving their educational objectives. Not only did they migrate to the United States in large numbers and concentrate in specific areas, thereby creating substantial constituencies for local politicians, but inasmuch as they had migrated partly for political reasons, they contained within their ranks substantial numbers of politically adept middle-class leaders. Germany, moreover, was a rapidly developing world power whose culture was validated by great scientific, artistic, and literary accomplishments. A case for German instruction could be made quite independent of the linguistic background of a specific immigrant group.

At the opposite end of the status continuum stood blacks and Orientals, who were often denied any access to public schooling. When blacks petitioned for schools in Atlanta in 1872, they were grudgingly given a couple of old rented buildings whereas over the next eighteen years ten new structures were built for whites.[7] The Chinese of San Francisco went without public education from 1871 to 1885, when a California supreme court ruling resulted in the establishment of a segregated school. Future concessions by local authorities to these relatively powerless groups came slowly and painfully.

Status politics significantly shaped nineteenth-century education, but recent historiography has not characterized its form correctly. The competition among ethnic and racial groups sharpened the demand for schooling and contributed to its dispersal at a rate far surpassing anything occurring in Europe. The offshoot of an experiment in political democracy was the provision of schooling even for cultural minorities. The exceptions to the pattern confirm this general relationship. When blacks and Orientals were deprived of their political rights, access to schooling was also denied them. Cultural imperialism in its most marked and dramatic form consisted not of compulsory instruction but of the *exclusion* of a group from public schooling.

Class Conflicts in the Late Nineteenth Century

Although status politics dominated much of the discussion over nineteenth-century schools, class distinctions also had their impact. However, class conflicts that occurred seldom pitted working-class groups against the public schools.[8] It is true that some working-class families kept their children out of school so they could work to augment the family income. But groups representing the working-class community supported the extension of compulsory education to cover a broader age range or more of the calendar year. Unions in Chicago, San Francisco, and Atlanta were among the foremost proponents of compulsory education. A plank supporting compulsory education appeared in all the platforms of the Illinois Labor Federation between 1884 and 1893. There is no evidence of any union opposition to compulsory education in San Francisco, and in Atlanta the Georgia Federation of Labor joined a broad coalition that finally secured passage of the legislation in 1920. In the eyes of labor leaders in Atlanta and Chicago, compulsory education was the concomitant of child labor legislation; both were designed to preclude the exploitation of young children by profit-minded capitalists, and both had the salutary side effect of decreasing the size of the labor force, thereby raising the price of unskilled labor. In 1890–91 working-class groups in Illinois did oppose a particular piece of compulsory-education legislation, but their opposition centered on the fact that the law required schooling in the English language. German Lutherans were so incensed by this insult to the legitimacy of their culture that they deserted the Republican party in droves and elected Peter Altgeld governor, thereby installing in office the most liberal regime Illinois ever enjoyed. Subsequently, both Lutheran and Catholic Germans wholeheartedly supported the passage of compulsory-education laws that did not include the restrictive language provision.

Manual training, drawing, singing, and other curricular innovations were welcomed by unions and immigrant groups. Instead of meeting worker resistance, these "fads and frills" were the object of a vigorous attack by the archconservative Chicago *Tribune*. According to the newspaper, physical culture, music, art, and German-language instruction were among the ways the schools were wasting the taxpayers' money. When the issue was taken up by the board of education, labor and immigrant groups led a counteroffensive in the spring of 1893. Germans were particularly resentful that instruction in their native language was considered a wasteful "frill." But, significantly, their support—and the support of laboring groups in general—was not limited to the German language but included the whole range of innovations that had begun to supplement the basic curriculum.

Working-class groups typically embraced many of the new "fads and frills," to which they thought their children had as much right as did children attending middle-class private schools, Reformers had a class bias, but the consequence of that bias was not the imposition of schooling on working-class children against the will of their parents. For urban educators, the central issue was not providing every street urchin with proper schooling but ensuring that schools attended by middle-class children were sufficiently attractive to compete with private schooling. As a result, middle-class children were given privileged access to scarce educational resources.

Organizational Interests of Schools

To understand the way these processes worked, the organizational interests of schools must be taken into account. Public schools after the Civil War were only beginning to establish themselves as the dominant form of education. Atlanta did not establish its public school system until 1872, and in 1865 San Francisco had only 138 teachers in twenty-nine schools. Although Chicago provided schooling as early as the 1830s and by 1853 had even created the office of superintendent, the consolidation of the system, including the passage of a state law requiring free education, did not occur until 1865. When in 1871 the Chicago fire destroyed one-third of the city's school buildings and reduced the remainder to homes for fire victims, it took two to three years before operations were restored.

This tenuously established public organization still had to justify its claims on the public purse. The common school did not develop automatically; it had to compete with alternative models of providing education. It chief competitor was a two-class, dual system of schooling. This arrangement, which persisted in Europe throughout the nineteenth century, provided education to the prosperous members of the community through private tutoring, academies, and boarding schools. Public schools were charity schools, which served a limited segment of those unwilling or, more likely, unable to pay for their children's education.

As organizations interested in their own maintenance and enhancement, schools sought to extend their services to the children of the middle class. If public schools were defined as charity schools for the poor, they would acquire the ignominious image reserved for almshouses and homes for the incurable. If they were to depend solely on the eleemosynary instincts of the public, they would have limited scope and be starved for resources. The drive for common schooling, with which Horace Mann was so closely identified, was thus not simply or even primarily a campaign to bring schooling to the masses. On the contrary, the campaign focused on making public schooling sufficiently attractive so that middle-class parents would choose these schools over private forms of education.

Although class bias in the distribution of access to education has yet to be fully documented, the importance urban school leaders attributed to secondary education gives us some valuable clues. Secondary schools after the Civil War offered a classical education to a limited, privileged segment of the population. Whereas primary education was being extended to three-fourths or more of the relevant age cohort, secondary schooling remained selective.

The most careful analysis of the class selectivity of high schools is contained in Selwyn Troen's study of Saint Louis schools. He shows, for example, that only 23 percent of the students in the Saint Louis high school in 1870 came from blue-collar families, whereas 51 percent of the pupils in the primary schools had fathers so employed.[9] On the other side, children from business and professional families constituted 43 percent of high school students, but only 29 percent of the primary school population.

Quite clearly, the Saint Louis high school had won the support of the city's middle-class residents, if perhaps at the cost of providing equality of educational opportunity for working members of the community.

The secondary schools in the cities we examined seem to be characterized by similar class selectivity. In Atlanta the high schools were open only to whites; a black high school was not built until 1924. In San Francisco in 1878 only 30 percent of the students in Boys' High School were sons of the working class (see chap. 3). The emphasis on secondary education is thus an indicator of the interest school policy-makers had in recruiting a middle-class clientele. In Atlanta, where the control of schooling was most carefully monitored by socioeconomic elites, this emphasis on secondary schooling was especially visible. Although a system of public schooling was not established until 1872, from the very beginning high schools were a constituent part of that system. At a time when just three elementary schools served the white children of Atlanta, two sex-segregated high schools—one for boys, one for girls—offered an almost exclusively classical curriculum. In Chicago a high school was established in 1854, even though as late as 1865 fewer than two-thirds of the schoolchildren of primary school age were in public schools. In San Francisco in 1870 only about half the children aged six to fifteen were in public schools, yet Boys' High School was opened in 1856 and Girls' High School in 1864. To be sure, some of the primary school children were being educated in Chicago's and San Francisco's parochial schools, but overcrowding, double shifts, and insufficient resources were a continuing concern to their parents. Indeed, the social composition of the high school became such a political issue in San Francisco that the superintendent was called upon to defend his policies in one of his annual reports. If the city of San Francisco was to attract "the best class" of respectable citizens, he argued, then it must maintain excellent educational facilities. At the same time the superintendent insisted that the high school was not a socially selective institution, though a rigorous analysis of his own data shows exactly the opposite (see chap. 3).

If nineteenth-century school officials conceived their primary missions to be training a docile work force, they could hardly have pursued their objective more haphazardly. Instead of concentrating their limited fiscal resources on the most deprived segments of the community, they ignored them until adequate facilities had been extended to the more favored. Instead of insisting on attendance in publicly controlled institutions, they allowed foreigners to go to their own schools. Instead of keeping potential troublemakers under their watchful eyes, the poorest, most outcast segments of the community went uneducated altogether.

In sum, class and status had much to do with the development of nineteenth-century educational institutions. For the most part, issues involved the distribution of educational opportunities among social groups.

In this regard the white Anglo-Saxon Protestant middle class did especially well. Yet other groups, eager to imitate the success of native-born Protestants, used their political influence to win concessions for their children as well. In this way public schooling became common schooling, eagerly sought by all segments of the society.

Increasing Class Conflict at the Turn of the Century

The issues in urban education began to change toward the end of the nineteenth century. Competition among ethnic groups for status and legitimation continued, but its visibility and intensity seemed to recede. At the same time the relationship of schools to the marketplace became an increasing concern, and class conflict took a somewhat different form. With the growth of secondary schooling, the connection between educational experience and later employability became more obvious. In addition, the growth of organizations representing people in their occupational roles occurred at what seemed an exponential rate. Businessmen's associations, chambers of commerce, labor unions, and especially professional associations all became politically active. The central issues were no longer compulsory schooling and foreign languages, but vocational education, teachers' salaries, rights and perquisites, and school finance.

These changes in urban education did not occur uniformly in all parts of the United States. Although the trends are evident in all three cities, the variations in the pattern of conflict also deserve consideration. Chicago provides perhaps one of the best examples of class conflict in urban education to be found in the United States. On the one side, the archconservative Chicago *Tribune* and an active set of business organizations, including the Chamber of Commerce, the Civic Federation, and the Association of Manufacturers, defined the interests of employers in broad, strikingly clear terms. On the other side, labor unions, allied with teachers' associations, militantly and at times effectively countered this coalition of business elites. Because nearly every issue in urban education was defined by these participants in class-antagonistic terms, Chicago provides the analyst with an ideal laboratory for observing the way participants understood the class impact of numerous reforms. What can only be inferred or guessed in more subtle political contexts is openly declared in Chicago's bitter class struggles.

Not surprisingly, Atlanta falls at the other end of the continuum. The issues that polarized Chicagoans were resolved in Atlanta with minimal reference to their class implications. But if the continuity between the nineteenth and twentieth centuries is greatest in Atlanta, modern political forces also were beginning to make themselves felt in what would become known as the capital of the "New South." In San Francisco, conflicts increasingly revolved around the intersection of education and the marketplace, but, unlike the situation in Chicago, they were not always defined in class-contentious terms.

The sources of increasing class conflict in education were multiple. Of greatest importance was the rapid growth of the secondary education sector during the three decades between 1900 and 1930. Only 4 percent of Chicago's school membership consisted of high-school students in 1900, but this percentage increased to 9.7 in 1920 and 17.6 in 1930. In San Francisco the percentage of students enrolled in high school increased at roughly the same rate. In 1900 it was also 4 percent, increasing to 9.5 percent in 1920 and 14.4 percent in 1929.

Historians have yet to provide an adequate explanation for the growth of secondary education at this time. Many attribute it to the educational needs of the new industrial economy, but comparable economic changes in Europe produced only modest effects on education there. For example, the estimated enrollment in all secondary schools per 10,000 of population in 1920 was 247 in the United States, but only 117 in Germany, 83 in England, and 61 in Sweden.[10] It is plausible that the American economy benefited by this differential in educational opportunities on the two sides of the Atlantic, but beneficial consequences are still not causes. If one takes a competitive view of the processes of educational change, one finds a more adequate explanation in the competition of interests of various groups and organizations in late-nineteenth-century America.

The most obvious beneficiaries of an expanding system were the educators themselves. Any expansion meant more jobs, more promotional opportunities, and a greater claim on public resources. In addition, educators found expansion of the secondary education sector especially inviting. Not only were older children often thought to be more interesting to instruct, but secondary education's associations with classical culture and its connections with universities gave it a certain prestige.

Ethnic and racial groups also had an interest in expanding secondary education. As schools increasingly became public instead of private, it was difficult in a politically democratic society to deny them to all who demanded educational opportunity. Each group wanted access to a public institution that was supplying services to others. In addition to parental demands expressed through nationality and racial groups, labor organizations were interested in extending education into adolescence. As part of their drive to limit the supply of workers, labor organizations favored the extension of educational provision as the preferred alternative to early employment.

This period was also marked by the growing power of political organizations representing occupational interests. Business, labor, and the new middle-class professions discovered that group action was a valuable tool for defending their particular interests, and they used their influence in education as in other policy areas.[11] Each of these groups had their own distinctive sets of interests; no stable alliance among any two of them was able to determine policy choice in all situations; instead, outcomes in particular instances fluctuated as different coalitions came together in an ever-changing series of uneasy alliances. On particular questions, those who seemed to have the greatest stake in the issue had the greatest influence over the outcome. On some issues working-class groups had great influence; on other occasions they had almost none.

Compulsory Education and Child Labor Laws

Labor's clearest victory during this period concerned compulsory education and child labor laws. Campaigns for such legislation had been spearheaded by labor groups since the 1880s, but it was only after 1900 that this goal was consolidated throughout the country. Characteristically, Chicago was the first of the three cities to operate under state legislation redirecting children from the labor market to educational institutions. Legislation in California gave San Francisco the authority to enforce compulsory education only after a strong campaign from 1907 to 1911. In Georgia, child labor and compulsory education were among the primary goals of the labor movement throughout the first two decades of this century, but it was not until a firm alliance was formed between labor and a number of middle-class reform groups that satisfactory legislation was finally approved. Opposition came from rural Georgia and from industries wanting to achieve a more competitive position with the North. As one cotton mill owner argued, "The movement in favor of this legislation is inspired in New England . . . for the reasons . . . that they want to destroy the competition which arises by the erection of new mills in the South."[12]

Labor's decisive victory on this policy issue, even in the South, must be attributed in part to its declining significance for business. As the American economy became more urban, more productive, and more capital intensive, and as the need for manpower was more readily satisfied both by natural increase and by waves of immigrants, the demand for child labor declined. The most successful industries found child labor wasteful and inefficient, and the smaller, more labor-intensive industries no longer had the political power to withstand the labor-reform drive.

Labor was also advantaged by the coincidence of its interests with those of school reformers. Now that schools had been clearly established as something more than just charitable institutions, school people had achieved their own autonomous base of political power. In alliance with the reform-minded women and men of the new professions, and with labor's support, they could campaign for the extension of public authority to include the entire range of the school-age population. Moreover, the definition of what was school age could be regularly raised.

Vocational Education and Fiscal Policy

If labor's greatest success was in the area of compulsory education, it could also be reasonably satisfied with the outcome of a second dispute that marked this period—the question of vocational education. This curricular innovation was originally introduced as manual training, a reform designed to develop the physical and mental capacities of the "whole" child. As time passed, business interests were more or less successful in redefining manual training as schooling for a particular form of employment.[13] Businessmen were in fact so insistent that public schools offered little of commercial value in their instruction that they sought to create vocational schools separate and apart from the public school system.

Labor rightly suspected that vocational education separated from public schools could come under the close administrative control of industrial interests. They feared that children would be trained for positions in particular factories and indoctrinated in antiunion ideology so they would provide a steady, low-cost source of productive labor for dominant commercial and industrial interests in particular localities. Although trade unions did not object to vocational education per se—indeed, they thought it desirable that children be equipped with skills appropriate to the economic world in which they would be living—they vigorously objected to business-dominated schools. If vocational schools were not to be run by the trade unions themselves, then the public schools should be given jurisdiction.

As with many issues, the conflict between business and labor over vocational education was fought with greatest intensity in Chicago. A well-organized business community, with the expert assistance of former superintendent of schools Edwin G. Cooley, campaigned aggressively for a separately administered system of vocational education. In a community where many issues were defined in class terms, the trade unions not only vigorously objected but succeeded in establishing the principle that vocational education was to be an integral part of the public system of education. Business and labor could only play an advisory role in policymaking.

Labor's success must once again be attributed to the coincidence of its interests with those of the school system as an organization. Had vocational education been set up under separate administrative auspices, secondary education would have been divided between classical and vocational. And the segment with the greatest growth potential would not be in the hands of public-school administrators. A rival competitor for public loyalty and taxpayer resources had to be destroyed at its very conception. The school system, in an alliance with other professional groups and with labor support, was once again able to extend its jurisdiction. At the same time, its standing as an independent, autonomous system of political power was being enhanced.

Although the battle over vocational education was fought most vigorously in Chicago, the outcome in the other two cities was much the same. With backing from both business and labor, vocational education was incorporated into the curriculum of both Atlanta's and San Francisco's secondary schools in the early decades of the century. The growing numbers of students in secondary schools almost ensured that some such curricular modification would occur. But in all three cities vocational instruction was left in the hands of school officials.

One of the consequences of this decision was that vocational education was concentrated on training a few for highly skilled trades instead of training large numbers for factory life. Recent research on vocational education in the three cities has shown that its curriculum never took the form most desired by large-scale corporate interests.[14] What mass production industry needed most were semiskilled workers who could efficiently carry out repetitive tasks. Public schools, however, had an organizational stake in promoting a far more prestigious form of job training. If vocational education were to become attractive to teachers, parents, and students, it would have to provide access to highly skilled craft employment.

The interests of schools and trade unions once again seem to have coincided. Schools could provide training for plumbing, electrical work, carpentry, bricklaying, and other trades. Education in these areas would lead to relatively stable positions in the most highly paid blue-collar jobs. Since the strongest unions organized workers in just these areas, the unions and teachers could establish mutually accommodating relationships. Vocational schools rapidly became politically powerful institutions that attracted able graduates of the city's primary schools. In Atlanta the technical high school even became the primary point of access to Georgia Tech University. Two generations later reformers would be less concerned about vocational schools that provided dismal, low-grade instruction leading only to dead-end jobs than they were about the limited access to these schools available to minority groups.

Labor had the least success in conflicts over financial policy. In all three cities the schools were constantly starved for financial resources. Schools were the most costly of all locally provided public services, and wage increases in this labor-intensive sector could dramatically affect local tax burdens. In all three cities business and commercial interests continually resisted tax increases. Although the financial resources available to the schools continued to grow, in the three cities this was the single issue that created the most political controversy.

Not surprisingly, teachers were the group most concerned about adequate financing. Because salaries were so low, the teaching force in all three cities was overwhelmingly female. But even though they were socially and politically vulnerable, women teachers regularly agitated for salary increases. In the first two decades of this century the school boards in all three cities questioned the legitimacy of teacher organizations. Organizational activity was treated with suspicion, and overt links with the trade union movement provoked special board hostility.

Once again the conflicts were most intense in Chicago. Not only did the Chicago Teachers' Federation develop strong ties with the Chicago Federation of Labor, but it also identified numerous instances of underpayment of taxes by Chicago businesses and utilities. Board members closely allied with Chicago's well-organized commercial interests responded in 1915 with the Loeb Rule, which outlawed the affiliation of a teacher organization with the union movement. Teachers, together with their labor and reform allies, countered by securing the passage of compromise legislation that guaranteed teacher tenure.

Ethnic and Race Issues

Although school politics had become increasingly marked by class conflict in the first decades of this century, questions of race and ethnicity did not instantly disappear. Especially in the South, race relations remained so significant a concern that class issues were never vigorously articulated. And in San Francisco the controversy over school governance split the labor movement into its Protestant and Catholic parts. Even in Chicago, Mayor William "Big Bill" Thompson used ethnic antagonisms to full effect in his efforts to regain control of the schools. Yet status relations among ethnic groups had become sufficiently stabilized so that they no longer remained the primary basis of conflict. Orientals were eventually allocated a legitimate place in the California school system, and secondary education was finally conceded to the blacks of Atlanta. The processes of Americanization had progressed to the point where instruction in the English language was confirmed as an integral part of public education. Catholics had adjusted to the idea that schools legitimizing their religion would have to be privately financed and church-controlled.

These changes occurred most slowly and painfully in Atlanta. Concessions to black education continued to be made only grudgingly and in response to active group pressure. For example, in 1916 the school board decided to eliminate the seventh and eighth grades from black primary schools and to substitute some form of vocational education. Blacks responded to the insult by organizing an Atlanta chapter of the National Association for the Advancement of Colored People (NAACP), which insisted to board members that equal educational facilities be provided, including a high school for black adolescents. When the board refused these demands, the NAACP organized a campaign against the next school-bond issue, succeeded in securing its defeat, and used this leverage to arrange a compromise with the board, which laid the groundwork for the black high school that opened in 1924.

Race issues in Atlanta handicapped the formation of modern class cleavages of the sort that divided Chicago's polity. For one thing, the (all-white) labor organizations were antagonistic toward the black portion of their working-class constituency. They therefore often came under the influence of conservative leaders, who established accommodating relations with Atlanta businessmen. At times trade unions were even part of what was known as the "conservative" faction in city politics, though the difference between "conservatives" and "progressives" often seemed to rest largely on family relations and personal contacts. Also, teacher organization was hardly assisted by the ease with which the school board could play white teachers off against black ones. When the board in 1919 hiked the dismal wages black teachers were receiving to fifteen dollars a month, they reduced white teachers' pay to cover the cost.

Just the year before in San Francisco, a major, ethnically based conflict had occurred in the midst of an attempt to replace an elected school board with an appointed one. When the Protestant principal of the city's technical high school dismissed students on the grounds that they would soon be attending parochial schools, the predominantly Catholic school board "fired" him. This action precipitated protest in the local community served by the high school and agitation by the Public Schools Defense Association and the American Protective Association, which took this occasion to mount a more general anti-Catholic campaign. Among Protestants in general, the action taken by the school board was so offensive that many voted in favor of a reform measure that replaced this elected board with one appointed by the mayor.

The controversy illustrates once again the way ethnic conflicts could interrupt a politics of class. Initially, the reform had been uniformily opposed by teachers and trade unionists, who believed it was a plan by the business elite to capture control of San Francisco schools. Presented to the voters in these terms, it had been soundly defeated. But once Protestant voters felt insulted, the religious identifications of the old school board became a central political fact and the reform won voter approval.

The Question of School Governance

But while ethnic conflicts persisted, the increasing importance of class-related issues finally resulted in a change in school governance. Decentralized, ward-based, patronage-focused, lay-controlled school boards were gradually replaced by centralized, citywide, professionally directed, reform-oriented boards.[15] These changes have attracted the attention of many analysts, but they have frequently been misunderstood. The reforms in school governance were not dictated by the interests of native-born business elites, as many have thought.[16] Business. interests were well served under the decentralized system that had flourished in previous decades. Instead, the changes were wrought by the combined efforts of labor, professionals, and some business leaders, all of whom would find the problems that concerned them better handled by a centralized, professionally administered system. As ethnically based distinctions yielded to class- or market-based distinctions, the appropriate political institutions for resolving school issues were altered.

School governance provoked the greatest controversy in San Francisco, and at first glance it seems to provide a striking instance of reform sponsored by a business elite. The Claxton Report, which called for governance reform, was prepared just before World War I at the instigation of a group of university women and endorsed by prominent business groups. Opposition came from ethnic communities, trade unionists, the old patronage-ridden school board, and the teaching staff. But before the Claxton Report's recommendations were adopted, the picture had become far more complex. In the first place, the recommendations themselves addressed a significant administrative problem. Authority over San Francisco schools was formally divided between an elected superintendent, on the one hand, and a full-time, paid four-member board of education on the other. Teachers were uncertain which individual or group was their formal superior. Second, the reforms called for an unpaid, lay board appointed by the mayor, an organizational structure that in Chicago had allowed for a good deal of variation in political control. Unless one could predict the outcome of mayoral elections, one could not be certain which social groups were to benefit from the new arrangements.

The political processes themselves added to the complexity of the situation. When the Claxton recommendations were first proposed to the voters, they were defeated. Later the recommendations were modified somewhat, making them less offensive to the teaching staff. In their new form, they were supported by the trade unions, which in subsequent years were always conceded at least one position on the seven-member board. When the complexity of the situation is taken into account, the changes in San Francisco's school governance seem less an instance of business-imposed reform than a conjoint sharing of power by the new business-labor-professional group triumverate. The role of San Francisco's powerful trade unions in this controversy is particularly significant in this regard. Since they had developed a comfortable relationship with the old superintendent, their first temptation was to resist changes in government structure. But in the end they found it difficult to object to a more centralized and

administratively more efficient system to which they would be given continued access.

The power that an unpaid, appointed school board gave to a big city
mayor was particularly evident in Chicago. Indeed, William Hale Thompson used his power of appointment to weaken the Chicago Teachers' Federation (CTF). After winning the 1915 mayoral election and declaring that
he would stay aloof from school-board matters, he delayed making the
customary new school board appointments[17] so that board member Jacob
Loeb and his supporters could pass the Loeb Rule. This rule, specifically
designed to break the strong affiliation that the CTF had with the Chicago
Federation of Labor (CFL) forbade teachers to join unions or organizations
affiliated with unions.[18] Labor and teachers vehemently attacked it, and the
superior court of Cook County ruled that it violated teachers' rights. Mayor
Thompson, the Loeb board, and the Illinois Manufacturers' Association
(IMA) stood firm on the other side of the issue.

Loeb next tried another rule, one that was more specific in listing
forbidden organizations; the teachers won another court battle, and Loeb
finally just submitted a list of seventy-one teachers he wanted fired. The
board fired almost all of them, many of them officers of the CTF, and at this
point Chicago's most prestigious reformers became outraged.[19] The
ongoing battle fed directly into efforts to restructure the Chicago schools
that were being undertaken in the state legislature. The reformers and the
teachers supported one bill and Thompson and the IMA supported another,
which was essentially a statement of the status quo. Since both sides had
been weakened by the fray, the final result was a compromise bill, sponsored by school-board member Ralph Otis. But once again, school reform
was the product of the efforts of labor and professionals to find a more
appropriate way of resolving school issues, not a vehicle for serving the
interests of business elites.

School reform became a major issue in Atlanta politics in 1897. After a
series of conflicts between school board and city council, the mayor and his
supporters on the city council terminated the appointments of all but one
member of the existing board, reduced the size of the board, and appointed
a new board that cut teachers' salaries, reduced the number of board
employees, and drastically lowered board expenditures. A modern curriculum with specialized instruction was introduced into Boys' High School,
and a manual training program was authorized for the city's elementary
schools. Power shifted from the board to the superintendent as the number
of board committees was reduced and an assistant superintendent was
appointed. Corporal punishment was abolished.

Although some of these steps were classic reform moves, they were
hardly the work of dominant social elites imposing their values on a resis-

tant working class. In contrast to the old school board, which contained some of the most prestigious members of Atlanta's social elite, the new board consisted largely of self-made men whose success owed much to their political connections (see chap. 6). Aided by the requirement that each ward be represented on the board, the connections between schools and city hall became closer and more congenial under the new regime.

Much of the reform energy came from Atlanta's desire to provide progressive leadership for a "New South." The mayor who spearheaded the reform was the same man who had led the Atlanta Exhibition, and his key appointee to the school board, "Hoke" Smith, was later to be elected governor on a platform advocating progressive reforms. Apparently Atlanta's emerging middle class felt the school system needed "modernization" so that the city could keep pace with developments in the North. But if the movement had essentially middle class origins, opposition came primarily not from working-class groups but from Atlanta's old, established social elite.

CONCLUSIONS AND PLAN OF THE BOOK

In a society that was economically and socially stratified but politically pluralistic, schools could achieve legitimacy only by separating themselves, as institutions, from particular groups and factions. Schooling was not only accepted but given perhaps unwarranted esteem by almost all segments of society, largely because it was not clearly wedded to any one group. Public schools were not charity institutions; neither were they exclusive prerogatives of the rich and well-to-do. Public schools did not offer a narrowly sectarian curriculum, nor did they refuse to legitimate the culture of ethnic minorities when these groups could muster sufficient political power. Public schools did not offer adolescents only a classical education; nor did their embrace of vocationalism subordinate all other curricular goals.

During crucial, formative periods, schools were generally responsive to those with the most political power. Middle classes received the most favored educational opportunities; strong parties had valuable patronage opportunities; the English language was strongly preferred above all others; and racial minorities were treated shamefully. But schools, as institutions, also seemed to recognize that their long-range survival required them to extend their services to as many supporters as possible. Instruction in the German language was provided to this large and politically vocal immigrant group; many school people developed close associations with trade unionists; and even racial minorities were finally given some access to education.

Conflicts over school policy did not have predictable outcomes. In Atlanta and San Francisco governance reforms were instituted, only to be modified and revised a few years later. Chicago vocational education policy represented a compromise among a multiplicity of interests. So did the resolution of the controversy over "fads and frills." The winners in one political contest were the losers in the next. No one social group held sufficient economic and political power to dictate the course of school policy.[20]

The ultimate winners in such an uncertain contest were, of course, the schools themselves. As organizations, they could only prosper from contests and conflicts among competing interests. Because almost every group felt they had some access to the institution, few groups attacked public schools per se. These were the politics of institutionalization, the processes by which the school system became an organized system of autonomous power.

Chapter 2 analyzes the politics of school finance. In our view it is remarkable that this issue, so important to schools in nineteenth-century cities, has been all but ignored by recent educational historiography. When money matters are considered, one finds that labor continually supported the public school and that business leaders, instead of being the sustainers of education, often opposed its expansion. One also finds that reformers, though concerned about efficiency, gave the schools more fiscal support than did machine politicians.

We show in chapter 3 that curricular reforms occurred because schools, eager to build a broad base of support, changed their mode of operations whenever new, rival institutions were being established in substantial numbers. It was in part because the middle class was turning to private day and boarding schools for their secondary education that the public schools were eager to add a high school to the existing elementary program. It was in part because Germans were establishing their own schools with instruction in their native language that the public schools were prepared to teach in German as well. It was in part because business began establishing its own vocational schools that manual training and vocational education became a part of the public-school curriculum.

The question of "fairness" in the allocation of school resources and in the recruitment of teachers is the subject of chapter 4. Did native-born Americans control the school system and give most of the benefits to members of their own group? Did immigrant groups use their access to the local political machine to redirect school resources to their community? Or were all groups in the city treated more or less alike, thus allowing the school system to distance itself from the interests of any particular group? Using quantitative information from previously unexamined sources, we find a school system more open, more responsive, and more "fair" than could have been anticipated on the basis of previous accounts. Apparently the complex pluralistic politics of urban America kept schools from becoming the captive of any special set of group interests.

Racial minorities were the major exception to this pattern. As chapter 5 shows, both the blacks of Atlanta and the Orientals of San Francisco were given separate, inadequate facilities or completely excluded from education. We attribute this largely to the political isolation of these racial minorities. In contrast to the European immigrants, who were absorbed fairly quickly into the country's participatory political framework, immigrants from Africa and Asia were subjected to political discrimination and political exclusion. The difference between the political condition of European immigrants and these racial minorities is worth emphasizing, not only because it explains in part the racial trauma our nation continues to endure, but because it shows how dependent the educational progress of the European immigrant was upon a participatory political system. If immigrants from Europe had been treated politically in the way that racial minorities were, it is doubtful that America would have had, in the 1920s, the world's largest and most inclusive educational system.

In the second part of the book, we turn to urban educational reform. In chapter 6 we show that reform in Atlanta was opposed by members of Atlanta's highly conservative "Bourbon" elite, not by groups and organizations representing the city's working class. Chicago's Otis Law, which provided the most significant structural changes in the city's school governance and administration before World War II, is the subject of chapter 7. The law itself was a compromise that accommodated a wide range of group and political interests. But in the conflict that preceded the compromise, it proved especially significant that reformers were in alliance with the teachers and with labor, while business and machine influences worked together on the other side. Chapter 8 analyzes the contrasting policies of four superintendents and one school board president, all considered reformers. One of these, Edwin Cooley, turned out on closer inspection to be hardly a reformer at all, even though in a good deal of the published literature he is treated as a quintessential member of that select group. On the other hand, Ella Flagg Young, who is seldom today discussed as a leading early reformer, forged close alliances with all of Chicago's major reform groups. William McAndrew of Chicago, Joseph Gwinn of San Francisco, and Robert Guinn of Atlanta provide still other perspectives on the meaning of reform.

The financial crises of the 1930s are discussed in chapter 9. We have found that the reform triumphs of earlier decades could not be sustained in times of fiscal constraint. In Chicago the political machine, business, and labor formed an alliance to maintain public-school solvency, isolating teachers and reformers in the process. In San Francisco the state rescued the city's schools from a similar fiscal disaster while, locally, a pluralistic style of politics reasserted itself under a school board appointed by a machine-connected mayor. In Atlanta it was labor that was isolated, as teachers exchanged their support for that of an increasingly education-minded business elite. In our concluding chapter we suggest that the great growth and reform of America's urban educational system, though begun during the years 1870 to 1940, was realized only after World War II.

2 Political Support for the Free School

In a landmark decision in June 1982, the United States Supreme Court, in *Pyler v. Doe*, ruled that the state of Texas had violated the constitutional rights of illegal alien children by denying them a free public education. For the first time a sharply divided high court, in an opinion written by Justice William Brennan, indicated that illegal aliens are entitled to equal protection of the laws under the Fourteenth Amendment to the Constitution. This "Amendment extends to anyone," said Brennan, "citizen or stranger, who is subject to the laws of a state and reaches into every corner of a state's territory." While states may withhold benefits from those who are in the United States illegally, legislation punishing children for "a parent's misconduct . . . does not comport with fundamental conceptions of justice."[1]

At issue was a Texas law, enacted in 1975, that forced illegal alien children to pay tuition to attend public schools. Brennan's opinion, focusing on the consequences of such a restrictive law, noted that "the stigma of illiteracy will mark them for the rest of their lives. By denying these children a basic education, we deny them the ability to live within the structure of our civic institutions and foreclose any realistic possibility that they will contribute in even the smallest way to the progress of our nation." He further added, "It is difficult to understand precisely what the state hopes to achieve by promoting the creation and perpetuation of a subclass of illiterates within our boundaries, surely adding to the problems and costs of unemployment, welfare and crime."[2]

Brennan's opinion, written in response to a case brought by the Mexican Legal Defense Fund, was widely applauded in the Hispanic community, which had regarded the Texas law as challenging their status as equal citizens of the United States.[3]

On the other side, Chief Justice Warren Burger, in his dissenting opinion, stated that "the court points to no meaningful way to distinguish between education and other governmental benefits. . . . Is the court suggesting that education is more fundamental than food, shelter or medical care?"[4]

The premises upon which the opinions of the high court rested reflect arguments about the value and role of public education made over 150 years ago. Brennan's concern that children denied a basic education were also being denied the ability to live within the structure of our civic institutions harks back to colonial New England. According to educational historian F. T. Carlton, this same concern was held more than a century ago by two quite different "elements"—well-educated leaders and the laboring classes—who urged that free institutions could not long exist or could not progress without wide diffusion of education.[5] Brennan's view was anticipated most eloquently by Robert Rantoul, a Massachusetts civic leader, in an 1839 address: "A self-governing people without education is an impossibility; but a self-governing people, imperfectly and badly educated, may continually thwart itself, may often fail in its best purpose, and often carry out the worst."[6] Just as the Hispanic community cheered the Brennan decision, so working-class leaders applauded this view 150 years earlier. Writing in 1831 in *A Manual for Workingmen*, Stephen Simpson penned the following:

> Indeed, to conceive of a popular government devoid of a system of popular education is as difficult as to conceive of a civilized society destitute of a system of industry. This truth has been generally received in this country, and never, I believe, directly denied; although its force has been attempted to be evaded by the rich, who have heretofore, unfortunately, been our sole law makers, through the odious system of charity schools—the bare idea of which impresses a consciousness of degradation, and leads to results the very reverse of those that ought to be produced by popular instruction.[7]

If Brennan's view was anticipated by Rantoul and Simpson, Chief Justice Burger's dissenting opinion also reflects early-nineteenth-century arguments of a more conservative nature. In questioning whether the court was placing the value of education above that of food, shelter, or medical care, he was in effect echoing an argument stated in 1850 by critics like the *New York Tribune*: "the backbone of the opposition [to free schools] is hostility to be taxed to school other men's children—that is, to the free school principle in any form."[8] Another argument against taxation for common schools was found in a lecture given to the New York Study Club. "Who," asked the speaker, "would want to pay taxes to educate children that should never have been brought into the world? Why should the thrifty pay for the shiftless? I am not so un-christian as to say that the child once here should not be cared for. But so long as tax-payers pay for expensive playgrounds, etc., the children of the poor will increase like rabbits in a burrow."[9]

Curiously, some revisionists find themselves in the same bed as the chief justice. As Carlton observed decades ago, "Liberty to the radical is assumed to be non-interference with the individual; protection and tax-supported schools look to government interference."[10] Although the precepts of radical philosophy would hardly be embraced by Justice Burger and his fellow dissenters on the Supreme Court, his argument, like that of many revisionists, dissociates the state from responsibility for its citizens. This argument, too, has roots in events that occurred a century and a half ago. In Massachusetts in 1839, a new state government asserted that the board of education was trying to introduce supervision into the schools, to increase the power of the central authorities at the expense of that of the local districts, and in effect, to "Prussianize" the schools.[11] The argument is based on the right of the citizen to educate his children or not, as he pleases, and to live free from restraint of any kind. As Carlton, points out, "It would not be difficult to find arguments advanced in opposition to labor unions, collective bargaining, or an eight-hour day, which rest upon the same foundations and repeat almost identical phrases."[12]

The bitterness of the arguments for and against free public schools, with accusations of immorality, illegality, irreligious tendencies, and socialism was intense in the nineteenth century.[13] But the center of the storm was without doubt paying to educate other people's children. It is thus instructive to analyze the political alliances that formed around the issue of free schools in the nineteenth century.

First of all, we will look at the state of the nineteenth-century school, which people did not flee from, but rather flocked to. A demand for services by all classes, with which the schools were unable to cope, was combined with government arrangement that made the schools responsible to meet service demands with money given them by the city council. For its part, the council had to balance the needs of the schools against the need for other civic services. We shall find that in these disputes the working class generally supported public education. They were joined by school leaders motivated not only by altruism and a concern for social order but also by an interest in organizational expansion. In opposition were elements from the business community and often the Catholic church, the former because businessmen opposed taxes that increased business costs and the latter because it already supported a network of parochial schools. Finally, we will examine the role of political parties in the battle for free schools. Generally speaking, American political parties supported public education, particularly after popular enfranchisement and the growth of large working-class concentrations in urban areas. With an appointed school board as well as an appointed superintendent responsive to the party in power, city hall had a great deal of influence on the fiscal well-being of the school system. Under city administrations run by municipal reformers, schools fared much better than under administrations run by political machines. This pattern is particularly easy to see in San Francisco, where the fiscal fortunes of the schools followed the bouncing ball of politics from reform to machine and back again. The effect of city hall on school politics in Chicago and Atlanta is also evident: in Chicago the machine was closely connected to business interests, and in Atlanta government was dominated by white elites, making it difficult for the working class to press their demand for schools.

THE STATE OF THE NINETEENTH-CENTURY SCHOOL

Analogous to the 1982 conflict over the education of illegal aliens was the nineteenth-century conflict over educating everyone in the society instead of the few who could afford to pay for the privilege. The conflict was exacerbated by the dramatic growth of urban areas and a concomitant growth in the number of children who wished to attend school. Who the schools should serve, what sorts of services should be offered, who should pay, and how much were all unresolved issues, and with the advent of compulsory education the question of school financial policies was even more hotly debated.

Tables 2.1–3 show the expansion of the schools in Atlanta, Chicago, and San Francisco. In the seventeen years from 1878 to 1895 the average daily attendance (a smaller figure than enrollment) of the schools of Atlanta more than quadrupled; in the twenty-six years from 1870 to 1896 Chicago's average daily attendance grew by 140,700 children, a sixfold increase; and in the thirty-six years following 1872, San Francisco's schools nearly doubled in size, an increase of 14,247 children. Although all cities experienced rapid growth, if one looks at per-pupil expenditure and the number of pupils per teacher, the tables show an interesting difference in commitment to funding the public schools. From 1878 to 1895, per-pupil expendi-

TABLE 2.1 Expansion of the Atlanta Public School System, 1878–95

| Year | Total Expenditures ($000s) | | Expenditures per Pupil | | Average Daily Attend-ance | Pupils per Teacher | |
	Cur-rent Dollars	Con-stant Dollars[a]	Cur-rent Dollars	Con-stant Dollars[a]		Blacks	Whites
1878	38.1	92.0	10	25	3,667	91	63
1882	55.3	133.5	11	25	4,256	69	64
1885	76.3	198.0	10	27	5,571	—	—
1890	137.5	357.0	11	28	8,413	—	—
1895	138.6	388.5	9	26	14,767	118	65

Source: Atlanta Board of Education, *Annual Reports, 1878–95.*
[a]1947–49 = 100.

TABLE 2.2 Expansion of the Chicago Public School System, 1870–96

Year	Total Expenditures ($000s)		Expenditures per Pupil		Average Daily Attendance[c]	Pupils per Teacher
	Current Dollars	Constant Dollars[a]	Current Dollars	Constant Dollars[a]		
1870	527.7	973.2	21	39	25,300	47
1875	662.1	1,406.0	20	43	33,000	47
1880	691.5	1,671.1	16	40	42,400	47
1885	1,093.3	2,837.7	19	49	58,000	45
1890	4,706.3[b]	12,215.0[b]	53[b]	136[b]	89,600[b]	33
1896	6,334.3	17,755.5	38	107	166,000	38

Source: Chicago Board of Education, Annual Reports, 1870–96.
[a]1947–49 = 100.
[b]Large increases in all columns due to annexations.
[c]Figures are rounded.

TABLE 2.3 Expansion of the San Francisco Public School System, 1872–1908

Year	Total Expenditures ($000s)		Expenditures per Pupil[b]		Average Daily Attendance[c]	Pupils per Teacher[d]
	Current Dollars	Constant Dollars[a]	Current Dollars	Constant Dollars[a]		
1872	667.3	1,299.0	36	70	17,588	36.6
1879	858.2	2,147.9	29	73	26,376	41.9
1885	800.0	2,076.4	24	62	31,110	47.2
1891	950.2	2,466.2	28	73	30,121	39.1
1896	1,084.4	3,039.7	32	90	31,414	40.1
1901	1,261.8	3,536.9	37	104	32,733	37.7
1908	1,809.0[e]	4,695.2[e]	54[e]	140[e]	31,835	35.5

Sources: San Francisco Superintendent of Public Instruction, Annual Reports, selected years.
[a]1947–49 = 100.
[b]Total per-pupil expenditure was computed by combining current expenditures and debt service.
[c]Includes high school, commercial high school, polytechnic high school, grammar school, primary school, kindergarten, and special schools.
[d]Teachers in high schools, grammar schools, primary schools, kindergartens, special schools, teachers of special subjects, and regular substitutes. Principals who do not teach are excluded, as are unassigned day substitutes, evening-school and normal-school teachers and substitutes for evening and normal schools.
[e]Figures reflect the reconstruction efforts of the school department after the earthquake and fire of 1906.

ture in Atlanta remained pretty much constant, and in fact it underwent a slight drop from 1890 to 1895. Although we were unable to obtain separate per-pupil expenditure figures for blacks and whites, the steady overall pupil-expenditures figure may well mask an increase in expenditures for white pupils accompanied by a decline in those for black pupils. Within the strictly segregated system, the pupil/teacher ratio in black schools deteriorated badly while the pupil/teacher ratio in white schools remained essentially the same (table 2.1). By 1895 whites experienced a pupil/teacher ratio of 65 to one, while blacks suffered in classrooms with a pupil/teacher ratio of 118 to one.

In contrast to the very low and relatively stable level of per-pupil expenditures in Atlanta, expenditures in Chicago and San Francisco were much higher but rose and fell over time, as did the number of pupils per teacher. In 1885 Chicago spent nearly twice as much per pupil as did Atlanta, while San Francisco's expenditures were nearly two and one-half times as much. With their greater resources, the school systems of Chicago and San Francisco both paid teachers more and reduced the size of the average class. By the mid-1890s the number of pupils per teacher had dipped to about forty or less in the northern cities, while in Atlanta's white schools the ratio remained at sixty-five to one. But if Chicago and San Francisco provided substantially higher levels of service than Atlanta, that level was not uniform across the decades. In Chicago the level per-pupil expenditure steadily increased until 1890, when the annexation of a large suburban area induced very rapid increases in educational expenditure. At the same time the pupil/teacher ratio dropped significantly. In San Francisco levels of per-pupil expenditure remained constant from 1872 to 1891, with a drop in 1885, but rose rapidly thereafter. Pupil/teacher ratios changed inversely in much the same fashion.

What we see as figures on paper posed real problems for schools, which never quite managed to keep the supply of classrooms and teachers equivalent to the demand for education. The first year the Atlanta schools opened, white enrollments exceeded school capacity by nearly 50 percent. Those who did manage to enroll almost universally found themselves in overcrowded classrooms, instructed on part-time schedules by untrained or poorly trained teachers. The board showed very little concern for blacks, who had to rely on schools run by northern missionaries and the Freedman's Association in the years immediately after the Civil War, which sometimes operated on triple shifts to handle as many pupils as possible. The limited concessions made to blacks involved accommodations that were poorly constructed and quickly became overcrowded.[14]

Overcrowding was also the main issue in Chicago annual school reports. Every report from 1870 to 1895 spoke of the large class size and the number of pupils in rented rooms or on half-day sessions. Officials also conjectured about the number of children who were either out on the streets or in private schools because public facilities were inadequate.

School officials adopted several policies for dealing with population pressure. In Chicago, the earliest strategy for coping with influx was to draw up waiting lists, allocating pupils to classes as vacancies occurred.[15] By the mid-1870s this approach was replaced by the more elaborate procedure of instituting half-day sessions and using rented rooms.[16] As a result, few children were actually denied admission to Chicago's public schools, though many had shortened school days or were housed in unpleasant surroundings.

In San Francisco also, school officials devised measures to accommodate the large number of pupils who sought seats in the classroom. After eight days' absence, pupils were dropped from the rolls and others were given their places.[17] San Francisco school officials were well aware that crowded, dilapidated facilities deprived many children of an adequate education. They had often witnessed the scene described by an irate parent in a letter to the *Bulletin* in 1885. The child entered the eighth grade and was put in a "low-ceiled room about fifteen by twenty-five feet in size with dirt and cobwebs plentiful. With him in this pestilential recess were seventy-nine others."[18]

The demand for schools was there. But though public-school leaders wished to build and expand to meet that demand, government approval was required to fund both capital and operating expenses. Consequently, school finance became enmeshed in conflicts over local government priorities and the tax burden the public should be expected to bear.

INTRAGOVERNMENT CONFLICTS OVER SCHOOLS

With the services schools should offer still under debate, with voters distrustful of the financial management of many public institutions, and given the volatile character of a nineteenth-century economy that was marked by frequent periods of recession, discussions of school expenditures were often translated into calls for retrenchment. Schools were particularly vulnerable to cutbacks because they were not fiscally independent. Even though school boards were responsible for spending the money necessary to sustain the school system, these boards were dependent on the city council for funds. At best, city councils had to balance the needs of the school department with the needs of other city departments, making it difficult to meet pressing enrollment demands. At worst, the school board's lack of fiscal autonomy allowed political machines in cities like Chicago and San Francisco to raid the public-school treasury.

In Atlanta the political system was dominated by the "leading citizens" of the city. Lawyers and businessmen were especially well represented among office seekers, and this elite domination was reflected in the membership of the school board as well. The members of the board were appointed by the city council, "by virtue of the respect which stemmed from their wealth or success, or by virtue of their political activity."[19] Between 1869, when the first school board was appointed, and 1881, members of the board were uniformly business and professional men, and they included several of Atlanta's wealthiest and most eminent citizens.[20] Many men served more than ten years on the board, and five, including the first board president, served more than twenty years.[21] This domination of Atlanta's governing structures by the "Bourbon elite" created a tendency toward conservatism and even inertia in response to the growth issues confronting the Atlanta school during these years (see table 2.1).

Because the city council and the school board both had members drawn from the more prosperous classes of Atlanta, conflicts that emerged between them had no apparent class overtones but were instead problems of political authority. The city charter vested full authority over the school system in the school board, but the city council retained power over appropriations. These conflicts emerged in the first years of Atlanta's school system and persisted well into the twentieth century.[22] The fiscal permissiveness of the school board in matters of building construction, teacher salaries, and the addition of new subjects to the curriculum was criticized by the councilmen, while the school board, anxious to meet public demand for increasing services, attacked the callous disregard for the educational needs of Atlanta's children shown by the penurious council. Tensions between the two groups reached crisis proportion in 1897, culminating in the dissolution of the school board and the city council's appointment of a smaller and politically more responsive board.[23]

The school board in San Francisco was no freer to make financial decisions than the school board in Atlanta. It not only was powerless in determining the amount of its revenue, it was also restricted in designing and drawing up its budget. Responsibility for decisions on school finances was divided among the state legislature, the board of supervisors, and the board of education and remained so until 1927. A look at the major sources of school revenue gives some indication of the extent of this divided control. Revenue was derived from interest from the state school fund, the statewide school tax, city and county taxes, taxes voted at special elections, and the poll tax.[24] The board of education did not have control over setting any of these rates, and the numerous ceilings imposed on each revenue source restricted its actions. The city and county taxes were expected to supplement the amount available from the state, and they fluctuated according to what was available from other sources, including rental and sale of school properties. A legal ceiling of thirty-five dollars per census child, based on the average daily attendance of the previous year, was expected to cover both operating and building expenses.[25]

The school department was required to submit expenditure requests a year before the funds would be needed. Because of burgeoning enrollment, the board consequently found itself unable to meet unexpected expenses.[26] In addition, regulations governing school finance were closely bound up with state and local politics, and restrictions became even more cumbersome after 1877 when the state legislature barred all San Francisco municipal departments from spending more than one-twelfth of the total anticipated revenues in one month.[27]

In Chicago, some of the school board's financial responsibilities were delegated directly to it by the state legislature, and some of them were shared with the city council. Among the responsibilities the board handled on its own were the rental, furnishing, and maintenance of school buildings, the employment of teachers plus determination of their salaries, and the direction of the routine, day-to-day operation of the schools. These obligations had to be met with "cash on hand," since deficit spending was strictly prohibited by 1872 legislation. The school board's financial control was further weakened by decentralization within its own internal governance structure. A standing committee on finance and auditing oversaw expenditures, with approval by this committee considered approval by the entire board. Over the years the number of committees on the board proliferated, however, and it became customary for individual committees to have de facto control over expenditures in the areas under their purview. This decentralization made it difficult to exercise rigorous control over expenditures or to carefully compare different areas of expenditures.[28]

The responsibilities the board shared with the city council included the authority to sell or rent school lands and to manage the fund created as a result of past sales and current rentals.[29] The school-lands fund had been established when Chicago's city government was formally organized; the sale of the lands was to provide an operating fund for the schools. In the period after the Civil War, this school-lands fund contributed only a small portion of total revenues, leaving taxation and bonding as the two most important sources of school monies. Because it did not provide a greater share, the school fund was the most controversial source of financing. Problems surrounding the rental and sale of school lands frequently raised questions about the relationship of the school system to the business community, and particularly about the competence and disinterestedness of the public bodies charged with promoting the welfare of the schools when it conflicted with business interests. Even as early as 1870, the rental of school lands was being used as a political plum, and when the properties were appraised that year, the city council reduced the appraised value by half. In addition, the school lands had become a partisan as well as a class issue, with Republicans accusing Democrats of reducing their value to help "secessionists."[30]

So in all three cities, attempts to finance schooling generated highly predictable patterns of institutional conflict. On the one side, school boards, regularly faced with escalating enrollments and crowded classrooms, insisted that expenditure increases were vital. On the other side, city councils or other government bodies that were reluctant to raise local taxes charged the boards with waste and inefficiency. With the responsibility for providing services divided from the responsibility for raising revenues, this pattern of contention was hardly escapable. Each side knew best the domain for which it was primarily concerned, and each failed to perceive clearly enough the difficulties the other faced. No wonder school finance became the most bitterly contested of all local issues.

SUPPORT FOR AND OPPOSITION TO FREE SCHOOLS

In political circumstances where the struggle for school expansion was so bitterly contested, it was important for the school to be able to count on support from leaders, groups, and community organizations. Which segments of the urban population gave schools their consistent backing? Where did the social sources of opposition stem from? Were working-class groups attacking the schools for waste and extravagance? Did they attempt to forestall elite efforts to impose schooling on their children, as much of the revisionist writing might lead one to believe? Or did labor unions become stalwart defenders of the free school? How about businessmen? Did they see the free school as a cost-efficient means of providing a better-educated work force? Or did they oppose the rapid increases in the cost of public education?

The Working Class and Trade Unions

Carlton, in his turn-of-the-century study, attempted to categorize groups into supporters and nonsupporters of public education. Although recognizing that no group was unanimous in its opinion, basically he found supporters to be "Citizens of the Republic, workingmen, non-tax payers, Calvinists, residents of cities." Those who did not support tax-supported public education were "Residents of rural districts, taxpayers, members of exclusive or ultra-conservative classes, Lutherans, Quakers, etc., possessing a mother tongue other than English, proprietors of private schools."[31]

Carlton's findings are at odds with a number of studies that appeared some sixty-five years later. Far from finding the workingman to be a supporter of public education, these researchers believe he was a victim. Michael Katz, for example, claims that "school committees were unashamedly trying to impose educational reform and innovation on this reluctant citzenry. The communal leaders were not answering the demands of a clamorous working class: they were imposing the demands; they were telling the majority, your children shall be educated, and as we see fit."[32]

If one recognizes that within the working class, as within the middle and upper classes, there were varying views of the value of public education, then it is obvious one can find instances of working-class opposition to free schools, and especially high schools. Some such opposition can be found even among trade-union writings. But most union leaders believed that education was the greatest hope for bringing about social equality. Indeed, labor leaders were often proud to claim primary responsibility for the development of the nation's public schools, as, for example, Samuel Gompers did in his testimony before the United States Commission on Industrial Relations in 1914:

> It is not generally known that to the organized labor movement of Massachusetts belongs the credit of establishing public schools in Massachusetts and the general public school system as it has since developed. Prior to that time there were schools which children of poor parents could attend but attendance at such schools carried with it the stigma of the poverty of the parents. Such poverty was a stigma then. The labor movement of Massachusetts secured the enactment of a law removing as a requirement for attendance at these schools that the parents of the children must declare that they could not afford to pay for the tuition of their children. Thus came into existence the first public school in the United States.[33]

While this claim may have exaggerated the power of labor in antebellum Massachusetts, and while one should not overemphasize the political strength of trade unions even in big-city politics of the late nineteenth century, there is little doubt that labor was both rhetorically and substantively committed to free public education. For example, the preamble to one San Francisco union's constitution had as one of its principles that members "keep a watchful and jealous eye upon our common school system, so that it may even be preserved to us and future generations in all its original strength and purity."[34]

In part, labor's enthusiasm for education simply reflected the wider societal belief that schools were important for political democracy and social change.[35] But labor had more immediate objectives in making the case for expanding public schools. For one thing, schools removed from the labor market young children who, by working for minimal wages, seemed to depress the general wage levels.

Slightly after the turn of the century, the Atlanta *Journal of Labor* began a major campaign to enact child labor legislation. Calling it a humane, wise, and just act, the Georgia Federation of Labor urged the soon-to-be-convened Democratic convention to enact child labor laws, striking "the shackles from the limbs of the factory child-slaves."[36] The campaign continued through 1906, when the Georgia legislature passed a child labor bill.[37] During this period, the *Journal of Labor* published articles tying together child labor and education:

> There is one defect in our law [the 1906 child labor legislation], however, and the same is true of practically all of the states that have compulsory education, and that is the provision which permits a child, the sole support of indigent parents, to be relieved from school attendance and allowed to labor. . . . Experience has demonstrated that the majority of claims for exemption are not bona fide, and are the product of parental avarice rather than necessity. . . . It is far more important that the child should be given an education and be made a useful citizen than that the parent eke out a miserable existence through the meagre earnings of an infant when the parent can be as well or better supported by the state.[38]

The campaign for public education thus went hand in hand with the campaign against child labor. Labor also favored the expansion of free public institutions that serviced the broadest possible segments of society. To the extent that such public institutions were instituted, trade-union leaders believed, their people would have the same opportunities the wealthy enjoyed. An attempt in 1878 to abolish the teaching of foreign languages in the San Francisco public schools, for instance, led the Turners' Union to remark that the change would "rob the poor man's child of an equal opportunity with the rich man's at acquiring an education in harmony with the modern idea, and tend to make the poor man poorer and the rich man richer."[39] The Illinois State Federation of Labor (ISFL) in 1884 called for "the prohibition of the employment of children under fourteen years of age in workshops and schools except as applied to industrial schools," and for "the adoption and enforcement of a compulsory education system." Although absent from the 1885 and 1886 platforms, a child labor plank reappeared in 1887, 1888, 1892, and 1893. The compulsory education plank also appeared in all the available platforms between 1884 and 1893.[40] The ISFL also included a free textbook plank in its 1885, 1887, 1888, 1892, and 1893 platforms.[41]

Reflecting the sentiment that education should be available to all and that the cost of textbooks should not be an inhibiting factor, the free textbook issue was discussed frequently in the labor press during these years. There was considerable agreement among the papers that free textbooks should be provided to pupils in the public schools. Rationale for the position was based on the strong antimonopoly sentiment that pervaded public discussions during this era. The *Knights of Labor* asserted that "the system is in the hands of a set of conscienceless sharks and is made the means of unmercifully fleecing parents, so that though our schools are nominally 'free,' the constant demand for new books at monopoly prices

constitutes a heavy tax on education."[42] The American system was compared with the Swiss, in which textbooks were free. Book manufacturers
were accused of using "bribery, corruption and bulldozing to prevent any
legislation that would interfere with their grasps on the people's pockets."[43]
They were charged with using newspapers to mold public opinion and to
create a misleading impression of popular support for their position.[44]

The solution the labor papers proposed was some form of state production of textbooks. Periodically, legislation calling for the state manufacture
of textbooks was introduced in the legislature. Those who opposed it argued
that state interference would destroy competition, to which the labor paper
the *Rights of Labor* (formerly *Knights of Labor*), replied that competition
was impossible "under the present reign of trusts."[45] The paper also went to
some lengths to show that the cost of production was far below the price
charged for schoolbooks and was within the capacity of the state to
absorb.[46]

The manual training issue also illustrated labor's commitment to a
broadly based educational system. "Much of the degradation of labor,"
asserted the *Knights of Labor*, "may be traced to ignorance, and this is
caused to a great extent by sending young children out into the world to
battle for bread before they have been taught anything that will put them
on even ground with their fellows."[47] The paper lauded the platform of the
Farmers' Alliance party, which called for "a public school system that will
be practical, based on moral, manual and intellectual training that will
include the dignity and necessity of honest labor."[48]

Two years later the issue of manual training was raised again by the
Knights of Labor. "The American employers of our great industrial armies
do not afford our boys and girls fair opportunities to learn skilled trades,"
the paper said. It argued that little instruction was imparted to young
employees in the shop, and that foremen were hired not for trade proficiency, but for the capacity to drive men—overworking and underpaying
them. The solution, in the view of the *Knights of Labor*, was to establish free
manual training and public technical schools "on the same footing as the
schools of natural science, medicine, law and the fine arts." These "must
replace the old private and family apprenticeships." The main opposition
to such a plan was "the satanic press of the 'protected,' tax-gathering
plutocracy," who called this socialism. The paper observed that "our entire
system of public schools is socialistic in principle although not in practice,"
and that the people are "getting aroused to the necessity of universal
industrial education in public schools."[49]

Labor signified its support for free schools through its emphasis on the
need for adequate taxes to support them. In Chicago, those who refused to
support the expansion of the public-school curriculum were "the mil-
lionaire element of society that never patronizes the public schools, and

that is always on tender hooks for fear it may be excessively taxed."[50] In San Francisco, an 1897 controversy led labor unions to object to a proposal limiting municipal taxes to one dollar on each hundred dollars of assessed value. Among the arguments against the limit was one claiming that "working people and small traders and manufacturers . . . have children to educate and cannot send them to expensive private schools."[51] Labor support for school expenditures was also evident in its position on school bonds. In late 1899 a major controversy erupted over whether the city should float bonds for the construction of a large "panhandle park" adjoining Golden Gate Park. Citizen improvement associations and the Merchants Association lobbied in favor of the bonds while labor groups argued that schools should receive a higher priority than the park project. In a letter to the *Star* the Labor Council stated that "it needs but little thought from a workingman's standpoint, as his children are always the sufferers, to show the necessity of more school houses."[52]

Atlanta's labor movement was less active than those of Chicago and San Francisco, in part because late-nineteenth-century Atlanta was dominated by the "leading citizens" of the city. Their predominance in city politics is accounted for in part by the persistence of at-large, citywide voting for all municipal offices. School board members were appointed by the city council. Candidates for the city council were obliged to live in the ward they proposed to represent but were elected at large, and so had to campaign in every ward in the city. The principal motivation behind the retention of city wide election of candidates in Atlanta was that black voters represented a majority in the fourth ward and a near majority in the third. Ward-based election of councilmen would have been likely to result in the direct representation of the black community in city government, a prospect unattractive to white citizens of all classes.[53]

The preservation of city wide elections had the effect of limiting the power of Atlanta's white working class to elect its representatives to office, because the strength of a large working-class constituency in some wards was more than offset by strong support in others for elite candidates. In an important election in 1888, for example, in which the upper-class Citizens' Ticket was strongly challenged by the working class People's Ticket, the latter slate carried the first ward and made a strong showing in the heavily black third and fourth wards but suffered a substantial defeat city wide in all races because of heavy majorities for the Citizens' Ticket in remaining wards.[54]

Even though working-class organizations were largely ineffective in electing working-class candidates to city offices, by virtue of its substantial voting power labor was courted by all candidates for office, and representatives of the working class were frequently included among the Citizens' Ticket candidates. As a rule, representation on the ticket of leading citizens was the only way the working class could win political office at this time. Although there were a number of direct challenges to elite candidates from slates formulated and supported by organized labor, none of these challenges was successful until well after the turn of the century. Labor's lack of influence over school policy should not be taken as evidence of working-class opposition to schools, however. Indeed, labor's political weakness helps account for both Atlanta's low level of educational expenditure and the severe crowding experienced by white and black children.

Business

Although the working class viewed education as the most viable road out of poverty, large numbers of taxpayers had doubts about education as a remedy for the country's social problems. Among the most vocal opponents of free schools were business elites. The political strength exercised by white business and professional elites in Atlanta has already been discussed. The question that remains is whether business attitudes in San Francisco, and especially in highly industrialized Chicago, were similar. In Chicago, particularly, events like the Haymarket Riot of 1886 had brought to the public's mind such issues as anarchy, rebellion, and citizenship. In these two cities it might have made sense for business to make the educational investment necessary to ensure a pool of well-trained workers who would be schooled not to rise up against the capitalist system. But if such calculations made sense to some, Chicago and San Francisco businesses were far from being unanimously prepared to bear a large tax burden for the sake of the public schools. Even though some businessmen may have seen "schooling . . . as a means of producing the new forms of motivation and discipline required in the emerging corporate order," business leaders remained unenthusiastic about educational expansion, offering it little support in times of prosperity and coming out in strong opposition in periods of economic uncertainty. Whether or not they were "alarmed by growing labor militancy," as some have suggested,[55] business leaders were especially concerned about excessive school expenditures in recessionary periods (when labor militancy was more likely).

The idea of expanding, ever more costly public schools found few friends among San Francisco's wealthiest citizens. When school expenditures came under close public scrutiny, the Merchants Association, in its *Review*, called the school department a "municipal calamity." It noted that "proportionately, no city spends more money upon its public school system than San Francisco, yet few cities receive less in return.[56] Despite the "exceedingly generous appropriation" given the department, "thousands of boys and girls were turned away for lack of room at the opening of the present term."[57]

The response of the business community to school bond issues and special taxation was in accord with its belief that fiscally the schools were irresponsibly managed. "Economical administration and a decent saloon license," claimed the *Review*, "would probably provide sufficient revenue."[58] Special taxes frequently were tied up for years in litigation.[59] However, some members of the business community came to accept the need for bond issues to provide funds for building schools when it became apparent that "no head of a family in ordinary circumstances would care to live here [if new schools are not erected]."[60] But basically, through the turn of the century, business favored lower expenditures, arguing that schools could live within the budgetary restraints that had been imposed upon them since the early 1880s.[61]

Business in Chicago was equally unwilling to support heavy school taxes and instead insisted on economies of all sorts. The costs of schools theoretically could have been placed largely on the business community, since business rented many of the lands that constituted the school fund. But in the late nineteenth century they contributed only between 8 percent and 10 percent of the total per year,[62] far less than many groups felt they should provide.

In 1872 control of the fund passed from the city council to the board of education. Finding many of the properties underassessed and paying lower interest rates than those publicly announced, the board accused the council of mismanagement, claiming that "persons who look on the School Fund as public plunder took advantage of this."[63] Back rents were successfully collected, but an attempt to increase the appraisals embroiled the board in a protracted dispute with major business interests occupying the lands. After an intense battle, in which the judge initially ruled in favor of the lessees, an out of court compromise was negotiated.[64]

Controversy over school lands in Chicago reached its greatest intensity in the mid-1890s when, in anticipation of the 1895 appraisal, several tenants began to push for ending the system of land reevaluation and replacing it with a fixed or graduated rental scheme. Some tenants, including the Chicago *Daily News* and the Chicago *Tribune*, managed in this way to renegotiate such favorable terms on their leases that Illinois governor Altgeld accused them of "waving the flag with one hand and plundering the public with the other."[65] The *Tribune's* attorney was both president of the board of education and a member of the committee that negotiated the paper's new lease.[66] Writing at the time of the controversy, one commentator observed that

> The board admitted that the appraised valuation might fall below what the property would bring in the open market were it free from all incumbrances. . . . even an untechnical examination of the leases is sufficient to show that the finance committee feels very tenderly toward the tenants.[67]

Although other attempts would be made to increase the school fund by reassessing rental properties, the fund never yielded a substantial operating revenue, since it would have been at the expense of key Chicago businesses.

Catholics

While the rental of school lands was mainly an issue in Chicago, Catholic opposition to tax-supported public schools was more general. Many immigrants were Catholics and chose to send their children to Catholic schools even though they paid taxes that helped support public schools. And while non-Catholics were unhappy about giving money to schools in which religion was an integral part of the curriculum, Catholics were equally unhappy about having to support schools they did not use.

The intense discourse over spending public money on parochial schools was elevated to the national level in the 1870s and 1880s, causing divisions within both the Republican and Democratic parties. In 1875 President Ulysses S. Grant declared that every child in the land should have a common-school education free of sectarianism.[68] In the same year James Blaine, one of the aspirants for the Republican presidential nomination, introduced a constitutional amendment forbidding public funds to sectarian schools. It passed the House but failed to pass the Senate, where the Democratic majority, interpreting the amendment as an attack on Catholics, defeated it.[69]

With only a few exceptions, Catholic opposition to the free school continued throughout the century. Some church leaders like Father Peter Yorke of San Francisco claimed that the state had no business interfering in the private life of the family, which he felt it was doing with its insistence that all taxpayers support public schools.[70] Others did not object to the free school in principle but believed that public funds should be allocated for parochial schools too. An editorial in the San Francisco *Monitor*, the official archdiocese newspaper, claimed that "[while] the state should place primary education within reach of all its citizens and . . . the majority of schools should be public or under the supervision of the State, . . . it is an injustice to those Catholics, Methodists or Episcopalians who, through religious convictions refuse to make use of the public schools, to refuse help to those institutions which alone they can use—thus imposing on them a double tax for the education of their children."[71]

The times that Catholic opposition was not voiced were those exceptional moments when public money was made available for parochial schools. One of these exceptions occurred in the early days of the San Francisco schools when an ordinance provided that schools "formed by the enterprise of a religious society in which all the educational branches of the district schools shall be taught . . . should be eligible to receive public funds."[72] This provision was ruled illegal by the state legislature in 1852. Nevertheless, the following year the state superintendent of public instruction recommended that the state school law be altered to allow some public funds to finance denominational schools that were helping to ease the burden of educating the state's children. The result was the passage of the Ward School Act in 1853. In San Francisco this meant that the Catholic schools would once again be eligible to receive public funds. There were three such ward schools in San Francisco between 1853 and 1855, providing education for 1,421 pupils in the primary and grammar-school grades. These schools received nearly forty thousand dollars during the two-year period that the law remained in effect.[73] In 1855 an amendment to the law required that teachers in parochial and convent schools pass an examination and obtain a public-school certificate before the school could receive public funding.[74] The nuns in charge of the Catholic girls' school did not take the exams, but the lay male teachers who taught at the boys' schools took them and were appointed by the school board.

A second exception occurred in 1870, when the state legislature granted fifteen thousand dollars to schools run by the Presentation Sisters. Considerable opposition was engendered, with the *Bulletin*, a leading newspaper, calling the bill "one of the most objectionable passed by the Legislature" and labeling it a threat to the existence of nonsectarian schools.[75] Despite this isolated incidence of public funding for Catholic schools after 1855, a repeat of the ward-school experiment was never again put on the city agenda.

In the absence of its ability to obtain public funding for its own schools, the Catholic church spent the later years of the century attacking the expansion of the school curriculum. Based on its objection to the "double tax," the church argued that the public school was an institution that taxed "the poor for the benefit of the wealthy."[76] The *Monitor* suggested that the schools try to save money by paring down the scope of the curriculum and by eliminating high schools. The paper found it "no wonder that the laboring poor are filled with discontent at beholding this and many other injustices done them, nor will it remove this discontent to say to the poor man, the high school is open to your child as well as those of the rich, for he cannot make use of the privilege for many reasons sufficiently obvious."[77] The *Monitor* applauded the attempt by a state senator to introduce a bill "providing for the exclusion of music, drawing and languages, except English, from all schools maintained at the public expense."[78]

The one institutional expression of potential working-class opposition to public schools thus came from the Catholic church. It may be argued, on the basis of this evidence, that the church spoke for a pervasive workingman's view that schools had little value. It may be that the church voiced a widespread view that schools offered little hope for economic advancement for working-class children but instead were designed by elites to "domesticate" the poor. It may be argued that it was the church, not the trade-union movement, that best expressed working-class opinion about public education. All these arguments are possible, but in our opinion they are in the end unconvincing for several reasons. First, the Catholics themselves concentrated their own limited resources on providing religious based education for their parishioners. Their success in creating an institutional rival to public schools in many working-class neighborhoods is inconceivable apart from a belief common to priest and parishoners alike that education was not only an aid to salvation but also a step toward a better life in this world. Second, the Catholic church was always willing to withhold its criticism of public schools any time it could receive some government aid for itself. Indeed, the public schools might have gained more in fiscal terms at an earlier date had they been more willing to work cooperatively with their fellow educators within the Catholic church. Finally, Catholics criticized the public schools not for giving working-class children education they did not need but for limiting access to the high schools to middle-class children.

All in all, Catholic opposition to public schools must be understood as basically a function of the church's own organizational interests. Hoping to maintain its own parish schools in the face of an increasingly well-endowed competitor, the church quite astutely did its best to keep its public-school rival from becoming overwhelmingly strong.

The Role of Political Parties in the Development of Public Education

Not only has the persistent effort by working class groups to obtain free public education been misconstrued by the revisionists, not only have the business community's and the Catholic church's positions on public education been misinterpreted, but the support of political parties and the contributions of "reformers" to the development of public education have also been incorrectly portrayed. Inasmuch as workers in northern cities could— and did—vote, worker concerns, whenever expressed by community groups, trade unions, or independent political parties, commanded the attention of the regular political parties. At various times these voters channeled their concerns through independent labor parties, including the United Labor party, the People's party and the Workingmen's party of California. But as strong as the educational commitments of independent workingmen's parties were, it was "the Democratic boss and his machine" that "towered over" politics in the late nineteenth century.[79] Revisionist literature has identified the political machine as an essentially working-class institution, while its nemesis, the municipal reformer, is characterized as a middle-class do-gooder driven by the twin goals of social efficiency and social control. Samuel Hays asserts, for example, that the municipal progressives were a small group of upper-middle-class elites who wished to replace ward-based "friends and neighbors" politics with a more "efficient" government run by the best-educated, best-qualified people.[80] The 1898 San Francisco city charter is referred to "as the first and crucial step in the process by which San Francisco's business and professional elites worked to translate their corporate ideal into social reality."[81] Machines, on the other hand, have been treated as devoted friends of the poor and immigrants. Among the many services they supposedly provided were direct relief for the poor, as well as information and influence for families unfamiliar with the red tape and overlapping jurisdictions of city agencies.[82] In cities where machines dominated school politics, bosses and their subordinates sometimes mediated between their constituents and the official school system. In addition, "through jobs and contracts in the schools the machine sometimes offered paths of social mobility to groups that otherwise might have been excluded."[83]

If these characterizations are correct, then the expectation with respect to school finances would be that the machine would use its political muscle not only for distributing patronage, but also for underwriting, somewhat profligately perhaps, a growing school system. Tightfisted reformers, with an accountantlike view of efficiency, could be expected to have attacked "unnecessary spending" in the system. Under reform regimes, school expenditures would have declined and pupil/teacher ratios would have increased.

In order to ascertain the evidence for these interpretations of urban machines and their reform opponents, we looked at policy outcomes in San Francisco, where political machines, reform movements, and third-party movements alternated in their control of city hall, providing an unusual opportunity to study the effects of changing political coalitions on the fiscal well-being of the schools. Our findings did not confirm the revisionist interpretation of municipal politics. Instead, as shown in table 2.3, pupil/teacher ratios worsened and expenditures per pupil declined between 1879 and 1885, when the machine was politically dominant, not rising to their 1879 level again until 1891, when the power of the machine had begun to wane rapidly. Only after that date did per-pupil expenditures increase and classroom crowding ease.

The relationship between these changes in the economic well-being of the San Francisco public schools and the balance of power among San Francisco's political forces is graphed in figure 2.1. The graph adopts the characterization of San Francisco's nineteenth-century politics developed by T. J. McDonald (1979), who has written a careful analysis of municipal politics and finance in San Francisco during this time. McDonald divides the period 1870 to 1910 into five distinct political periods—the People's–

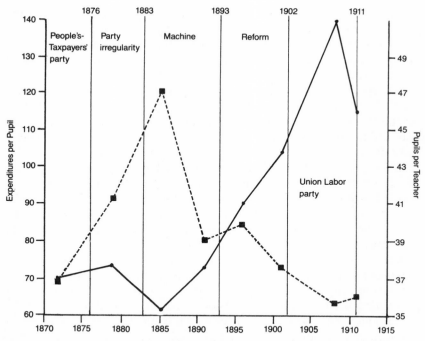

Fig. 2.1. Expenditures per pupil and pupils per teacher, by political era, San Francisco 1870–1911. *Solid line*, expenditures per pupil, in constant dollars; *broken line*, pupils per teacher. From San Francisco Superintendent of Public Instruction, Annual Reports, 1870–1911.

Taxpayers' party, party irregularity, the machine, reform, and the Union Labor party. From McDonald's account and others, it can be said that by 1885 Boss Buckley's star was rising steadily.[84] By 1890 reformers were gaining in influence, and in the last years of the century they were in power.

The school-expenditure data show that the single period in nineteenth-century San Francisco when the public schools suffered a precipitous decline in per-pupil expenditures was the era when Boss Buckley's machine was in firm command. Constant-dollar per-pupil expenditures fell from a high of seventy-three dollars in 1879 to just sixty-two dollars in 1885. Although they did climb again, they did not increase beyond their 1879 level as long as Buckley remained in power. When reformers took control after 1891, school expenditures per pupil went up steadily, reaching ninety dollars four years later and climbing to over one hundred dollars per pupil by the end of the century. Consistent with this expenditure pattern, the pupil/teacher ratio rose dramatically when the machine was in power in the early eighties. By 1885 there were as many as forty-seven pupils per teacher. No wonder the school crisis was a central political issue in that year. But after reformers took command the pupil/teacher ratio declined steadily, reaching a level of thirty-nine to one by the beginning of the last decade of the century. In short, detailed analysis of expenditure levels in nineteenth-century San Francisco hardly shows that reformers were more concerned about cost-cutting and penny-pinching than were the city's machine politicians.

Political bosses frequently professed their support for education, of course. Christopher M. Buckley, who entered San Francisco politics as a Republican but became a Democrat when fortune dictated, claims in his "Memoirs" that "if there was one thing more than another that I desired to keep absolutely aloof from politics, it was the conduct of the public schools. I wished them maintained in the highest degree of efficiency for a reason personal to myself. All my life I have had to feel the lack of early opportunities of learning. I went through the grammar school, and had to let it go at that. When my historian asked me where I acquired what he was pleased to call my gift of correct English speech, I had to tell the blunt truth—behind the bar of a saloon."[85]

Buckley's rule reached its zenith in 1885, though he continued to be a political force until as late as 1890. During these years it appeared that Buckley's support for the public schools had turned into the public schools' "support" of Buckley. Even while he was cutting school expenditures and leaving teachers with ever-larger classes, he found good "use" for public education. In October 1884 the San Francisco *Chronicle* compiled a list of accusations against the school board: teaching positions in the department were sold, janitorships were hawked, votes on replacing textbooks were bought by publishers, contracts for merchandise were mismanaged, furniture was taken from the storehouse for political and personal purposes, carpenters in the school shop worked on private houses and were paid for it out of the school treasury.[86]

Well aware of these kinds of abuses, revisionists persist in believing that while patronage and corruption did exist, these were in fact mechanisms by which the needy and poor were served. Rather than creating a municipality structured by the needs of the middle and upper classes, the urban boss is said to have spent public funds on working-class and ethnic demands, offering access to jobs and better services. Our data on school expenditures, which show more rapid school expansion under reform leadership, run counter to this view. Significantly, so does McDonald's quantitative study of San Francisco municipal expenditures, which analyzes the effects of bosses and reformers on municipal spending in general during the late nineteenth century.

McDonald's research attempted to ascertain whether changes in general expenditure levels by the San Francisco city government were determined by increasing industrialization and other socioeconomic factors or by changes in political power that occurred in the forty-six years from 1860 to 1906. Three different patterns were possible: (1) Socioeconomic forces in the city were of fundamental importance, and changes in political power would have little effect on expenditure levels;[87] (2) Political factors would affect expenditure levels: as political machines and professional politicians gained power, expenditures would increase, while reform "efficiency" would lead to expenditure cuts. One study of San Francisco had, without investigating actual expenditure patterns, actually made this claim about the politics and finances of San Francisco;[88] (3) Political factors would affect expenditure levels: as reformers gained power they would spend more to provide a complete set of public services, whereas machine politicians, having a different concept of the general interest, would seek to minimize business discontent by keeping taxes low. This third pattern is the one we found in San Francisco school politics.

McDonald found, first of all, that expenditures climbed steeply during the period of reform governance, which began fiscally in 1893 and continued through 1902.[89] As can be seen in figure 2.2, whereas general fund expenditures were about $2,300,000 in 1892, they rose as high as $3,800,000 by the turn of the century and higher in the next decade. By comparison, expenditure levels under machine rule (1883–92) hovered between $1,900,000 and $2,300,000, a relatively constant figure over a decade of significant change. Clearly, reformers were more willing to draw upon the

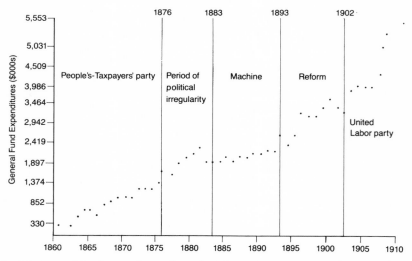

Fig. 2.2. General fund expenditures by political era, San Francisco, 1860–1910. From McDonald 1979, 177.

public purse than the machine politicians had been during the preceding decade.

These differences, to be sure, could be a function of social and economic factors rather than any difference that can be attributed to politics per se. To test for this possibility McDonald included in a single regression equation four economic variables—value added by manufacturing, number of workers per manufacturing plant, area of the city, and population density—together with information on what political regime (machine, reform, taxpayer, etc.) was in political power. He discovered that when economic factors were taken into account expenditure levels during the machine era were $1.10 less per capita than what was expected, while during the reform era they were $.75 more per capita. If these numbers seem small, it is only because at this time overall per capita expenditures were very low. McDonald himself explains that the political variables were about as important an explanatory variable in his analysis as were the economic factors. In his words,

> the "machines" were more fiscally conservative and the reformers more expansionary. . . . While campaigning against the machine's extravagance, the reformers of the 1890s added more expenditure then they subtracted. . . .
>
> The conclusion is quite clear and both statistically and historically significant. Not only were there expenditure differences between the eras, but these eras also produced an effect independent of industrialization and urbanization. The expansion of municipal government, in short, was not simply the result of underlying social change, but also of the decisions of political actors. Indeed, the independent effect of politics . . . was frequently larger than that of the other variables.[90]

McDonald's interpretation of these findings is that machine politicians believed fiscal conservatism was the key to political legitimacy; therefore they held to the concept of a limited budget. Corruption existed, but it was to be kept in the private sector, a matter between franchise seekers and members of the party. "In return for their services supporters may have received certain favors; neither, however, was financed from the public sector."[91] (It should be noted, however, that the public did pay for political corruption, even if not by means of the municipal budget. For instance, rates paid to well-connected utility companies such as the Spring Valley Water Company, which for some time had a monopoly on water supply to the areas around the city, were said to be usurious.)

On the other hand, reformers, including James Phelan and several San Francisco merchants, believed that "the public purse" should be "harnessed to the broad goal of economic development."[92] Consequently, the reform era effected an across-the-board increase in expenditure over that of the machine period. Phelan improved the sewer system, bought supplies for the hospital and the almshouse, built new schoolhouses, and planned new parks. McDonald concludes his study with an observation on the "irony" of municipal reform. He notes that Hays accuses reform of effecting changes that stifled democracy, all in the name of democracy. But the case of San Francisco suggests that reformers, while campaigning for economy, spent more money on the public sector. By comparison, the machine had been penurious.[93]

CONCLUSION

Free schools have always been a sought-after prize. Both the Hispanic community in 1982 and workingmen in 1882 fought for them, aided in their quest by liberals and by municipal reformers. Working-class support extended to compulsory education, and labor showed a willingness to bear the taxation burden of such an institution. People sent their children to the schools, which found it almost impossible to match supply to demand.

The schools' ability to respond to the need for services in the nineteenth century was hampered by the divided authority over school expenditures. The school board was responsible for spending the funds, but it had to obtain them from the city council. Boards in the nineteenth century were dominated by businessmen, some of whom saw schools as a necessary evil that forced them to pay for the education of other men's children, a nineteenth-century objection echoed by Chief Justice Burger in his 1982 *Pyler v. Doe* dissent.

Objections to paying for the education of other men's children were also voiced by the Catholic church. But in contrast to the anti-public-education position of the business community, the church did not object in principle to free schools. Because Catholics wished to give their children a religious education, however, they established a vast network of parochial schools that needed support. They objected to the "double tax" parishioners had to pay. While certain church leaders like Father Peter Yorke of San Francisco felt the government had no business interfering in people's private lives, which he felt it was doing by insisting that the public pay to support public education, the times when the church was not outspoken against public education were times when parochial schools were given public funds. Quite clearly, the church's objection to tax-supported schools was more practical than principled and, in any case, did not reflect any heightened sense of class consciousness among the religious authorities.

Nineteenth-century political parties, whether machine or reform, acknowledged the electoral power of the working class by supporting public education. But in contrast to their rhetoric, expenditures for schools during machine administrations at times actually dropped, while expenditures during reform administrations generally increased. Usually considered a friend of the working class, the political machine instead used school lands and funds to the advantage of political friends or wealthy businessmen, who in turn paid members of the machine some sort of fee. Reformers, on the other hand, talked the language of efficiency but built up the bonded indebtedness of the city by improving hospitals, roads, and schools. In San Francisco, schools never fared better than under reform administrations.

3 The Politics of Curricular Change

Public school systems in late-nineteenth-century urban America faced increasingly complex organizational problems as extensive immigration and continued industrialization created a more diverse clientele. New bases for group mobilization were constantly forming, forcing the schools to redefine their purposes and pedagogical philosophies. When powerful groups began to establish competing institutions, the public schools responded with modifications in their own practices as part of their continuing effort to enlarge their sphere of influence and achieve a monopoly on educational services.

The expansion of the curriculum was one way the public schools attempted to build a wider clientele and develop a broader base of support. Foreign languages were introduced into the schools of polyglot cities like Chicago and San Francisco in response to the demands of large and influential ethnic groups. Middle-class and upper-middle-class parents, whose children did not need to work to supplement the family income, found public schools receptive to their request for secondary schooling. The introduction of manual and vocational education responded to increasing business demand for labor with specialized skills.

These educational innovations were not without their critics, of course. The introduction of foreign languages (usually German and French) was opposed by other ethnic groups, by the Catholics in San Francisco, and by some school officials who felt it was a pedagogically unsound departure from the aims of common schooling. Attacks on secondary-school expansion were mounted by those who opposed the diversion of resources from primary to secondary schools. Manual training was resisted by school officials committed to the traditional curriculum.

There was also more generalized opposition to curricular expansion. This opposition gained momentum in periods of financial crisis when calls for expenditure cutbacks were coupled with attacks on the extravagance of employing special teachers. Underlying the movement for retrenchment was a philosophy of education fundamentally at odds with the organizational interests of the public school system. Those who labeled the increasing differentiation of the curriculum "fads and frills" believed the function of public schools was to provide practical education in the narrow sense of imparting the basic knowledge needed for citizenship and, in later periods, minimal functioning in the labor market. Others who stood steadfast behind curricular expansion argued that if the public schools did not provide instruction in special subjects, children would be forced to attend private institutions or do without. Thus the public school system's defenders contended that preserving the quality and clientele of the public schools, on the one hand, and the ideal of equal opportunity, on the other, mandated that they offer an extensive and varied curriculum.

In all of these disputes school officials attended primarily to their most urgent organizational interests. If external groups were strong enough to establish institutions that could someday rival the "common school," their concerns were given preferential treatment. When Germans began educating their children in German-language schools, public schools experimented with bilingual programs. To attract middle-class pupils away from private day and boarding schools, well-endowed public high schools were established. When businessmen set up their own vocational schools, the school system soon followed suit. In short, whenever social groups demonstrated such strong commitments to educational objectives that they began creating institutions that might compete with the "common school," the public school modified its curriculum accordingly.

In virtually all these diversifications of the curriculum, educators received the support of trade unions and other working-class-groups. In general, the trade unions accepted the ideal of the common school and viewed with suspicion any efforts to curtail its curriculum, financing, or scope of operations. Labor supported foreign-language instruction, expansion of secondary schooling, and the addition of manual training and vocational programs. Unlike some businessmen and other large property owners, labor leaders generally felt the benefits of their innovations outweighed their potential costs to local taxpayers. And unlike Catholics, who had their own schools to sustain, union leaders believed the best route to working-class advancement was a unified program of popular education. So continuous was labor support for the expansion and diversification of the public school that it is difficult to imagine today's complex, autonomous urban school system apart from it.

FOREIGN-LANGUAGE INSTRUCTION

The introduction of foreign-language instruction in the public schools of both Chicago and San Francisco occurred in response to the efforts of politically powerful ethnic minorities who sought to maintain continuity with their native cultures. School officials, nonetheless, had reasons of their own for favoring the policy. Quite apart from any pedagogical objective, the inclusion of foreign languages was consistent with a strategy of institution building that required seeking support for the public schools from the city's ethnic groups. Thus, while bilingual education as practiced in the nineteenth century was in part a by-product of the pluralist accommodation that characterized this era,[1] it was also directly related to the school system's organizational need to expand.

Their large numbers in the population created potential for significant political leverage on the part of immigrants to the nineteenth-century American city. In San Francisco, French- and German-born residents constituted 11.5 percent of the population by 1870. At the same time, German-born residents alone made up 17.7 percent of Chicago's population.[2] The organizational activities of these groups enhanced their political power. In both cities, Germans were leaders in trade unions and political parties and showed a particular interest in school politics. During 1871–73, for example, 16.7 percent of the seats on the San Francisco school board were filled by members of German descent.[3] The capacity of these groups to establish private educational institutions in competition with the public schools increased the effectiveness of their demands.[4] When several German organizations pressed for the inclusion of their language in the Chicago public schools in 1865, the school board approved German-language courses in one school as an experiment. The next year the board elaborated a general policy on the teaching of German, stipulating that if 150 parents requested it the language could be taught in each of the city's divisions.[5] Demand was so high that within a year of its first proposal this quota was met and German was taught throughout Chicago. By 1870 there were 2,597 pupils studying German in the Chicago public schools.[6]

San Francisco's public schools initially went even further than Chicago's in providing language instruction for the city's major ethnic groups. In 1865 the first Cosmopolitan Schools were opened, offering instruction in both French and German. In these schools most subjects were taught in French or German from the earliest primary grades, and English was taught as a second language. However, soon after they were opened, the Cosmopolitan Schools were reorganized and thereafter studies in English occupied a greater portion of the pupils' time.[7] Nonetheless, in 1871 there were 5,395 pupils in San Francisco's Cosmopolitan Schools, all of whom spent some time studying French or German.[8]

The school officials who supported foreign-language instruction spoke not only of the benefits of preserving traditional cultures but of the importance of bringing immigrants into mainstream public education. In 1877 San Francisco's school superintendent argued that although French and German were not essential to the curriculum of common schools, they were a necessary concession to the "foreign elements of our society." Before the

Cosmopolitan Schools were opened, he said, "hundreds of children of foreign parents were attending private schools in order that they might receive instruction in the language of the "Fatherland." Now they are found under the care of American teachers, and being molded in the true form of American citizenship."[9] Chicago school officials also realized that German instruction could draw German pupils away from the private schools and into the public schools. The chairman of the committee on German language noted that "the number of private schools now to be found in every nook and corner of the city will decrease, and the children of all nationalities will be assembled in the public schools, and thereby be radically Americanized."[10]

The teaching of foreign language in public schools had its opponents from the outset. Other ethnic groups who objected to preferential treatment for the Germans or the French were one source of opposition; the Catholic church was another. In San Francisco the Catholic newspaper contended that "there is no good reason why French or German should be taught in the public schools any more than Irish or Russian."[11] Some school officials also objected to the teaching of languages on pedagogical grounds, arguing that chldren who were not native speakers did not learn enough to benefit, and that language instruction at an early age was so difficult it actually harmed the child.[12] In San Francisco the Cosmopolitan Schools remained a focus of controversy into the early 1870s. French and German were offered in all the city's public schools by 1873, but the next year, in a dramatic turnaround, the board eliminated foreign-language instruction and closed the Cosmopolitan Schools. Even the *Monitor*, the Catholic newspaper that favored the move, noted that the dismissal of French and German teachers "was rather suddenly and discourteously accomplished."[13] The change, though rationalized in financial terms, seems to have been the result of the election of a Republican nativist majority to the school board.[14] But the elimination of foreign language instruction did not last long. The next year public protest, particularly among the German community, led to the reestablishment of the Cosmopolitan Schools.[15] Attacks on the Cosmopolitan Schools continued throughout the 1870s, but the most decisive blows to the teaching of foreign languages in the public schools came when the issue became entangled in efforts to cut back school expenditures toward the end of the decade.

The financial crisis of the late 1870s had indeed brought hard times and bitter criticism to San Francisco's public school system. As early as 1876, the school budget had been squeezed, and local newspapers had blamed extravagant expenditures for the problem. In this economic context, the Catholic newspaper the *Monitor* raised curricular issues anew, selecting as its targets instruction in German, French, music, and drawing. The paper charged that instruction in these subjects was disproportionately expensive and benefited only a handful of pupils who were not required to leave school at an early age to work:

> The most strenuous advocates for State secular education will acknowledge that the rudiments of a sound English education—reading, writing, and arithemetic, with perhaps a little history and geography—are all the State should be called upon to provide for by taxation. No objection should be made to also teaching the other branches, the luxuries as we may fairly call them, but they should be made special charges upon those who want them and they should cost the city nothing.[16]

Catholics were joined in their opposition to the extravagances of special subjects by a majority of the state legislators, and in 1877 legislation calling for the abolition of instruction in foreign languages and music passed both houses of the state legislature. However, the bill was not enacted because the governor failed to sign it.[17] When a state senator from San Francisco tried the following year to introduce a similar bill, San Francisco school officials sent a delegation to Sacramento to express their point of view, and leaders of the German community rallied crowds at a mass meeting to demonstrate their support for the Cosmopolitan Schools.[18] This public pressure, plus insistence by the legislative committee's chairman that children had the right to learn languages in the common schools (rather than having to attend "private and high class" institutions for them), caused the bill to be dropped.[19] Sensitive to the cries of retrenchment yet generally in favor of foreign-language instruction, the school board voted to eliminate special language teachers in the earliest primary grades.[20] Foreign-language instruction was continued in many of the schools but was conducted by regular classroom teachers. In this way the school system was able to retain its organizational commitment to attracting culturally distinct groups but at the same time to eliminate some of the costs involved.[21]

The move did not silence the school system's critics. A nativist paper, the San Francisco *Argonaut*, added its voice to the denunciation of special subjects. It termed the school system "an extravagant and costly sham . . . a fraud . . . a crime" and charged that "we are spending money to teach one class of foreigners languages while another is threatening to burn our city. We are spending money to educate in music and drawing and other accomplishments the children of men who are prowling our streets and defying our laws."[22] The leading reform newspaper, the *Bulletin*, criticized school expenses along much the same lines as the *Monitor*. It first laid out its conception of the proper tasks of the public schools: "the main object of the common school system has been to give the rising generation a thorough grounding in the English language and those accomplishments which form the basis of ordinary commercial intercourse. Anything ulterior to this may be regarded as foreign to any public obligation and belonging solely to private considerations."[23] By these standards, the course of study of the San Francisco public schools needed "considerable judicious pruning." Once again, "special subjects" were singled out for criticism. The *Bulletin* charged that the introduction of French and German into "certain schools which have been designated 'cosmopolitan schools,' [has] converted the latter very largely into 'class' institutions." It finally recommended that because of the expense, "every branch not strictly consistent with the accepted idea of what popular education ought to be" should be eliminated.[24] Eventually, opponents of foreign languages, though they lost many battles, would win the war.

In the early 1880s the San Francisco public school system was one of many municipal departments to have its budget cut. As a consequence, it trimmed its curriculum along the lines recommended by critics. Special teachers of French, German, music, drawing, and bookkeeping were discharged.[25] As a result the number of pupils studying foreign languages declined throughout the 1880s; in 1879, 2,917 took German or French; in 1882 the number fell to 1,885, and in 1888 it was no more than 1,635. The number of grammar or primary schools offering foreign-language instruction also shrank from nine in 1875 to seven in 1879, and to only four by 1882.[26] Although the decline was hastened by political opposition to foreign-language instruction, it must also be recognized that as time passed the schools had less of a stake in German and French instruction. Private schools teaching the children of immigrants in their native tongues failed to develop, and San Francisco's public schools, no longer faced with competition from this sector, could afford to narrow their curriculum to English-language instruction alone.

In Chicago, foreign-language instruction also blossomed as an issue in the midst of economic and fiscal difficulties. The first volley in the "war on the fads" was shot by the Chicago *Tribune* in early 1893, with an editorial urging that the salaries of teachers specializing in "ridiculous" subjects such as "singing, drawing, mudpie-making and modern foreign languages should be cut to the lowest figure."[27] The attack was then carried forward by several members of the board, including Alfred S. Trude, who was incidentally the newspaper's attorney as well.[28] The city council, responsible for approving the school budget, became involved by passing a resolution requiring that the board of education's budget be itemized before council approval would be granted.[29]

Initially, the definition of fad was unclear, but in February the *Tribune* chose to specify the German language in another editorial attacking unnecessary subjects in the public schools.[30] The inclusion of German in the controversy was of crucial importance in its development. Chicago's German community was a politically potent force that only a few months earlier had succeeded in electing Governor Altgeld to office. City elections were just a few months off, and board members had little desire to arouse the ire of the Germans.[31]

The German community was quick to react to the *Tribune's* attack. Leaders of the community convened mass meetings and sent vocal representatives to school-board sessions.[32] The board sought to protect itself—at first by delaying any action on the issue, then by proposing a separate resolution on each subject included in the "special subjects" area. The *Tribune* responded by accusing board members of logrolling to protect their "pet fads."[33]

Representatives of the labor movement next became involved as proponents of the fads. Led by Thomas J. Morgan, the Trades and Labor Assembly first adopted a neutral, fact-finding attitude and urged the board to delay action on the special-studies issue. However, in mid-March the labor group came out squarely behind special studies, claiming that the children of workers "are just as much entitled to study music, delsarte, physical culture and have a knowledge of form and shape as those . . . of the wealthy."[34] From then on the labor spokesmen joined the representatives of the German community and women's organizations in attendance at board meetings and mass rallies in support of the fads. Chicago's only profad newspaper, an immigrant-oriented paper entitled the *Inter Ocean*, also began an earnest campaign to save the special studies.[35]

The school board, through various evasive tactics, avoided discussing the fads—especially the German-language issue—until well after the late-March mayoral election.[36] It then produced a compromise that was more or less acceptable to all sides. First the school board decided by a vote of eleven to seven to eliminate German instruction from the four primary grades but to keep the language at the higher grade levels. Many of those who opposed other fads voted to retain German instruction in the higher grades. This resolution seems to have been acceptable to the German community; the editor of the most important German newspaper had in fact endorsed such a plan in his mayoral campaign. Prominent Germans were also guaranteed a veto over future school-board appointees by Mayor Harrison and thus were given insurance against further incursions into German-language instruction.[37]

In the meantime, the Committee on School Management hammered out a solution to the teaching of other special subjects. The committee's report, adopted unanimously by the board, noted that the special studies had great educational value and stipulated that the time devoted to them should be reduced but not eliminated.[38] The board's action seemed acceptable to all parties. Public agitation over the fads had waned after the decision concerning German-language instruction and was not renewed when the board announced its decision to reduce the time devoted to other special subjects. The *Tribune* applauded the board for taking action to secure more classroom space. Although the controversy over special studies continued throughout the late 1890s and early 1900s, the board decision marked the end of the war on fads as such.

The "fads and frills" conflict is especially interesting because it pitted two basic theories of education against each other. To the *Tribune* and its supporters, these curricular developments interfered with the common school's primary purpose—to inculcate the minimum amount of education that would prepare the children of workers for low-skill occupations and nonauthoritative political roles. The common school, the paper said, should provide for the "children of the masses" and "education for bread-winners." "The ideal of a common school education . . . means to lay the foundation of a practical education . . . enough to fit the child for ordinary work."[39] This meant restricting the curriculum to the rudimentary subjects. Special subjects were "costly luxuries" that "fritter away" the pupils' time.[40]

Organized groups of workers, on the other hand, embraced these curricular reforms and the ideology of "objective" or "scientific" education they represented. In the view of Thomas Morgan, the most articulate educational spokesman of organized labor in the 1890s, the realization of the democratic ideal of government by consent of the people required the "widest, deepest, and best education of every member of the state and nation."[41]

Many unionists also thought that education should provide working-class children with the kind of craft-related skills that, as mechanization progressed, were increasingly difficult to acquire in the workplace. Thus in early 1893, in response to attacks on the special subjects by the *Tribune* and others, the machinists union sent the following petition to the board of education: "the Machinist Union respectfully urges the utmost practical extension of the principle of manual training in the public schools, and respectfully insists that the coeducation of hand and brain will produce better workmen and better citizens."[42]

While the opponents of special studies viewed them as more appropriate for private schools or for more advanced students, the labor movement defended their place in the primary grades, which was as much of the public school system as most children ever experienced. Morgan was fond of pointing out that only 22 percent of the workmen's children ever went beyond the fourth year of school, so that unless the other 78 percent received drawing, singing, and these special studies in the primary grades, they would never get them.[43] The attempt to limit special studies to the higher grades was seen by unionists as an expansion of the educational oportunities open to wealthy families at the expense of the "common schools." In the words of Henry D. Lloyd, a leading figure in labor politics, "In places like the nineteenth ward, there are not enough school rooms for children, while in wealthier portions of the city, there are expenditures for high schools. The attack on fads is a continuation of this same policy."[44] Just as the postponement of quality education to higher grades was unacceptable to labor spokesmen, so was its relegation to parochial and private schools.[45]

Two aspects of the conflict over "fads and frills" deserve emphasis in conclusion. First, in marked contrast to the portrait of curricular reform painted by some writers,[46] public school expansion encountered opposition from business and financial interests but enjoyed popular support. The strongest backing for curricular innovation came from labor and ethnic groups. Second, the outcome was a characteristically pluralist compromise in which all sides felt their interests had been taken into account. As business leaders urged, the most costly aspects of the innovations were curtailed, especially during periods of financial retrenchment. But the principle of a diversified curriculum in general, and foreign-language education in particular, was never conceded. Indeed the school system, always eager to expand its role, would in the future find new ways to diversify its operations and broaden its social support.

SECONDARY EDUCATION AND THE STRATIFICATION OF THE PUBLIC SCHOOL SYSTEM

The early establishment of high schools can also be understood as an organizational response to a competitive environment. In this case public schools were concerned not about alienating any well-organized ethnic interest but about attracting a diffuse middle-class population that still generally preferred private day or boarding schools to any public institution. Anxious to avoid "charity schools," educators realized that building the "common school" required, above all, the commitment and loyalty of this diffuse middle class. Yet the pursuit of this goal seldom pitted school officials against working-class groups. On the contrary, trade unionists tended to support public secondary schools, seeing these institutions as the main channel of economic opportunity for children of working-class families. Secondary-school officials had more to fear from business and taxpayer opposition, especially in times of fiscal constraint, for, just as foreign languages could be defined as a frill, so a classical secondary education could be defined by penny-pinching conservatives as beyond the proper scope of a publicly supported institution.

Because public schools sought middle-class support, high schools were quickly established in most cities. When public schools were opened in Atlanta in 1872, two sex-segregated high schools claimed a share of scarce educational resources even at a time when primary schools remained grossly overcrowded. Chicago's initial high school, the first in the nation to include both boys and girls, opened in 1856. San Francisco's Boys' High School opened the same year, and its Girls' High School opened less than a decade later. School officials always spoke in egalitarian tones when defending the public high schools against the charge that they had an elite bias. Yet San Francisco's superintendent contended in 1880 that the need to attract "the best class" of respectable citizens required support for secondary education.[47] A Chicago superintendent also argued along these lines, suggesting that "the wealth of the city" that had "furnished the means for the elementary education of the majority" had a right to claim "the higher advantages it seeks" in secondary schooling.[48]

Nineteenth-century high schools were not the mass institutions that developed in the next century. In Atlanta enrollment remained small, growing from only 295 students in 1874 to 638 in 1890.[49] Average daily attendance in Chicago's public secondary schools was only 2 percent of the population aged fourteen to seventeen years in 1870 and only 6 percent by the 1890s.[50] No more than 4 percent of San Francisco's public-school students were in the high schools at any point in the nineteenth century.[51]

The socioeconomic status of high-school students also revealed the selectivity of the institutions. Students in San Francisco's high schools "came in general from upper middle-class homes in the city. In 1867, 45 percent of the students had fathers who were merchants or professional men, while only 15 percent came from the many homes of unskilled or semi-skilled workmen in the city. Children whose parents came from non–English speaking countries seldom attended high school."[52] Data on parents' occupations supplied by the students at Boys' High School show that children of artisans and workers were poorly represented in the school (see table 3.1). Because the figures are based on students' identification of their parents' occupation, they do not neatly coincide with census categories and should be interpreted with caution. Nonetheless, it is clear that in 1878 and 1883 both semiskilled and unskilled workers were greatly underrepresented among high-school students' parents. High-white-collar workers were greatly overrepresented among the students' parents. In 1878, 43.8 percent of the children listed high-white-collar occupations for the parents, and in 1883, 39.0 percent did so. These numbers greatly exceed the 5 percent white-collar employment in the entire city.

One of the reasons working-class children were poorly represented in the nineteenth-century public high school was that few working-class families could afford to forgo the immediate income that would be lost by keeping young workers out of the labor market. In addition, school policy contributed to the exclusiveness of public high schools. Until 1881 strict entrance exams in Chicago enforced the notion that the high school was an institution distinct from the elementary school with its policy of universal admis-

TABLE 3.1 Employment of Parents of Boys' High School Students,
San Francisco, 1878–90

Occupation	Percentage of Parents Employed		Occupation as Percentage of Work Force
	1878	1883	1890
High white collar			
and merchants[a]	43.8	39.0	5.0
Low white collar	27.7	40.7	25.7
Artisans and			
skilled workers[a]	14.9	12.7	28.4
Semiskilled workers	9.6	4.3	27.9
Unskilled workers	4.0	3.3	12.9
Total percentage	100.0	100.0	99.9
Total employed (n)[b]	249	300	144,082

Sources: San Francisco, *Superintendent of Public Instruction, Annual Report*, 1878, 81–82, 1883, 14–15.

[a]The categorization of occupations follows Thernstrom as cited in Erie (1975) with two exceptions. Merchants are all grouped in the high-white-collar category because it is impossible to determine the amount of property they owned and thus to divide them on this basis into the high- or low-white-collar categories. Artisans are all grouped with skilled workers because it is impossible to determine whether they owned their own shops and thus should be categorized as small proprietors in the low-white-collar category.

[b]The 1878 total excludes thirty-six parents who are listed in the original source as having no employment, and the 1883 total excludes many widows and retired persons as well as those who could not find work. The totals also exclude several listings that are impossible to classify such as "agitator," "paperwarehouse," or "vinegar and pickle works." For most of these it was impossible to tell whether the parent owned or was employed in the enterprise listed.

sion. Although San Francisco's early high schools did not have admission requirements other than graduation from grammar school, in the 1870s school officials grew concerned about the number of "unqualified pupils" who, according to the principal of Girls' High, were "a tax on the public, a terror to the teachers, and a discredit to the school."[53] In 1879 the deputy superintendent, contending "that the High Schools contained at least a fourth more scholars than ought to be there," favored a separate standard for grammar-school graduation and high-school admission. On the other hand, the view that secondary education was appropriate for all students was also expressed. Even after the separate standard of admission was set in 1880, the principal of Boys' High School criticized this policy, arguing that the high school should be seen as "but a continuation of the Grammar School."[54]

The heavy emphasis on a classical curriculum also discouraged attendance by a broad clientele. Atlanta's Boys' High School provided a purely classical course of study throughout the nineteenth century. Chicago's secondary schools offered three distinct programs—classical, English, and normal—until 1875. San Francisco's Boys' High School concentrated on preparing students for college. The opening of the University of California nearby drew away many of the school's students because a high-school diploma was not required for admission until 1884. Nonetheless, the goal of providing a basis for higher education exerted a strong influence on the curriculum of San Francisco's Boys' High School.

The select student body of public secondary schools and their heavy emphasis on a classical curriculum provided occasion for controversy, with critics charging that the public high school was an elitist institution. School officials staunchly defended secondary education against these attacks. With its classical curriculum, the secondary school seemed the pinnacle of public education, an inspiration to pupils in the lower grades and a means of attracting the "best class" of students, who might otherwise attend private boarding or day schools. In spite of the low representation of their children among high-school students, working-class groups joined the supporters of public secondary education because they viewed public education as their main chance of obtaining a better life for their children.

Attacks on secondary education were more successful during periods of financial stress. In San Francisco, as the financial crisis of the late 1870s deepened, the social unrest that accompanied depressed economic conditions prompted many to blame popular discontent on education. John Swett, principal of Girls' High School, cited the source of public criticism—hard times, high taxes, and the feeling that "vice, crime, idleness and poverty are the results of overeducation."[55] Critics included the San Francisco *Call*, which argued, "There seems to be no good reason for introducing into public education a learning which belongs appropriately to an academic course."[56]

The high schools became a major focus of this attack partly because San Francisco's secondary school system was in a precarious position. The use of state funds for secondary education was forbidden by the state constitution, so high-school expenditures were a disproportionate drain on the local school system's resources. The *Call* editorialized that "a very small proportion [of students] can devote their time to study the fourteen years required to go through the entire course," and thus the paper questioned whether "it is equally the duty of the taxpayer to furnish the means for the high education which but one hundred would avail themselves of." The *Call* contended that sufficient schooling to enable students "to perform the ordinary duties of citizenship was necessary, but that beyond that level other considerations must justify the expenditure of public funds on secondary education."[57] The 1878 San Francisco superintendent's report summarized these concerns:

> Some hold that higher education is a luxury, and should be enjoyed, if enjoyed at all, as other luxuries are, by those who are able to pay for it. Others think that the middle and lower classes are educated to discontent, if they pass beyond the grammar school. Still others object that High Schools are maintained at public expense for the educational support of the children of the wealthy; that in fact, the middle and lower classes are not largely represented in the High School.[58]

In support of the high schools, the superintendents and principals argued that the poor must have an equal chance at education in order to maintain "open avenues of success" and "prevent the existence of an aristocracy of education."[59] The interest of the state in securing both intelligent supporters of republican government and a prosperous citizenry called for public secondary education. School officials endeavored to prove that high schools drew students from a cross section of the community and were a force for equality. In 1880 the superintendent said:

> an examination of all the state and city reports at hand, which represent nearly every section of the Union, proves, beyond a shadow of a doubt, that the children of mechanics, tradesmen and laborers attend the High Schools in a ratio equal to their attendance in the grammar schools. . . . If the opposition in certain quarters to the liberal maintenance of High Schools should take on the character of a warfare against the secondary system of education, the main strength and support of the system would be drawn from the ranks of the poor (i.e., people of moderate circumstances).[60]

Although the superintendent's own data indicate that workers' children were underrepresented in the public high schools (see table 3.1), school officials seem to have been correct in their assertion that working-class parents defended the public high school as necessary for educational equality. Representatives of working-class organizations took just such a stand at the state constitutional convention of 1879. There a delegate from the Workingmen's party, argued that "if the state can only provide for the education of its children to a limited degree, then from that point on must education be limited to children of the rich".[61]

Although the debate over high schools continued throughout the 1880s, the school board, instead of cutting secondary-school expenses, made the curriculum of the high schools more practically oriented. The addition of commercial classes and, later, the establishment of a separate Commercial High School in the mid-1880s silenced the critics and protected the expanding organizational prerogatives of San Francisco's public school system. The superintendent revealed that the new school was designed to meet the demands of parents and businessmen who claimed that public schooling did not teach children skills appropriate to business. "The Commercial High School," he said, was established "for our graduates from the grammar school who cannot afford or do not wish a three-year scientific or classical course but . . . [would like] such instruction as will help them make a living."[62]

With this decision, repeated and affirmed in subsequent decades, the importance school officials placed on organizational expansion becomes even more apparent. Faced with a choice between a classical curriculum for a small, elite segment of the population or a more differentiated curriculum serving a wider range of the teenage population, public schools seldom hesitated. They increasingly welcomed children of working-class, immigrant groups to the high school, and they increasingly softened admission requirements and broadened their curricular offerings. Vocational education was soon the central curricular issue for the public schools.

Manual Training, Vocational Education, and the Relation between School and Work

In the view of Lawrence Cremin, the 1876 Philadelphia Centennial Exposition was a tribute to industry and an acknowledgement of its success in "the world wide competition for industrial supremacy."[63] The relation of education to progress was one of the exhibition's main themes, and the education display included examples of tools from Russia. Seemingly interesting only to a few craftsmen, these tools marked the beginning of a far-reaching pedagogical change in American education because they represented a systematic, "progressive" way to teach the skills necessary for learning a trade. One of the American educators attending the exhibition was Calvin M. Woodward, a faculty member at Washington University in Saint Louis. While teaching a course in applied mechanics, Woodward decided to have the students make wooden models in order to illustrate a particularly difficult point. When the college carpenter came in to help supervise the work, Woodward realized the students were unable to use tools in even the simplest way. Putting first things first, he began teaching tool work, not with any immediate vocational goal in mind but as an important component in learning larger concepts.[64] During the 1870s Woodward became an outspoken critic of the public schools, challenging them to recognize the need for teachers of manual as well as cognitive skills.

Woodward's challenge of "educating the whole boy" did not go unmet. William T. Harris, the former Saint Louis school superintendent, argued that Woodward's ideas were a "dangerous survival of Rousseauism" because they failed to distinguish between higher and lower faculties in the individual. Harris noted that "marbles, quoits, baseball and jackstraws" were educative as well as tools, but that did not mean their place was in the classroom. To Harris, the difference between manual education and teaching general subject matter was "the difference between a piece of baked bread, which nourishes for the day, and the seed-corn, which is the possibility of countless harvests."[65]

While educators debated these issues in pedagogical terms, the organizational interests of public schools greatly shaped the eventual outcome. As the school system expanded its secondary-education role, its curriculum inevitably adapted to its new clientele. In addition, public schools could not ignore the increasing number and prominence of nonpublic institutions offering one or another form of vocational training. Prodded in separate directions by business and by labor, the public schools accepted Woodward's arguments, not necessarily because they were pedagogically sounder than Harris's, but because they made institutional sense.

Establishment of Rival Institutions

Many business leaders were among the most vigorous and effective proponents of manual training and vocational education in the late nineteenth century. They not only had the desire to see a better-trained work force, but they also had the resources to establish rival institutions if the public school system did not fulfill this need. Chicago's business community began to agitate for manual training earlier than San Francisco's. In 1881 the Citizens' Association of Chicago, whose members included some of the most important businessmen in the city, issued a report criticizing the public schools for failure to provide "practical training, that training of hand and eye which would enable those leaving our schools to be useful and productive members of society almost immediately after leaving high school."[66] At the same time, the Chicago *Tribune* took up the cause. For over a year, weekly articles advocating "practical education," "manual training," and "industrial education" in the public schools appeared in the paper. In 1882 several prominent businessmen including Marshall Field, Richard Crane, George Pullman, and John Crerar began efforts to open a private manual training school. Over the next two years the plans were carried out by the Commercial Club, and in 1884 the Chicago Manual Training School was opened. Although the school's curriculum included some traditional academic subjects, its major focus was on the use of "shop work" to train both the hand and the mind. In establishing the school and maintaining close watch over it as members of its board of directors, Chicago's leading businessmen were interested in more than educational reform. As one observer who was close to the leaders at the time put it, "being men of large experience in practical affairs they recognized that the destruction of the apprenticeship system would tend to a decline of American industrial power, hence they . . . founded this school to secure better mechanics—more skillful workers in iron and wood."[67]

By the early 1890s, San Francisco's business community also showed considerable interest in industrial training. Instead of pressuring the public schools to reform their curriculum, leading businessmen concentrated on founding private industrial arts schools. The Lick school opened early in the decade and offered training in the machine trades. At the same time, an endowment had been procured from a leading San Francisco merchant, J. Clute Wilmerding, who desired to found a school where "our boys shall be trained to earn a living with little study and plenty of work." The major business organization in the city, the Merchants Association, mounted a drive for donors to supplement the endowment. When it opened at the turn of the century, the Wilmerding school offered a course of instruction geared primarily to the building trades. Both the Lick and the Wilmerding schools were private institutions but did not charge tuition. These actions by the local business community prompted changes in school policy concerning manual training.

Response of Public Schools

Although public schools in time responded to the challenge these rival institutions posed, educational leaders in Chicago and San Francisco were initially divided in their estimation of the inherent value of manual training. As early as the 1870s, some school officials in both cities proposed altering the curriculum to incorporate more practical subjects. Among the educators who supported the idea of manual training in the public schools was California state superintendent Ezra Carr, who argued: "I hold it to be a correct principle that while the common school does not aim to make farmers or mechanics, but leaves this to special schools, that it is the business of the common schools (which educate the masses of the industrial population) to teach the elements of technical knowledge both scientific and artistic."[68] Similarly, in 1877 Chicago's school superintendent spoke of the necessity to change the curriculum, saying that students should be provided with "a wider intelligence and a more facile hand," including "manual skill" and the "habits of industry."[69]

At first most educators neither heeded these calls for modernization nor responded to appeals to national pride. Although the bulk of the educational community accepted the notion that schools had a utilitarian function, many officials felt this did not require specialized education for trades. Tradition-minded school officials recoiled at the suggestion that the curriculum should be so differentiated, seeing such attempts as a violation of the common-school ideal. The same California state education convention that heard Superintendent Carr urge the introduction of industrial education into the public-school curriculum voted for a resolution stating that "the attempt to combine practical instruction in agricultural and mechanical pursuits with the course of study in our public institutions of learning, except for purposes of illustration or experiment, is erroneous in theory and a failure in practice."[70] A committee appointed to study the matter reported on some of the difficulties that would arise were such schools established. Workers "would risé in rebellion against a course which, if carried out, would result in flooding the country with a class of workmen entering into direct competition with them." Furthermore, such schools would probably produce poor workmen due to "irregularity of attendance [and] a lack of interest in the work, [imposed at] an age at which manual labor is usually irksome and to a certain extent unnatural." When the full convention adopted a resolution proposed by the committe, it "deprecated any and all attempts and projects to divide up and fritter away our but too scant school fund on experiments of doubtful value or expediency."[71]

Whereas in San Francisco the 1870s and 1880s were a period of debate concerning the place of vocational education in the public schools, by the 1890s the introduction of manual training was a fait accompli. We have already seen that the board had established a Commercial High School in 1883. A decade later it also formed a Committe on Manual Training, which recommended that manual training be provided in two or three of the city's high schools and in half of the grammer schools. The report stated that "such training does not attempt to manufacture mechanics, but to give practical ideas to all pupils . . . and to obtain proper respect for manual labor."[72] It was clear that educators were influenced by the efforts of businessmen who set up private institutes training pupils for specific trades. Private efforts, they argued, "stand upon a plane above the reach of a majority of boys . . . for one boy they may educate and save, thousands get away." If the public schools were to establish a sufficient manual training department, the vast majority of pupils would benefit. Thus, spurred by competition from private industrial schools, educators began to recognize that "if we are to carry more pupils beyond the grammar schools we will find the greater proportion of them attracted to the business and manual training courses rather than the classical."[73] During these years, the board oversaw the construction of the Polytechnic High School, which was equipped with machine-forging, carpenter, and wood-turning shops, laboratories for physics and chemistry, and rooms for mechanical and freehand drawing. The superintendent called the offering an "act of justice" to boys who desired to enter mercantile or industrial life.[74]

Thus manual training was fully incorporated into the public-school curriculum only when educators became convinced it was necessary to attract and hold a new organizational clientele. Yet efforts to relate the public-school course of study more closely to the needs of the workplace brought the school system critics as well as supporters. As the concept of manual training became more clearly defined in school policy, many of those who had supported it in principle attacked it in practice. Businessmen who emphasized the skill-specific aspects of vocational education criticized the pedagogical formulations that appealed to school officials but seemed extravagant to businessmen. As manual training became identified more closely with preparation for specific trades, the labor movement began to perceive threats to its control over the labor market and apprentice system. The issues identified by the various sides would continue to be addressed in the early twentieth century, and eventually the federal government would enter the vocational-education debate through the Smith-Hughes Act of 1912.

The Voice of Labor

Although school officials were prompted to expand their vocational programming largely in response to the growing number of rival private institutions, their actions were not taken in the face of organized labor opposition. While the trade unions were sometimes ambivalent about the value of vocational education, their support steadily grew as the idea became increasingly popular. In the end labor, which feared the formation of "scab factories" controlled directly by businessmen, became one of the most vigorous proponents of publicly controlled vocational education.

Initially, labor was uncertain about vocational training. While recognizing the failures of the existing apprentice system in recruiting new workers, it nevertheless saw the system's abolishment as a threat to labor's control of recruitment and as a setback to its gains in higher wages and better working conditions. But vocational education was very popular and seemed to fill a need, and the question for labor eventually became not whether to have it, but how to run it and what should be taught.

As early as the 1880s, *Truth*, the leading labor paper in San Francisco, expressed admiration for manual training schools, consistent with its more general position that "schools must be free and the education of all compulsory and uniform and . . . [provide] practical useful knowledge."[75] A number of prominent labor leaders argued more specifically for vocational training. In the words of John Hittel, writing in the San Francisco *Alta*, "if America is to compete with England, Germany and France in the industrial production or in the honors of the inventions and scientific discoveries of the future, her children must be more highly educated. Improved industrial schools are indispensable . . . to prosperity and progress."[76] Basically most working-class organizations had been early supporters of some kind of manual training, and as early as the first years of the 1870s the Mechanics Deliberative Assembly had recommended to the state legislature a bill proposing that "labor schools be attached to the public school system."[77]

In Chicago, the rhetoric of working-class support for manual training reflected the broad social struggles in which labor was involved at the time. Manual training was seen as an important way to bring about the "justice that was due to a class that has heretofore been discriminated against in the matter of education."[78] The *Knights of Labor* urged that "those who are destined to labor for a living should be given a chance to learn the use of tools and machinery at schools provided by the state, the same as the state now provides an education in the higher branches to those who are now preparing for professional life."[79] Indeed, the paper went so far as to blame the failure to enact universal industrial education on the "satanic press of the 'protected' tax-gathering plutocracy."[80]

By the turn of the century labor's diffuse support for vocational education became more focused. As businessmen rallied behind former Chicago school superintendent Edwin Cooley's proposals for a separate system of vocational education, labor formed a close alliance with other public-school officials on behalf of a "common school" that would provide both academic and vocational training. The pedagogical justification for linking industrial and traditional education emphasized the value of conjoint training of hand and brain. But the labor-school alliance was held together by forces more powerful than any educational philosophy. Labor recognized that it could have greater influence over the curriculum of public-school programs than it could have over any separate set of institutions closely watched by business elites. School officials, still concerned about the formation of rival institutions, welcomed labor support. That the alliance was largely successful in shaping the terms of the Smith-Hughes Act of 1917 testifies not only to its own power but also to the prestige public schools had achieved by this time.

CONCLUSION

Curricular expansion in the public schools occurred in response to demands from different groups that had the political power to force such an expansion or that had the resources to set up competing systems unless their demands were met. These external pressures caused conflicts within the school system itself as well as conflicts between the schools and various societal groups. The ideology of a common, undifferentiated public-school curriculum, the legacy of Horace Mann, was a strong influence on educational thought throughout the nineteenth century, and some school officials were unwilling to accept anything other than the traditional curriculum. Yet schools gradually adapted to the diverse demands of the larger community.

In this larger community, major conflicts over the purposes of public education were regularly manifested. Chicago's "fads and frills" controversy, involving foreign languages, arts, and music, found business interests and much of the local press propounding the view that education should be limited to the basic, practical subjects. Labor took the stance that all children were entitled to "enrichment" courses and that if the public schools did not teach them they would not be available to the children of the working class. Because of its large numbers and politically adept leadership, the German community was able to have its language taught in the public schools.

The secondary schools were also established in spite of critics who argued that as long as the primary schools were not adequately financed there was no money available for elite secondary institutions. In addition, critics attributed the social unrest of the times to overeducation of the masses. But in the course of these debates, organized groups representing workers supported an expanding high school. Even though their children did not attend the high schools in large numbers, these groups viewed education as giving their more able children a chance for a better life. Educators themselves provided unflagging support for the secondary schools, although controversies did erupt from time to time over the issue of whether high schools should be separate institutions or extensions of grammar schools.

The public schools did not attempt to establish manual trade schools until industry took the lead and opened a number of institutes. Attempts were then made to incorporate manual training into the more traditional curriculum by teaching skill-oriented courses such as woodworking. When these types of courses were attacked by businesses who wanted schools to limit their program to trade-specific, practical skills, labor groups once again defended the schools against conservative criticism.

In periods of financial recession, of course, cries for retrenchment could be heard from large sections of the community. At such times those who wished to limit the size and range of public schools pressed their case with special vigor. Although it was not eliminated, foreign-language instruction was cut back, as were other special studies such as music, drawing, and more pedagogical forms of manual training which did not conform to the rising expectation that the curriculum should be made more practical. Consequently, by the end of the century the debate over the purposes of public education was subtly shifted from questions of cultural incorporation and citizenship to those of compatibility with the demands of the labor market. Thus businessmen could attack foreign-language instruction, music, and some forms of manual training as frivolous departures from the fundamental purposes of public education at the same time that they called for additional courses in the practical skills required for growing industrial economies. Working-class and ethnic groups, on the other hand, defended the differentiated curriculum as an essential ingredient of a democratic society. At the same time, these groups sought practical courses that would widen avenues of economic opportunity. School officials, for their part, maneuvered to protect and expand their organization in the context of these changing political pressures.

4 The Politics of Resource Allocation

In the late nineteenth century, cities in the northern United States were places of extraordinary human diversity. As immigrants from all the countries of Europe and many other parts of the world made the United States their home, former villages became great metropolitan centers harboring large foreign concentrations. For example, in 1896 in the city of Chicago there were fifteen ethnic groups that had reached a size of at least sixteen thousand people, or 1 percent of the city's population.[1]

The way the schools adapted to this ethnic pluralism is a complex and contentious issue, and one of the questions with which the "revision" of American educational history has concerned itself. Some revisionists explain an increasing level of school attendance among Chicago's immigrant groups as a complex adjustment to a capitalist wage-labor system; that is, immigrants saw the connection between education and well-paid jobs and thereby were forced to take an extremely utilitarian view of education.[2] Others discuss the issue of inequality, engaging the reader with anecdotes about ethnic discrimination and conflict in the schoolrooms of Boston and New York.[3] Still others present scattered quantitative information on expenditures for the education of children of different socioeconomic backgrounds. Poorer children, they purport to show, not only go to school for fewer years but are treated less benevolently when they are there.[4] The harshest claim of all comes from Michael Katz, who believes not only that the children of the affluent "get the best marks and the best jobs," but also that the questioning of dominant social and industrial values is precluded by the very structure and purpose of American education.[5]

Yet few studies have found a way to systematically assess how schools as organizations responded in general practice to ethnic change. Instead we have been left with broad generalizations drawn from quite specific incidents and situations. But while ethnic and class discrimination certainly occurred in classrooms, and while many school leaders undoubtedly had mixed motives in desiring to educate foreigners, the pervasiveness of the problem of intolerance and its institutionalization in the public school system as a whole cannot necessarily be inferred from events in places like Beverly, Massachusetts, in 1860.[6]

One way to assess the historical level of ethnic discrimination more systematically is to estimate the way the nineteenth-century school system allocated its limited resources. Much valuable information on resource allocation is of course forever lost. We cannot use survey techniques to discern how pupils were allocated among classrooms within schools, how teachers related to individual pupils, or which children were given favored access to extracurricular activities. However, archival sources do allow for some gross estimates of school practices, and in the absence of more refined information these are worth exploring. In this chapter we shall focus on two indicators of school allocative policies: the pupil/teacher ratio in individual schools and the characteristics of the teaching staff. These data will allow us to consider the evidence that bears on three understandings of how the school system responded to European immigration. These understandings or perspectives we shall identify as native dominance, pluralist, and universalist.

The native dominance understanding claims that people born in the United States and others of Anglo-Saxon descent (for convenience we shall call them Anglos)[7] were able to maintain control of public schools despite the influx of new immigrants. In the view of these analysts, Anglos maintained control of the schools because of their greater wealth, their better education, and their historical control of strategic institutions such as the state legislature and the school system itself. Bowles and Gintis state that "the unequal contest between social control and social justice is evident in the total functioning of U.S. education. The system . . . provides eloquent testimony to the ability of the well-to-do to perpetuate . . . an arrangement which consistently yields to themselves disproportional advantages, while thwarting the aspirations and needs of the working people of the United States."[8] If this argument is correct, Anglos would have received more than their share of the resources of the public school system. That is, Anglo children would have attended less-crowded classes, more education dollars would have been spent on them than on the children of the immigrants, and Anglos would have held more and better jobs in the school system, in proportion to their numbers in the population, than did immigrants.[9]

The pluralist perspective claims that certain powerful immigrant groups wrested control of the city's schools away from the native-born Americans and arranged the distribution of resources so that their own children received a disproportionate share. In the late nineteenth century, for example, Germans constituted one-third of Chicago's population and were in a position of influence within the labor union movement. During this period the Germans succeeded in introducing their native tongue into the public schools as a second language, something no other ethnic group had been able to accomplish. If this view is generally correct, the more powerful immigrant groups would have received the best treatment from the school system. In Chicago, where the Irish and the Germans were politically the best connected, one would expect the children of these groups to have enjoyed higher expenditures per pupil, less-crowded classrooms, and a larger percentage of the available teaching and administrative positions.

The universalist perspective suggests that the bureaucratization of school systems led to the adoption of a norm of universalism in the distribution of school resources. Professional educators, it is contended, tried to remove the control of schools as far as possible from the realm of political parties, placing decision making in the hands of professionals instead. Since the norm of educational opportunity for all was the justification for professional control, bureaucracies would not have discriminated against or in favor of particular groups in their allocation of public resources or their recruitment of staff. Rather, as the basis for universalist decision making one would find examples such as the following formula, used to allocate teachers to districts and individual schools in Chicago in 1968: "In the elementary school the class size from room to room should not deviate any more than is absolutely essential. As a "rule of thumb," the class size from room to room should not deviate by more than 10 percent—15 percent as a maximum. In a large school this deviation should be far less than the 10 to 15 percent."[10]

In addition, conflicts within the organization would be better managed if all members of the organization subscribed to the norm of universalism. Outside actors would be more easily controlled, and demands by specific groups for special treatment could be more easily buffered. Given this view of the nineteenth-century school, the distribution of resources among groups would be fairly equal. Children of all ethnic groups would study in classes of roughly the same size, and teachers would be recruited from the ranks of all ethnic groups roughly in proportion to their numbers in the population.

Data that allowed for a test among these competing hypotheses were available in both Chicago and San Francisco. Both cities were the home of numerous ethnic concentrations that competed for power within their local political systems throughout the late nineteenth century, and both cities reported data on the allocation policies of the school system. Before presenting the information in detail, it may be helpful if we sketch our overall findings. In brief, the evidence with respect to pupil/teacher ratios is most consistent with the universalist perspective. Although schools varied greatly in average class size as a rapidly changing urban population placed uneven burdens on school resources, this variation was only slightly related to the ethnic composition of the school. If native-dominance theorists can be pleased that Anglos did slightly better than average, and if pluralists can applaud the slight success of the Irish, the findings in general best support the claim that schools were uninterested in (or incapable of) systematic ethnic discrimination. Jobs for adults were another matter. In patronage-ridden school systems, public employment was the currency of local politics, and who directed the school board had consequences for teachers and administrators. In the decade after the Civil War, native-born Americans dominated the political crap game, but by the turn of the century immigrant groups—the Irish and the Germans in particular—were making rapid gains. Native dominance eventually gave way to a more pluralist picture.

UNIVERSALIST SCHOOL POLICIES: THE EVIDENCE ON CLASS SIZE

Class size, as measured by average daily attendance (ADA) per teacher, was high in the nineteenth century, and classroom crowding was a concern of parents and school people alike. That overcrowding was the norm can hardly be contested; differences of opinion have arisen only with respect to its social correlates. To test the validity of the three perspectives on the public schools' treatment of immigrants, we obtained data relating class size to ethnic characteristics of the population in Chicago for the 1898 school year. We found wide variations in average class size among the city's schools. Class size for the 215 elementary schools in a random sample varied from 30.7 to 69.8 pupils per teacher. Examination of the data revealed no clear geographic patterns in the degree of crowding. Areas near the center of the city were no more likely to have crowded schools than were outlying areas. However, it was still possible that crowding was greater in ethnic neighborhoods than in Anglo neighborhoods, even though geographic patterns were difficult to identify.

Determining the levels of crowding experienced by pupils belonging to the various ethnic groups was a multistep process. Using data on pupil attendance by school from the superintendents' annual reports, plus lists of teacher appointments by school as recorded in the proceedings of the board of education, we were able to determine an average class size for each elementary school. Next we determined the distribution of ethnic groups among schools by making use of the school census taken by the Chicago school system in May 1898. In this census the school board reported the number of persons belonging to each of twenty-seven ethnic groups (including native-born Americans with native-born parents) residing in each of the city's more than one thousand precincts. (See the appendix to this chapter for a fuller discussion of the data sources and treatment.) Assuming that the ethnicity of the pupils in a school would correspond to the ethnicity of the population of the precinct where the school was situated, we used data from

215 of Chicago's 222 elementary schools.[11] The number of students of each ethnic group attending each school was estimated using the following formula:

$$S_{es} \quad = \quad (P_{ep}/P_p) * ADA_s$$

where
$$
\begin{aligned}
S_{es} \quad &= \quad \text{Students } (S) \text{ of ethnic group } (e) \\
&\qquad \text{in school } (s) \\
P_{ep} \quad &= \quad \text{Population } (P) \text{ of ethnic} \\
&\qquad \text{group } (e) \text{ in precinct } (p) \\
&\qquad (\text{precinct where school} \\
&\qquad \text{is situated}) \\
P_p \quad &= \quad \text{Total population } (P) \text{ of} \\
&\qquad \text{precinct } (p) \\
ADA_s \quad &= \quad \text{Average Daily Attendance } (ADA) \\
&\qquad \text{reported for schools } (s)
\end{aligned}
$$

Given these estimates of the number of students of each ethnic group in each school in the sample, we estimated the average crowding each group experienced by computing a weighted average using the following formula:

$$ADA/T_e \quad = \quad \sum_{s=1}^{215} (S_{es}/S_e) * ADA/T_s$$

where
$$
\begin{aligned}
ADA/T_e \quad &= \quad \text{Average Daily Attendance Teacher} \\
&\qquad \text{experienced by ethnic group } (e) \\
S_{es} \quad &= \quad \text{Estimated total number} \\
&\qquad \text{of students } (S) \text{ of ethnic} \\
&\qquad \text{group } (e) \text{ in school } (s) \\
S_e \quad &= \quad \text{Estimated total number} \\
&\qquad \text{of students } (S) \text{ of} \\
&\qquad \text{ethnic group } (e) \text{ in all} \\
&\qquad \text{schools, obtained by summing} \\
&\qquad S_{es} \text{ estimates for each} \\
&\qquad \text{school} \\
ADA/T_s \quad &= \quad ADA/\text{Teacher for school } (s) \\
&\qquad \text{computed as follows:} \\
&\qquad ADA \text{ for school divided by} \\
&\qquad \text{number of teachers in school}
\end{aligned}
$$

When the data were analyzed according to these formulas, the results showed little difference in school crowding among Chicago's ethnic groups. Table 4.1 divides Chicagoans into six major categories—Anglos, Irish,

TABLE 4.1 Average Class Size for the Largest Ethnic Groups,
Chicago, 1897–98

Group	Average Daily Attendance per Teacher	Group as Percentage of City Population
Italians	46.9	1.2
Anglos[a]	47.6	32.1
Irish	47.7	13.4
Swedish	48.3	6.0
All others[b]	48.5	20.7
Germans	48.9	26.5

[a]Includes American, English, Scottish, Welsh, and Canadian.
[b]Includes remaining immigrant groups listed in table 4.3.

Swedish, Germans, Italians, and all others (including Poles, Russians, Norwegians, Bohemians, and all the smaller groups listed in table 4.3). Except for the Italians, who were included because the literature has identified them as an ethnic group particularly subject to educational discrimination,[12] these were the largest and most politically prominent groups in late-nineteenth-century Chicago.

But even though the political competition among these groups was sometimes fierce, the allocation of school resources among them was essentially the same. On the average, the Italians had two pupils per classroom fewer than the Germans, and the other three groups—Anglos, Swedish, and Irish—fell in between, all averaging about forty-eight per classroom. One should not conclude from these findings that the Italians were especially favored, because the percentage of Italians in the sample precincts is too small to allow for a precise estimate. One can say with considerable confidence, however, that variation in crowding in Chicago's schools was largely unrelated to the ethnic background of the pupils.

Another way to analyze the information collected is to divide ethnic groups into Anglos, Irish, persons from other northern European countries, and those from eastern and southern Europe. As can be seen in table 4.2, such an arrangement of the information also reveals little difference in the treatment of children from varied ethnic backgrounds. While the Anglos had an average class size of 47.6 and the Irish 47.7, the eastern and southern European groups, the most recent and supposedly the most poorly treated of the immigrant groups, had an only slightly larger average class size of 48.1. Clearly, the data support a universalist rather than either a pluralist or a native-dominance interpretation of the school system's allocative behavior.

The variation in class size increases as one divides the data into smaller

TABLE 4.2 Average Class Size for All Ethnic Groups, Chicago, 1897–98

Group	Average Daily Attendance per Teacher	Group as Percentage of City Population
Anglos[a]	47.6	32.1
Irish	47.7	13.4
Eastern and southern Europeans and others[b]	48.1	15.8
Northern Europeans[c]	48.8	38.7

[a]Includes American, English, Scottish, Welsh, and Canadian.

[b]Includes Bohemians, Chinese, blacks, Greeks, Hungarians, Italians, Lithuanians, Mexicans, Polish, Russian, Spanish, mixed, and other (see table 4.3 for further explanation).

[c]Includes Belgians, Danes, French, Germans, Hollandish, Norwegians, Swedish, and Swiss.

categories. When all twenty-seven ethnic groups into which the Chicago survey divided its respondents are separately analyzed, the results, as shown in table 4.3, reveal that the most favored group averaged nine fewer pupils per classroom than did the least favored group. But while stating the finding in this way suggests considerable ethnic variability, more careful examination of table 4.1 cautions against making any claim that ethnic groups were treated differentially. In the first place, much of the range is accounted for by three deviant cases—the Lithuanians, who had a class-size average of 3.6 more than any other group, and the blacks and the Mexicans, who had the smallest class-size averages. When these unusual cases are put to one side, the variation among groups is 46.8 to 49.6, or fewer than three pupils per classroom, well within the 10 percent range of variation the Chicago public schools felt was permissible as late as 1968.

These unusual cases, moreover, could very likely be due either to sampling error or to various defects in the historical data set. Two of the extreme cases are ethnic groups that consisted of less than 0.1 percent of the population in the sample precincts. Estimates based on such a small percentage are not sufficiently reliable to warrant any substantive interpretation. And the third unusual case, that of the American blacks, who, according to this data set, were in the most favored schools, must be interpreted cautiously. It may be that blacks, who worked as servants for some of the city's wealthiest residents, were domiciled in adjacent areas and their children thus lived in parts of the city where the class size was smaller. But while this is a possible explanation, it is equally likely that blacks, constituting only 1.4 percent of the population in the sample precincts, were also not present in sufficiently large numbers to permit a reliable estimate. In any case, even if the data are taken at face value, blacks had only four fewer

TABLE 4.3 Average Class Size for Twenty-seven Ethnic Groups, Chicago, 1897–98

Group	Class Size	Percentage of Population
Blacks[a]	43.9	1.4
Mexicans	45.0	0.008
Mixed[b]	46.8	0.3
Italians	46.9	1.2
Russians	46.9	2.1
Canadians	47.5	1.9
Greeks	47.5	0.1
Americans	47.6	26.4
Irish	47.7	13.4
Others[c]	47.7	0.09
Welsh	47.8	0.2
Belgians	48.0	0.11
French	48.0	1.2
Polish	48.1	5.2
Scottish	48.1	1.2
Chinese	48.3	0.13
English	48.3	2.4
Swedish	48.3	6.0
Danish	48.5	1.2
Germans	48.9	26.5
Hungarians	49.0	0.2
Hollandish	49.1	1.0
Swiss	49.1	0.2
Norwegians	49.4	2.5
Bohemians	49.6	4.8
Spanish	49.6	0.03
Lithuanians	53.2	0.08

[a]These are called "colored" in the data. We are assuming they are black Americans.
[b]Mixed refers to those of mixed parentage.
[c]Others refers to groups not listed.

pupils per classroom than the median ethnic group. Overall, there seems to have been little discrimination among ethnic groups in the allocation of teachers among Chicago's public schools.

Several alternative hypotheses come to mind that could account for variation in class size. Distance from the center of the city might be one reason the most favored school had fewer than thirty-one pupils per classroom and the least favored nearly seventy. While we attempt no quantitative measure of this variable, visual inspection of the data nonetheless revealed no obvious relation between centrality of location and crowding. Data limitations precluded our examining another possible explanation—

the income or wealth of a neighborhood. But given the strong connection between ethnicity and income, it is unlikely that a more direct measure of wealth would have found strong relationships where ethnicity identified virtually none.

To us the most convincing explanation for our finding that ethnicity had such a weak correlation with crowding, even in the face of considerable unevenness in class size across the city, is that crowding was a more or less randomly distributed characteristic over which the school system had, in the short run, very little control. In the late 1890s neighborhoods changed rapidly as the city underwent one of its largest growth spurts. Immigrants were arriving faster than they could be counted, which gave urgency to a school census of the sort from which our data was taken. By the time the school board identified the need, planned a response, contracted for a new school building, supervised its construction, and drew new attendance boundaries, another neighborhood could well have become inundated by urban newcomers, causing great crowding in another part of the city. Information on social change, always scarce, was a particular problem for the nineteenth-century school system, which was both highly decentralized and without modern means of communication. It may well be that the only way Chicago school officials could have discriminated among ethnic groups, even had they wanted to, would have been to establish a separate and unequal set of schools for immigrants, a policy that cities in the South followed in the treatment of blacks.

PLURALIST SCHOOL POLICES: THE EVIDENCE ON TEACHER ETHNICITY

In his "Memoirs," Christopher A. Buckley, Republican boss of San Francisco from 1882 to 1891, mentions a young woman who called at the Buckley residence one evening with the information that she had been granted a teaching position in the school department. "I have been just a little slow in coming around, Mr. Buckley," she went on. "I was told to bring it to Mr. ——— (a friend of education), but I thought it would be ever so much nicer to give it to you in person and thank you for your kindness. Here is the $250." Buckley questioned her about the gift, to which she replied, "Why Mr. Buckley, you ought to know. That was the amount agreed on with Mr. ——— for getting me my lovely position as teacher in the public schools. All the girls who are appointed pay you, don't they?" Buckley, inquiring into the matter at once, went to a person of prominence who took deep interest in the school department. "See here, boss," said the friend of education. "Better not turn over these old affairs. One cannot tell what may be uncovered. But you can bank on one thing. Your name will never be mentioned again." Buckley's story concludes on the sobering note that the "friend of education" later turned out to be the main broker in the appointments scandals.[13]

Although Buckley's own role in this autobiographical account has probably been sanitized, the story illustrates the pervasiveness of the patronage
system in nineteenth-century urban schools. Jobs were obtained through
political connections not only in San Francisco, but also in Chicago and
other cities throughout the country. One superintendent said in an 1896
article on teachers in the *Atlantic Monthly*, "Nearly all the teachers in our
schools get their positions by what is called 'political pull.'"[14]

These anecdotes and observations, interesting as they are, do not identify the intensity or exact locus of patronage practices. Were politicians
particularly interested in higher-paid, influential positions such as that of
principal? Was patronage the means by which the Anglos maintained their
dominance? Or was patronage the mechanism by which immigrant groups
obtained a toehold in the educational system? Did patronage practices
decrease over time? Did the amount vary from one city to another?

In order to estimate the extent and focus of patronage in nineteenth-
century urban schools, the home addresses of teachers and principals,
obtained from the annual reports of the school system, were analyzed to
determine whether teachers lived in the political wards where the schools
they worked in were situated. According to most studies of machine-style
politics, in the nineteenth century political parties were highly decentralized organizations, with aldermen and ward committeemen holding great
discretion over public employment opportunities within their particular
wards. Since these political leaders were primarily interested in maximiz-
ing political support within their own neighborhoods, they had an incentive to recruit jobholders from their own communities. To be sure, such a
practice was not invariant. A teacher might win a job because her uncle,
living in another part of the city, had good political connections. Or a
particular ward committeeman might have influence outside his own
neighborhood or ward. Nonetheless, on average and taken all together, it
seemed not unreasonable to assume that where political patronage was a
more widely practiced form of recruitment for school positions, one would
find a greater tendency for teachers and principals to live and work in the
same political jurisdiction.

Disproportionate tendencies to live in the same ward one works in can
therefore be taken as an indicator of a partisan-based recruitment system.
As can be seen in table 4.4, such a tendency was pronounced for both
Chicago teachers and principals between 1867 and 1915. Even though
educators could have lived in any of sixteen wards in 1868, fully 30 percent
of the teachers lived in the same ward they worked in. Though teachers
could have lived in any of thirty-four wards in 1915, the percentage living
and working in the same ward remained at 21 percent, a particularly high
figure given the great enlargement of Chicago's boundaries and the improvements in mass transportation that had occurred in the intervening

TABLE 4.4 Percentage of Educators Residing and Working
in the Same Ward, Chicago, 1867–1915

Ethnicity[a]	1867–68		1882–83		1893–94		1914–15	
	Per-centage	N	Per-centage	N	Per-centage	N	Per-centage	N
	Teachers[b]							
Total	30	281	28	95	35	199	21	169
Anglo	31	234	31	63	34	118	22	90
All non-Anglo	28	47	19	32	36	81	20	79
Irish	33	15	29	17	24	31	22	32
German	30	10	17	10	34	36	18	33
Other	23	22	20	5	66	14	21	14
	Principals and Assistant Principals							
Total	46	39	41	91	30	180	19	178
Anglo	49	35	38	73	31	121	22	100
All non-Anglo	25	4	50	18	27	59	14	78
Irish	0	1	44	9	28	29	11	44
German	33	3	50	2	31	16	17	24
Other	0	0	57	7	21	14	20	10

Source: Chicago Board of Education, *Annual Reports.*

[a]Ethnicity determined by surname.

[b]Includes teachers of the German language. Figures for teachers for the years 1882–83 and 1893–94 are weighted, since teachers of the German language were sampled at a different rate than regular teachers for those years.

period. Until 1894 the better-paid, high-prestige principal's positions were even more likely to be held by someone living in the same ward, a finding quite consistent with contemporary claims that principals' appointments were especially likely to be influenced by political considerations.

Given the prevalance of patronage practices in both Chicago and San Francisco, and given that many have regarded the political machine as particularly responsive to the concerns of immigrant groups, it is interesting that teachers with ethnic surnames were no more likely to be recruited as either teachers or principals on the basis of political favoritism. In three out of the four years for which comparisons were made, Anglo teachers in Chicago were more likely to live in the neighborhood in which they worked. Even the Irish did not stand out as being especially likely to be politically connected. Nor were localist tendencies any greater for principals of ethnic than of Anglo descent. For San Francisco, available data allow for comparisons only in the years 1875 and 1885, but even at this early period sharp differences between ethnics and Anglos are difficult to discern (see table 4.5). Although in 1875 ethnic teachers were slightly more likely than Anglo teachers to live in the same ward as the one in which they worked, the

TABLE 4.5 Percentage of Educators Residing and Working
in the Same Ward, San Francisco, 1874–85

	1874–75		1884–85	
Ethnicity[a]	Percentage	N	Percentage	N
	Teachers			
Total	30	230	30	317
Anglo	28	163	34	196
All non-Anglo	34	67	23	121
Irish	33	21	21	72
German	25	20	28	29
Other	42	26	25	20
	Principals and Assistant Principals			
Total	27	44	32	59
Anglo	28	39	33	46
All non-Anglo	20	5	31	13
Irish	0	2	50	4
German	0	1	20	5
Other	50	2	25	4

Source: San Francisco Superintendent of Public Instruction, *Annual Reports.*
[a]Ethnicity determined by surname.

reverse was true in 1885. In general, it seems that patronage was as important to the city's Anglos as it was to the ethnics.

Although the nineteenth-century political machine has been romanti-
cized by some as a primary channel of political mobility for ethnic groups,
little besides anecdotal evidence has ever been produced in support of these
claims.[15] In fact, some of the more careful scholarship on political patronage and corruption has shown that machine-style politics thrived in New
York City well before the arrival of immigrant groups,[16] that patronage
practices flourished in non-ethnic cities as much as in cities where ethnics
predominated,[17] and that machine-style politics was in every way consistent with the well-established individualistic political culture that pervaded American society in the nineteenth century.[18] Political parties in
Chicago and San Francisco had as much incentive to keep the native-born
population politically satisfied as to capture the vote of the ethnic immigrant. Native-born Americans voted more frequently, were more aware of
the political stakes involved, and were courted by both the dominant
parties. Immigrants often were ineligible to vote, and when they did participate they often tied their fate to just one of the two parties, thus limiting
their leverage. There is every reason to believe, therefore, that Anglos were
as likely to benefit from the patronage system as were the immigrants.
Accordingly, the Anglo teachers were as likely to live in the politically

appropriate place as were teachers with ethnic surnames. Political pluralism prevailed in Chicago, but it was a pluralism at least as open to Anglos as
to any of the ethnic immigrants.

Given this openness of the political system to both Anglos and ethnics,
one should not expect to find either Anglo dominance of the teaching staff or
rapid inroads by in-migrating ethnics. Given the diversity of claims on
political leaders, the processes of change can be expected to have occurred
at a slow but steady pace. Thus when one looks at the composition and
structure of the teaching staff, one expects to find that no one of the three
understandings outlined earlier would quite capture the nuances of social
change in the city. The native-dominance perspective anticipates that
Anglos would be able to keep control of jobs in the school system, obtain
classes with favorable pupil/teacher ratios, and receive higher salaries. The
pluralist perspective expects immigrant groups to wrest control of patronage from the Anglos, obtaining more and better jobs. The universalist
perspective assumes that all ethnic groups will be represented proportionately in the ranks of teachers and administrators and be assigned
classes without regard to their ethnicity.

To test these alternative hypotheses we collected data on teacher ethnicity, class size, teacher salaries, and teacher residences within Chicago and
San Francisco for selected years during 1896–1915. The indicators of differential treatment of an ethnic group were the proportion of jobs obtained
by each group, the level at which members of each group were paid (i.e., job
status), and the size of the classes they were assigned, assuming that
teachers from favored groups would be assigned smaller classes.

Our data on jobs within the school systems, while less precise than the
data on ethnicity and classroom crowding in Chicago, indicate that by the
latter part of the century, members of larger ethnic groups such as the
Germans and Irish were able to obtain significant numbers of jobs within
the school system. Although they were not paid as well as their Anglo
counterparts, this appears to be mainly a problem of seniority. The Anglos
had been in the system longer and had risen to higher-paid positions. Over
time, new immigrant groups seemed to move closer to equality with the
Anglos.

To determine the numbers and types of jobs held by members of the
various ethnic groups, we inspected lists of teacher appointments from
Chicago and San Francisco. Data for Chicago are from the school years
1867–68, 1882–83, 1893–94, and 1914–15.[19] We collected similar data from
San Francisco for 1874–75, 1884–85, and 1910–11.[20] Ethnicity was determined by the country of origin of the individual's surname.[21] Since only the
large ethnic groups had many members, we used a consolidated set of four
ethnic groups to categorize the teachers. These groups were Anglos, Irish,

Germans, and others. (Since very few teachers were Swedish or Italian, these two groups were collapsed into the "others" in the analysis.)

To obtain a sense of how well the teaching staff represented a city's overall population, we compared the teacher ethnicity data with United States census data on the foreign-born. Although we do not have population data directly comparable to our teacher-ethnicity data, since the censuses determine ethnicity by place of birth whereas we estimated it by the national origin of the individual's surname, it is apparent that in both Chicago and San Francisco Anglos held a disproportionately large part of the early teaching jobs (see tables 4.6 and 4.7). Anglos constituted 72 percent of San Francisco's teaching force in 1874–75 and 83 percent of Chicago's teachers in 1867–68. Even if one assumes that in 1870 the native-born population in both cities was primarily Anglo, when the percentage native-born is taken together with the percentage of Anglo foreign-born, it is still obvious that the number of teaching positions Anglos held in the early period was disproportionately large compared with their numbers in the city population as a whole. By 1910, the assumption that the native-born population is primarily Anglo can no longer be made. At the same time, the number of teaching jobs as well as the number of principalships given to Anglo teachers steadily declines, becoming more proportional to their numbers in the city population.

Although the Irish started with few jobs, their numbers increased rapidly in both cities. In 1893–94, 14 percent of the teachers and 16 percent of the principals in Chicago had Irish names, roughly the percentage of Irish stock in the city's population at that time.[22] Irish representation continued to increase over the next two decades in both cities. By this time the Irish held 25 percent of the teaching jobs and 34 percent of the principalships in San Francisco, percentages that in all probability were greater than the percentage of Irish in the city as a whole.

Germans and particularly the "other" ethnic groups had a smaller percentage of teaching jobs through the 1880s. Germans were hired to teach the German language, but German-language teachers were only a small fraction of the system's teachers (1–3 percent). However, the number of principalships held by the groups does show a small increase, at least for the Germans in Chicago.

A similar pattern that shows how ethnic groups gradually worked their way into the system of public education emerged in an examination of salary levels. In 1882–83 teachers of German and Irish ethnicity in Chicago were paid less than Anglo teachers, but by 1893–94 this difference had narrowed (see table 4.8). The percentage of non-Anglo teachers who were paid the higher salary increased substantially, from 63 percent in 1882 to 80 percent a decade later. In 1893–94 the German principals were even with or

TABLE 4.6 Ethnicity of the City Population and of Public-School Educators, San Francisco, 1870–1911

Ethnicity[a]	Total Population		
	1870	1880	1910
Native-born	44%	58%	72%
Foreign-born	56	42	28
Anglo	6	5	—[b]
Irish	17	13	6
German	9	9	6
Other[c]	24	15	16

Ethnicity[d]	Educators		
	1874–75	1884–85	1910–11[e]
Teachers			
Anglo	72%	61%	54%
Irish	9	23	25
German	9	11	11
Other[c]	11	6	10
Number	247	339	265
Principals[e]			
Anglo	89%	77%	54%
Irish	4	7	34
German	2	8	6
Other[c]	4	8	6
Number	46	61	108

Sources: Percentage foreign-born figures are from the United States Census, Population, 1870, 1880, 1910. Data on ethnicity of principals are from the San Francisco Superintendent of Public Instruction, Annual Reports.

Note: Percentage totals may not sum to 100 because of rounding.

[a]Ethnicity determined by place of birth.

[b]Insignificant number.

[c]For a list of ethnic groups included in the "other" category, see table 4.3.

[d]Ethnicity determined by surname. All figures include native-born as well as foreign-born persons.

[e]Includes vice-principals.

ahead of the Anglo principals in terms of salary, while Irish principals were behind both the other groups (see table 4.9). Yet many more Irish than Germans were principals, particularly when their numbers in the population are taken into account, indicating that the Irish may have had the political power to obtain such positions even though they did not have the seniority to achieve the highest salaries. However, many Anglos still held principalships in Chicago, even in 1914–15, well after their share of the population had begun to dwindle (see table 4.7).

Salary patterns in San Francisco vary somewhat from those in Chicago (see table 4.10). In 1874–75 the few teachers of German background were actually better paid than the more numerous Anglo teachers or the few Irish teachers. By 1910–11 all the groups had moved up the salary scale, but the

TABLE 4.7   Ethnicity of City Population and of Public-School Educators, Chicago, 1867–1915

Ethnicity[a]	Total Population			
	1870	1880	1890	1910
Native-born	52%	59%	58%	68%
Foreign-born	48	41	42	32
Anglo	3	3	3	1
Irish	13	9	6	3
German	20	18	18	7
Other[b]	12	11	15	21

Ethnicity[c]	Educators			
	1867–68	1882–83	1893–94[d]	1914–15
Teachers[d]				
Anglo	83%	65%	60%	51%
Irish	6	19	14	19
German	3	11	20	20
Other[b]	8	5	7	10
Number	288	101	233	286
Principals and assistant principals				
Anglo	88%	80%	69%	56%
Irish	3	11	16	25
German	5	2	8	14
Other[b]	5	7	7	5
Number	40	95	193	183

Sources: United States Census, Population, selected years. Chicago Board of Education, Annual Reports.

Note: Percentage totals may not sum to 100 because of rounding.

[a]Ethnicity determined by place of birth.

[b]See table 4.3.

[c]Ethnicity determined by surname.

[d]Figures for teachers are weighted, since teachers of the German language were sampled at a different rate than regular teachers.

TABLE 4.8 Teacher Salary by Ethnicity, Chicago, 1882–94

Salary Range	Anglos	Non-Anglos Total[b]	Irish	German
		Ethnicity[a]		
1882–83				
$500–599	15%	37%	42%	47%
$600+	85	63	58	53
Number	77	35	19	11
1893–94				
$500–599	15%	20%	23%	27%
$600+	85	80	77	73
Number	120	74	31	30

Source: Chicago Board of Education, *Annual Reports*, lists of teacher appointments.
[a]Ethnicity determined by surname.
[b]Includes individuals with other ethnic surnames as well as Irish and German.

Irish were still somewhat behind the others in compensation. However, the difference in the compensation of the ethnic groups was minimal. Finally, the table shows that principals' salaries were also essentially the same regardless of ethnic background.

For San Francisco, information on the average class size at each school within the system enabled us to determine whether teachers from particular ethnic groups were discriminated against by being assigned to schools with more crowded classrooms. In general, the results indicated that non-Anglo teachers were no more likely to teach in crowded schools than Anglo teachers. The differences between the class size for Anglo teachers and that for Irish teachers (the next largest group of teachers in each of the three sampled years) were minimal, the largest difference being 0.5 (one-half of one student in daily attendance per teacher) (see table 4.11). Although Italian teachers were assigned somewhat larger classes in 1894 and 1910, even here the differences are modest; moreover, the number of Italian teachers in our sample is so small that the differences are not statistically significant.

Thus the investigation of teacher ethnicity, salary, and class size revealed a pattern of slow assimilation of new groups into the corps of teachers and principals. Though Anglos still held over half the teaching positions and principalships even in the early twentieth century, a more equal distribution of jobs was emerging. The Irish, the most powerful of the immigrant groups, eventually achieved a disproportionate share. Italians,

Swedes, and other recent immigrants whose native tongue was not English had much greater difficulty in securing employment as teachers. Once hired, teachers seemed to be assigned larger or smaller classes without regard to their ethnic background.

CONCLUSION

Taken together, the information presented in this chapter lends little support to the claim that the schools blatantly discriminated against ethnic, working-class groups. School resource allocation policies, as seen in levels of classroom crowding and the number of teaching jobs held by ethnic groups, provide us with the data to determine more systematically the real extent of institutionalized discrimination, at least in terms of resource inequality.

TABLE 4.9 Principal's Salaries by Ethnicity, Chicago, 1867–94

Salary Range	Anglos	Ethnicity[a] Non-Anglos			
		Total	Irish	German	Other[b]
1867–68					
$500–999	3%	0%	0%	0%	0%
$1,000–1,599	52	33	0	67	0
$1,600–2,199	42	50	100	33	50
$2,200+	3	17	0	0	50
Number	33	6	1	3	2
1882–83					
$500–999	36%	47%	70%	50%	14%
$1,000–1,599	29	21	10	0	43
$1,600–2,199	32	32	20	50	43
$2,200+	4	0	0	0	0
Number	76	19	10	2	7
1893–94					
$500–999	11%	17%	24%	0%	21%
$1,000–1,599	54	56	59	50	57
$1,600–2,199	14	14	3	38	7
$2,200+	21	14	14	13	14
Number	127	59	29	16	14

Source: Chicago Board of Education, Annual Reports, lists of teacher appointments.
Note: Percentage totals may not sum to 100 because of rounding.
[a]Ethnicity determined by surname.
[b]For a list of ethnic groups included in the "other" category, see table 4.3.

Three perspectives—native dominance, pluralist, and universalist—on how school systems adapted to the nineteenth-century influx of immigrants motivated our analysis. With respect to classroom crowding, our data were most consistent with a universalist perspective. There was little difference among the various ethnic groups in Chicago in the average daily attendance (ADA) per teacher experienced by the various ethnic groups. Although

TABLE 4.10 Teacher's and Principal's Salaries by Ethnicity, San Francisco, 1874–1911

Salary Range	Ethnicity[a]				
		Non-Anglos			
	Anglos	Total	Irish	German	Other[b]
Principals and Assistant Principals					
1874–75					
$700–1,599	23%	17%	50%	0%	0%
$1,600–1,999	48	33	0	50	50
$2,000+	30	50	50	50	50
Number	40	6	2	2	2
1910–11					
$700–1,599	33%	34%	32%	43%	33%
$1,600–1,999	36	32	32	29	33
$2,000+	31	34	35	29	33
Number	58	50	37	7	6
Teachers					
1874–75					
$500–799	38%	41%	48%	33%	41%
$800–899	27	17	29	10	15
$900–1,199	21	22	14	38	15
$1,200+	14	20	10	19	30
Number	178	69	21	21	27
1910–11					
$500–799	6%	10%	11%	0%	19%
$800–899	6	6	5	7	7
$900–1,199	38	48	56	34	41
$1,200+	49	37	29	59	33
Number	143	122	66	29	27

Source: San Francisco Superintendent of Public Instruction, *Annual Reports.*
Note: Percentage totals may not sum to 100 because of rounding.
[a]Ethnicity determined by surname.
[b]For listing of groups included in "other," see table 4.3.

TABLE 4.11 Average Class Size by Ethnicity of Teacher, San Francisco,
1874–1911

Ethnicity of Teacher[a]	Class Size		
	1874–75	1884–85	1910–11
Anglo	46.5	49.3	35.5
Irish	46.6	49.2	36.0
German	44.0	47.5	37.0
Italian	47.5	52.5	37.6
Other[b]	45.0	50.0	35.0
Average	46.1	49.2	35.8

Source: San Francisco Superintendent of Public Instruction, *Annual Reports.*
[a]Ethnicity determined by surname.
[b]For listing of groups included in "other," see table 4.3.

important differences did exist in our sample analysis of 215 schools (pupil/teacher ratios varied from less than thirty-one to one to nearly seventy to one), these differences are only weakly related to the ethnicity of the pupils. When the groups were clustered by language and cultural similarity, the resulting pattern was one of tightly bunched classroom-crowding levels, with culturally dissimilar southern and eastern Europeans experiencing slightly less classroom crowding than western Europeans. A more likely explanation for classroom crowding is that rapid population growth in particular parts of the city placed unusual burdens on particular schools.

The data with respect to teaching jobs and principalships are most consistent with the pluralist perspective. Teachers belonging to the larger ethnic groups increasingly received equal treatment during the late nineteenth century. Few non-Anglos held teaching or principal positions just after the Civil War, and those who did were poorly paid. However, later in the century, as increasing numbers of immigrants entered the cities, members of the new populations did obtain jobs in the educational system. Rather than a long-term pattern of favoritism, we see early discrimination giving way to increasing acceptance of the larger immigrant groups.

Neither on the issue of job discrimination nor on that of classroom crowding are our data consistent with the native-dominance perspective. By the late 1890s, schools attended by Irish pupils were no more crowded than those attended by Anglo pupils, and other large ethnic groups were not far behind. While the Anglos still held many teaching jobs late in the century, even after they were no longer the largest group, this was in part a function of their earlier predominance in the population. While immigrants who came to the United States were themselves rarely qualified to obtain jobs in the school system, their children, being educated in that system, were more able to compete for those jobs. Thus, as an immigrant population became established, its members increasingly competed for employment on an equal basis with groups of longer standing.

Finally, class size and the structure and composition of the teaching staff do not address the quality of the educational experience of children from various ethnic groups. Interaction within the classroom and between home and school was extremely important for student achievement in school, and it is entirely possible that in this context ethnic discrimination could be found. But the analysis of school resource allocation at least provides information about overall school policy in the treatment of immigrant children by a major public institution. Certainly the schools of Chicago and San Francisco treated European immigrants differently from the way the schools of Atlanta treated blacks. Even though black men and women in Atlanta eventually were hired to teach children of their own race, few other concessions were made by the board to the city's racial minorities. The pupil/teacher ratio for whites remained basically constant between 1878 and 1895, ranging only from sixty-three to one at the beginning of the period to sixty-five to one at the end. The pupil/teacher ratio in black schools fluctuated wildly from ninety-one to one in 1878 to no less than 118 to one in 1895 (see table 4.12). Black teachers, moreover, were placed on a sharply lower salary schedule than were white teachers.

Because they had the vote, immigrants in northern cities fared better than blacks in southern cities. Boldly inegalitarian treatment such as that which prevailed for blacks in Atlanta would have ruined the careers of northern politicians. Even in Atlanta, blacks fared better educationally when they could vote, and they lost ground late in the nineteenth century when white primaries were instituted. Since these points require elaboration, in the next chapter we examine the extent to which race politics and race relations in urban education were resolved differently from the way issues arising from European immigration were treated.

TABLE 4.12 Atlanta's Primary-School Enrollment by Race, 1878–95

Year	Black Primary Enroll- ment	White Primary Enroll- ment	Black Pupils per Teacher	White Pupils per Teacher
1878	1,269	2,081	91	63
1882	1,111	2,813	69	64
1885	1,533	3,659	NA	NA
1890	2,373	5,402	NA	NA
1895	4,705	9,042	118	65

Source: Atlanta Board of Education, Annual Reports, selected years.

Appendix

DATA RESOURCES FOR THE ANALYSIS OF CLASS SIZE IN CHICAGO, 1897–98

Every two years during 1872–1916, the Chicago school board conducted a census of the city's population to determine the number of school-age children. For two of these years, 1896 and 1898, ethnicity was reported. Population within each precinct was broken down into twenty-seven ethnic groups, listed in table 4.3. Members of twenty-four of these groups (the three exceptions being native-born Americans with native-born parents and the black and Chinese racial groups) were classified by whether they were foreign-born, native-born with both parents foreign-born, or native-born with one parent American-born and the other foreign-born. Assuming that the ethnic composition of the school would be similar to the ethnicity of the precinct in which it was situated, we used the May 1898 census data as a proxy measure for student ethnicity during the 1897–98 school year. The May 1898 school census is reported in the *Proceedings* of the board of education for 1898–99.

Chicago school attendance data, used in determining classroom crowding, was reported in the *Forty-fourth Annual Report* of the board of education, for 1897–98. We used the average daily attendance figures to determine the number of pupils in a school. To ascertain the number of teachers assigned to each school, we examined lists of teacher appointments for the upcoming school year as voted by the board of education at its June meeting and printed in its *Proceedings*. The June 1897 list of teacher appointments for the 1897–98 school year is printed on pages 640–58 of the 1896–97 *Proceedings*. Using this report, we counted the number of regular teachers assigned to each school. Head assistants, German teachers, special teachers, and others were not counted, since the ratio of regular teachers to pupils would be the best measure of class size.

We determined in which precinct each of the public elementary schools was located by using the following resources: addresses reported in tables of "School Sites—Location, Size and Value of Lots and Improvements" in several different school reports, school addresses reported in city directories, street guides contained in old city directories, plus period maps of streets, precincts, and wards. These were taken from the collections of the University of Chicago, the Chicago Historical Society, the Municipal Reference Library of the city of Chicago, and the Chicago Board of Election Commissioners.

DETERMINING TEACHER ETHNICITY AND HOME ADDRESS

For each school year in the two cities, lists of the names of teachers and principals working in the respective school systems were available. We selected random samples of both teachers and principals (see tables 4.6, 4.7, and 4.8 for sample sizes), then determined the ethnic background of each educator by looking up his or her name in Smith's *New Dictionary of Family Names*.[23] The first country listed after the educator's name was assigned as the country of ethnic origin. For the 1884–85 San Francisco sample, for example, 95 percent of the names were identified directly or under a variant spelling in Smith's dictionary. In the 1910–11 San Francisco sample, 90 percent were identified in this way.

Another step was necessary when a name did not have a direct entry and was not cross-listed under a variant spelling. Using Smith's *New Dictionary* and Dellquest's *These Names of Ours*,[24] we determined if the name contained any distinctive spellings or endings that would identify it with a particular national origin. For each of the San Francisco data sets mentioned above, fewer than 2 percent of the names remained unidentifiable after this second step. These names were assigned to the "other" category.

Educators in Chicago and San Francisco were randomly sampled using a fixed-interval method. A 25 percent sample, for example, was drawn by selecting every fourth name. Sampling rates were as shown in table 4.13.

Regular teachers and German-language teachers were sampled at different rates in Chicago in 1882–83 and 1893–94. The percentages and numbers reported in the tables are weighted to take into account the differing rates at which the two populations were sampled.

The home addresses for Chicago teachers were obtained from the *Annual Reports* of the board of education. For San Francisco, the superintendents' *Annual Reports* provided us with information on teacher addresses and the location of schools. Using ward maps printed in 1879, found in the collections of the Bancroft Library at the Berkeley campus of the University of California, we were able to ascertain in which wards teachers lived and in which wards schools were located.

TABLE 4.13 Percentage of Educators Sampled, San Francisco and Chicago

San Francisco	1874–75	1884–85	1910–11	
Principals and vice-principals	100%	100%	100%	
Teachers	50%	50%	25%	
Chicago	1867–68	1882–83	1893–94	1914–15
Principals and assistant principals	100%	100%	50%	50%
Regular teachers	100%	10%	6%	3%
German-language teachers	100%	100%	50%	none

5 The Politics of Race and Equity

Few chapters in educational history reveal the intensity of popular demands for public schools better than those that consider the race question. While the story in the three cities is largely one of frustration and denial, blacks, Japanese, and to a lesser extent Chinese minorities all repeatedly demonstrated their unalloyed desire for public education. Even the almost equally intense white resistance to minority demands clarifies the importance the public at large placed on education. Equal educational facilities were denied to minorities not just because school officials were racially biased, but because many whites from all classes actively challenged minority claims. Intergroup rivalry was so intense, and educational opportunity was valued so highly, that minorities could win concessions only when they had the political strength to do so. Most clearly, it cannot be said that any group of economic elites forced schooling on black and Oriental Americans.

The single most important determinant of the access to and quality of educational facilities particular minorities received was a group's political resources. If the group could not impose sanctions on elected officials, the schools were content to provide only the legal minimum, ignoring the barrage of pleas and petitions from the minority. In most cases, political resources were difficult to accumulate because racial minorities either were explicitly denied the right to vote or were left out of the dominant political coalitions. Consequently, they devoted considerable energy to finding alternative methods of influencing decisions about schooling. In a number of instances significant benefits were secured in this way, but devising and implementing new strategies required intense community organization and persistent pressure on school officials.

Within the overall pattern of discrimination, the experiences of minorities varied considerably. Blacks consistently demonstrated a strong and organized demand for public schooling, although the precise nature of their objectives varied. In the South, school desegregation did not become a focus of struggle until the 1950s. Instead, blacks used their meager political opportunities to wrest promises of better black schools from reluctant boards of education. In the West and North, racial integration reached the agenda much earlier. The cases of the Chinese and Japanese in San Francisco highlight the importance of political power in obtaining access to schools. Although the school board attempted to exclude both groups, the Japanese used outside leverage to challenge the policy successfully, whereas the Chinese suffered exclusion and separation for over eighty years.

Black Schools and Politics in the South

Atlanta was the only city of the three that contained a significant minority population—it was 40 percent black at the inception of its school system in 1872.[1] Unlike Chicago and San Francisco, Atlanta did not face overt demands to end racial segregation, which had been adopted when the public school system was founded. Integration was never contemplated; in fact, the inauguration of the white school system was briefly delayed by the presence of federal troops in Atlanta and the attendant fear that the Reconstruction government of Georgia would compel racial mixing in the schools.[2]

Blacks not only were educated separately from whites, they also were relegated to markedly inferior schools and were excluded altogether from secondary schooling until 1920. Little effort was made to close the gap between the number of schools offered to whites and those provided for blacks; between 1872 and 1900, ten new primary schools were built for whites, while only two were opened for blacks.[3] The overcrowding that plagued the entire system was considerably worse in the black schools. The pupil/teacher ratio in black schools was dramatically higher than that in white schools, and the difference continued to grow as the century drew to a close.[4] Double shifts were the rule in black schools, and there were always more blacks than whites who could not find places in school at all. The black schools were housed in buildings of lower quality, and in numerous other ways blacks had access to poorer facilities than white pupils. Likewise, black teachers earned much lower salaries than their white counterparts. For much of the nineteenth century, the lowest-paid white teacher received a higher salary than the highest-paid black teacher.[5]

Political Pressures Yield Modest Educational Dividends

Despite this bleak picture, the schooling available to Atlanta's black community might have been considerably worse had not the structure of local politics occasionally placed blacks in strategic positions where they could trade their votes for better educational facilities. This occurred three times in the nineteenth century—in 1871, 1888, and 1891—despite the best efforts of Atlanta's white political leaders to obstruct black political participation.

In 1868, the year blacks became eligible to vote, Democrats replaced the ward-based system of elections with at-large election of candidates for all city offices, a move that effectively prevented blacks from holding any positions within municipal government. However, a split in the Democratic party in 1870 made the vote of the Republicans decisive. The Radical Republicans reinstituted ward elections and actively sought to attract black support by advocating public education and by running the Reverend William Finch, a prominent member of the black community, for councilman.[6] During his one-year term Finch, reflecting the interest in public education prevalent in the black community, strongly supported the establishment of public schools that would presumably include blacks.[7] A newly formed board of education had made no plans for blacks on the grounds that free education for blacks was already available in the four schools operated by church and missionary organizations.[8] The city council of 1871 nonetheless pledged to provide teachers for the black schools if the trustees of the private black schools would put their buildings at the disposal of the board of education.[9]

By the following year the Democrats had patched up their differences and were once again firmly in control of city government. At-large elections were reinstituted, and black participation was discouraged by excluding blacks from Democratic ward meetings and primaries.[10] The school system, which finally began operating that year, provided no accommodations for blacks. Only under the persistent pressure of former councilman Finch and his Radical Republican supporters did the board of education negotiate the takeover of two privately owned black schools.

Over the next sixteen years, it took constant black pressure on the board of education to obtain even the most modest schools. In their efforts to persuade the board, black ministers offered their churches for sale or rent to the school board, which was reluctant to construct new buildings for blacks.[11] Even when buildings were offered at small cost, the board hesitated to allocate its resources to black schools. In one instance it turned down the offer of a free school building, claiming it could not cover the cost of the teacher to staff it.[12] After close to a decade of black petitioning, the board finally decided in 1880 to construct one new school for black children.[13] The next year one of the older schools, whose condition had been termed "dangerous," was replaced.[14] By the end of 1883 there were three black grammar schools, only one more than had existed when the school system had begun. The combined capacity of the three schools was woefully inadequate: the 1883 superintendent reports noted that only half of the black children who wanted schooling could be accommodated.[15]

Meager as these elementary provisions were, blacks were even less successful in acquiring access to public secondary schools. Black petitions for secondary schooling began the year the school system was established and continued unanswered until the 1920s. In 1872, former councilman Finch and several other prominent blacks requested that the board establish secondary schools for blacks or make an arrangement with Atlanta University to provide free secondary education to black students. The board turned down these requests, and black students wanting a high-school education had to pay tuition at Atlanta University.[16]

Confronted by a united white electorate, there was little blacks could do to obtain schools other than keep up steady pressure and hope for the best. Once cracks appeared within the white alliance, however, opposing factions used education as an issue to lure black voters into their camps. The political divisions that would allow blacks some influence in the 1888 election were already evident in 1886. In that year a coalition of workers, blacks, and anti-Prohibitionists proposed an alternative to the so-called Citizens' Fusion Ticket, which granted equal representation to both supporters and opponents of prohibition and would therefore defuse the question as a political issue. The People's Ticket, put together under the auspices of the Mutual Aid Brotherhood (the political committee of the Knights of Labor), differed from the Citizens' Ticket by only two candidates for city council; but the two alternative candidates were both foes of prohibition, and one was publicly acknowledged as the "candidate of the working men."[17] Divisions within the labor movement and the black community over prohibition undoubtedly weakened the People's Ticket candidates, and they both lost; nevertheless, the races were close.[18]

The divisions in the white community had sharpened by 1888. The election was marked by vigorous solicitation of black support by candidates from both tickets, the emergence of concerted black demands for direct representation in municipal government and the continuing battle over prohibition.[19] Supporters of the People's Ticket candidate, Walter Brown, organized a Committee of Seventy, nineteen of whom were prominent blacks. In exchange for their support, blacks demanded that four members of the board of education be black, that a school for black children be opened in the fifth ward, and that a member of council be from the black community.[20] The People's Ticket responded with a platform that promised the construction of schools for each race and "just treatment for all citizens." However, when questioned about how pledges to black voters would be fulfilled, Brown's vague reponses raised suspicions among blacks that the People's Ticket would not or could not live up to its promises.[21]

Meanwhile, the Citizens' Ticket was making contacts with blacks who would ultimately swing the black vote to its side. Hoke Smith, then president of the school board, approached a black leader who had organized a Committee of One Thousand in support of Brown and asked what it would take to win the black vote. After being told that a black school in the fifth ward would be the price of support, Hoke promised that it would be built and, in fact, paid for the site.[22] When the conservative Citizens' Ticket candidate was victorious, the board of education ordered the new school built.[23]

Blacks were placed once again in a broker's role in 1891 when the Citizens' Ticket received a strong challenge from the prohibitionist 1890 Club. For a second time, the Citizens' Ticket used the promise of additional black schools to win black support. Candidates for the ticket were selected by a Committee of One Hundred that included three black representatives, one of whom introduced a resolution for the establishment of additional schools for blacks. Once the resolution was adopted by the Citizens' Ticket, leaders set about mobilizing support for the ticket.[24] After its victory, the new administration purchased and repaired a building for the purpose.[25] However, this was the last time in the nineteenth century blacks were able to trade political support for concrete benefits. The following year the establishment of the white primary effectively excluded them from electing municipal officials in a city controlled by the Democratic party.[26]

In addition to seeking better facilities, blacks demanded that black teachers be employed in black schools. Although the board of education began receiving petitions requesting black teachers as early as 1874,[27] pressure to employ them mounted when the Civil Rights Act of 1875 failed to outlaw segretated schools.[28] Black leaders argued that black teachers would be more familiar with black pupils and would take more interest in them, consequently providing them with a better education.[29] There were, moreover, a growing number of graduates of black colleges willing and apparently qualified to teach.

These requests were initally resisted by a board that was both reluctant to replace white teachers and fearful that black instructors would use their positions to stir up racial unrest. However, some board members had begun to worry that the missionaries' teachings were subversive of established patterns of race relations in the South. Compared with this threat, hiring southern black teachers seemed preferable. One board member accused the missionaries of "poisoning the minds of the colored people and raising them so much above their proper position that they will not be house servants etc. any longer."[30] Another factor that weighed heavily in the decision to employ black teachers was the economy to be realized because black teachers could be paid substantially less. After considering these arguments in 1878, the board hired three black and three southern white teachers.[31]

Although black leaders and white board members were satisfied with this arrangement, a petition signed by several hundred black citizens protested the removal of the missionaries, suggesting that the ministers who led the movement to hire black teachers did not have a unified community behind them. Nevertheless, the ministers continued to press for the appointment of black teachers to all the city's black schools, and by 1887 all the teachers and principals in the black school system of Atlanta were black.[32]

The White Primary Slows Educational Progress

After the white primary was instituted in 1892, there was little incentive for white politicians to upgrade the education provided to blacks. Thus, from the turn of the century to the 1940s, improvements in black schools required substantial organization and persistent pressure by the black community. Although some advances were made, black schools continued to lag far behind schools for whites, and black teachers continued to be paid substantially less. To improve black schools and equalize teacher salaries, blacks had to devise tactics appropriate to the limited political power they retained. The most successful and innovative of these tactics consisted of voting down bond issues that did not allocate sufficient funds for black schools. However, substantial gains were not possible until blacks began to utilize the federal courts to enforce their rights. This outside source of power completely overturned established patterns of school politics that had existed since the end of the Civil War.

Despite the increased political leverage provided by these new tactics, the first half of the twentieth century saw only minor improvements and modest expansion of black schools. New schools were built, and blacks were finally provided with a high school, but compared with the facilities offered to white students, those for blacks were vastly inferior. A survey of the Atlanta public schools undertaken in 1922 found that eleven of the fifteen schools provided for blacks were "unfit for human habitation" and should immediately be evacuated, and that the remaining black schools should be replaced as soon as possible. Conditions were considerably better in the white system, where only 10 percent of the schools were said to be "uninhabitable."[33]

In the decade after the institution of the white primary, black participation in educational politics declined sharply. Fewer petitions were presented to the board of education, and those that were submitted were ignored now that white politicians were shielded from possible reprisals by black voters. After the turn of the century, however, black newspapers frequently denounced the inadequacies of black schools, deficiencies made particularly glaring by progressive efforts to upgrade white schools. However, black leaders continued to adopt a conciliatory posture toward the board, advocating tactics that presumed the good faith of white board members.[34]

Although most of these requests were ignored, small advances were made. Not all board members condoned the neglect of black public education. In 1908 the board president warned that the failure to provide public schools for blacks would lead to crime or, worse, that blacks would be taught notions of social equality in private schools run by northern philanthropists.[35] Accordingly, in 1909 blacks were not altogether excluded from the proceeds of the first bond issue that allocated part of its funds to building public schools. Voting on bond issues was one of the few avenues of political participation left open to the black community, and black leaders urged blacks to cast their ballots in favor of the bonds.[36] However, allocations given to blacks barely made a dent in their vastly overcrowded schools.

Blacks responded by intensifying pressure on the board of education, using their traditional tactics of delegations and petitions. Together with others, the Neighborhood Union, whose membership consisted of faculty wives of Atlanta's black colleges, undertook a six-month survey of Atlanta's black schools. Publicizing the wretched conditions the study revealed generated more petitions and delegations. Finally, in 1913 the board responded with plans to construct six new schools. At the same time, however, it made clear its own conception of black education by recommending that manual training and domestic science be added to the curricula of the seventh and eighth grades in black schools. The recommendation was justified by the need for "more industrially trained workers and fewer professionals among the Negro population."[37] Strenuous protest throughout the black community caused the board to abandon this plan, but in its place the board introduced a course of study that deleted the eighth grade from black schools.[38]

This decision was so provocative that it aroused a new spirit of militance among some black leaders. Although the older generation advised caution, representatives of Atlanta's growing middle-class black community responded more forcefully. Officials of a black-owned insurance agency wrote to the National Association for the Advancement of Colored People (NAACP) seeking advice and aid.[39] A group of black leaders composed a petition to the school board and sent a delegation that not only insisted that the board not eliminate the black eighth grade but "boldly demanded the Negro children [be given] educational facilities in every way the equal of those enjoyed by their white contemporaries."[40]

As a result of the delegation's appearance, the board backed down on its plan to eliminate the black eighth grade but ignored the petitioners' demands for equal treatment for black children. A decision was subsequently taken to finance improvements in the white school system, and a representative of Atlanta's fledgling branch of the NAACP appeared before the board demanding equal consideration for black children. He was told "with brutal frankness and considerable profanity that none of the bond money was to be spent on Negro schools and that there was nothing colored citizens could do about it."[41]

The cavalier attitude of the school board toward their requests helped produce a consensus on black opposition to the bonds. At the same time an NAACP investigation of the city charter revealed that approval of bond issues required the assent of two-thirds of the registered voters, rather than only of those who bothered to vote. The incipient branch of the NAACP began a voter registration drive that met with an overwhelming response in the black community.[42] The campaign was a success, and the black vote was large enough to defeat the bond issue both times it was submitted in 1919. A third issue was proposed in 1921, and this time the city council made sure of black support by promising improvements in the black elementary schools and the construction of a black high school. City officials met extensively with the numerous black organizations that had mobilized around the issue and the bond commission vowed that one-third of the bond proceeds would be allocated to black schools.[43] In the end considerably less was spent on the black schools than had been promised, but several new schools were constructed, and the first black high school in Atlanta opened in 1924.[44] After 1921, black support was required for approval of Atlanta's frequent bond issues, and in the twenties it was actively solicited by the school board and the leaders of the white community.

With the onset of the depression, the school board proposed to eliminate several black night schools and elementary schools. Vigorous protests reduced these cuts, but some reductions, particularly in the night schools, could not be prevented.[45] Nevertheless, considerable mobilization of the black community took place in the 1930s, and many new groups were formed that would later play an important role in school struggles and the larger effort to transform Atlanta's race relations. The NAACP grew stronger, and several new political organizations were founded, including the Atlanta Civic and Political League and the Colored Voters League of Atlanta and Fulton County. For the first time since 1870, black candidates ran for city office.

Accordingly, when in 1935 the city council proposed a new bond issue the black community was prepared. Mass meetings were held, a voter drive was launched, and the bond commission was pressured to apportion an equitable share of the funds to black schools. Despite these efforts, black schools received less than had been promised. When the city again proposed a bond issue in 1938, black leaders protested the small amount slated for black schools, and the Urban League organized a successful voter registration drive among blacks in order to raise the number of votes required for passage of the new bond issue beyond an attainable level. Refusing to admit they needed black votes to pass bond issues, Atlanta's white board proposed yet another one that allocated even less to the black school system. Once again blacks, under the leadership of the NAACP, the Civic and Political League, and the Baptist Ministers' Union, registered to vote and then refused to turn out at the polls. Since two-thirds of the registered voters had to approve the bonds, the second bond issue went the way of the first.[46]

Encouraged by this show of strength, black teachers launched a campaign to equalize salaries between the races. This issue had been simmering since the early 1900s, when the board of education devised a new salary schedule that raised the pay of white teachers by cutting that of their black colleagues.[47] Petitions, protest, and active support in the black community had surfaced sporadically over the next three decades, but it became particularly intense in the 1930s, when cutbacks in teacher salaries meant that black teachers were barely making a living wage. In 1938, when a concerted and organized campaign was undertaken by the NAACP, the tempo of the protest activity increased. Community support was mobilized with the formation of the Atlanta Citizens Committee for the Equalization of Teachers Salaries. The board, however, maintained that it would not be possible to equalize salaries. Finally, in 1942, with the backing of the NAACP and the Citizens Committee, a black teacher filed suit against the city in federal district court. The suit marked the entry of the federal government into local school politics in a decisive way, and in subsequent years key school issues were no longer resolved strictly, or even primarily, at the local level.

In short, Atlanta blacks acted in a political context that afforded them very little influence. But because education was a highly valued prize in the community, black leaders persistently sought ways of influencing the school board's decisions. They moved from "polite" strategies of petitions presented by leading citizens to more organized and vigorous tactics. Although tactics grew more militant, demands remained within the Jim Crow framework of "separate but equal." The intransigence of the white community finally led Atlanta's blacks to look for support outside the city. Once the federal government had entered the conflict, dramatically altering the balance of power, blacks began to voice demands that would eventually undermine the entire Jim Crow structure.

THE STRUGGLE FOR BLACK AND ASIAN SCHOOLING IN THE WEST

On the other side of the continent, in San Francisco, the different social positions of minorities and the fluid character of social relations in the American West led to somewhat different outcomes. The diverse sources of political leverage and varying attitudes toward public education of San Francisco's black, Chinese, and Japanese communites led each group to have quite different experiences in the city's public schools. Although blacks were originally placed in segregated schools, early on they were integrated into the larger system. The Chinese occupied a position somewhat analogous to that of Atlanta's blacks, but, practically devoid of poli-

tical resources and with a more ambivalent attitude toward public education, they were denied access to public schools for nearly fourteen years.
The Japanese present a unique case of a group without political leverage
within the city but with a strong demand for integrated public schooling
and the ability to exert political power at the national level.

Blacks Win Integrated Schools

The social and political position of blacks in nineteenth-century San Francisco was quite different from that of their counterparts in Atlanta.
Throughout this period, blacks made up less than 1 percent of the total
population of the city.[48] The number of school-age black children was less
than 0.5 percent of the total school-age population of the city.[49] Whereas in
Atlanta the entire social structure was predicated on white supremacy,
black-white relations had no such salience in San Francisco.

By 1860 San Francisco had built three segregated schools,[50] which were
marketly inferior to the schools attended by white children, and as in
Atlanta, blacks were barred from high schools. Compounding this inequality was the precarious status of black schools, which became glaringly
evident to San Francisco's blacks when the school board arbitrarily closed
two of these schools in 1868. No official reasons were given, but one school
director remarked that one of the schools was a "nuisance." "It was too
close to a white school on the same street."[51] Yet in 1875 the San Francisco
school board voted to abolish the segregated schools and allowed blacks to
attend the same schools as white children—something never contemplated
in Atanta. To account for the differences we must look at the sociopolitical
situation of San Francisco's black community.

Because of its small size, the black population of San Francisco had very
little political influence in electorial contests. In 1880 there were probably
fewer than 450 black voters in the city.[52] Without the history of slavery that
had existed in the South, San Francisco's white population had less defined
views on the appropriate social role for blacks. Against this indifference
were pitched the unceasing efforts of San Francisco's blacks to obtain
better education for their children. Although they had little electoral power
and slight chance of increasing their political influence, black leaders kept
steady pressure on the school board and the state legislature. In response to
such pressure the first black school was established in 1854 despite a lack of
legislative authorization.[53] Efforts—ultimately unsuccessful—then turned
to establishing secondary schools for blacks. Most of the early demands for
better schooling sought improvements within a segregated framework.
After the 1868 closing of two black elementary schools, however, blacks
launched a concerted campaign for integrated schools. Community meetings were held, petitions were sent to the board, a bill proposing school
integration was introduced in the assembly in 1872, and finally in 1872 a

test case was entered in the supreme court of the state.[54] Within three years the board voted to abolish the "colored school." There were no incidents accompanying integration, and the status of blacks in the San Francisco public schools remained unchanged until the post–World War II influx of blacks established a pattern of de facto segregation.

Exclusion and Isolation of the Chinese

The experience of the Chinese community was quite different. With virtually no political influence owing to treaties that prevented them from becoming citizens, San Francisco's Chinese were even more politically marginal than the black community. Moreover, because they constituted a larger portion of the population—9 percent in 1880 and still a larger percentage of the work force, up to 25 percent by some estimates—considerable opposition grew to their very presence in the country, especially among the white workers with whom they competed.[55]

The political weakness of the Chinese community was reflected in the schools made available to them. The first Chinese school opened in 1859 after thirty Chinese parents petitioned the board of education, but it closed three months later owing to "lack of funds."[56] Several months later it was reopened as a night school attended primarily by adults who wanted "to learn a little English, . . . to obtain lucrative positions as clerks and interpreters for their countrymen.[57] This left Chinese children without a public school. The Chinese night school operated until 1871, when the superintendent recommended that it be closed. It was not until 1884, under court order, that the board began to provide public education for Chinese children.

This exclusion was partly due to the comparatively low interest in public education on the part of San Francisco's Chinese community. Children constituted only a tiny percentage of the Chinese population in San Francisco, because Chinese immigrants were overwhelmingly single men seeking work in the United States but not planning to settle permanently.[58] They viewed public education as a way to permit adults to gain minimal competence in English in order to secure better employment. Then, as opposition to the Chinese in California grew, most other concerns became subordinated to the overriding issues of personal safety and the right to remain in the country. In addition, Chinese parents sought a traditional Chinese education for their children in private schools, which not only showed more respect for Chinese cultural values than did the public schools, but also gave the children an education that would be useful when they returned to China, a journey generally contemplated by Chinese families. Thus, while private-school enrollment figures indicate that education was in fact a high priority of Chinese parents, the Chinese did not insist on public education for much of the nineteenth century.[59] However, toward the end of that period, as a more permanent community began to establish itself, Chinese parents increasingly voiced demands for educational rights.

Before the turn of the century, the few Chinese requests for public education were routinely ignored. However, within this overall context of neglect the treatment of Chinese by the school board varied both with the general tone of Chinese-white relations and with the party in power. Setbacks in educational opportunities were especially severe when Democrats were in power. Indeed, the California Democratic party overcame the disasters that befell it during the Civil War only by taking a strongly anti-Chinese stance.[60] This position was especially valuable in solidifying its labor support, for white workers were increasingly hostile to the cheap competition the Chinese represented.

A look at some of the major decisions regarding Chinese schools reveals the interplay between the demands of the Chinese community, their relationship with the community in general terms, and the political party in power, as well as the changes in all these factors over time. The establishment of the first Chinese school in 1859 occurred before any organized or widespread opposition to the Chinese existed.[61] The closing of the school three months later coincided with the election of Democrat James Denman as superintendent of schools. The Chinese night school that opened several months later was the only educational facility available to the Chinese throughout the 1860s. It was sparsely attended, with an average daily attendance of approximately thirty students.[62] One notable controversy that arose during the course of the night school's operation reflects Chinese concern with the public schools. In 1866 fourteen Chinese merchants presented a petition to the school board asking that the Chinese schoolteacher be removed. The Chinese objected to "the strong Christian bias in his teaching methods and materials."[63] This demand was in fact favorably received by the Democratic superintendent John Pelton, and the board dismissed the teacher, replacing him with one more acceptable to the Chinese community. However, this action does not fit the typical pattern of Democratic behavior toward the Chinese; it is more a reflection of Pelton's strong belief in the importance of cultural pluralism than of any change of heart by the Democractic party.[64]

More characteristic of the growing anti-Chinese rhetoric of the party was the position of James Denman, who was first elected superintendent in 1869. In his campaign, Denman exploited the simmering resentment of San Francisco's workers toward the Chinese by taking a stand against the Chinese school. On Denman's recommendation, the school was closed. Three factors probably account for why this did not evoke any organized protest by the Chinese community. First, the intensity of anti-Chinese agitation at this time led the Chinese to adopt a "wait and see" attitude toward the schooling question. Second, a strong network of missionary schools offered an attractive alternative to public education. Third, the virulence of the anti-Chinese movement had dampened much of the Chinese interest in Americanization, making exclusion from public schools less important for San Francisco's Chinese residents.[65]

In 1877 a petition signed by thirteen hundred Chinese residents was sent to the state legislature requesting amendment of the state law to allow Chinese children to attend the public schools or "what we would prefer, that separate schools may be established for them."[66] Submitted as it was at the height of the anti-Chinese movement in California, it is not surprising that this request was ignored. Even Republicans who had been "soft" on the Chinese question began to advocate an end to Chinese immigration as the only way to restore industrial peace.[67] The only allies the Chinese had left were American missionaries, who defended the rights of Chinese residents to send their children to the public schools. However, the urgings of the Ministerial Union of San Francisco were rebuffed by the school board, which professed ignorance of any attempt by the Chinese to enter the public schools.[68]

Once the foes of Chinese immigration had achieved their aim with the passage of the first set of Exclusion Acts in the early 1880s, the Chinese community began to direct its attention to the rights of American-born Chinese, including the right to public eduction.[69] A new state law passed more than twenty years earlier had paved the way by declaring that schools should be open to all except children of "filthy or vicious habits" or diseased children.[70] On the basis of this law, the exclusionary policies of the board were challenged in court by Chinese parents who had tried unsuccessfully to enroll their daughter in the public schools. In *Tape v. Hurley* both the municipal court and the state supreme court ruled that the child must be admitted. City superintendent Andrew Moulder, a Democrat, rushed a bill through the state legislature designed to permit the establishment of segregated schools for "Mongolians."[71] With the passage of this bill, a separate school for Chinese children was established in San Francisco. However, attendance was sparse. In 1885 only 3.9 percent of school-age Chinese children were enrolled; and five years later the figure had climbed only to 8 percent.[72] After enduring years of vicious attacks by white residents and repeated rebuffs by the school board, most Chinese turned their backs on the public schools, preferring to send their children to missionary schools and private Chinese-language schools. Attendance at these institutions was more than four times that of the public schools.[73]

With its right to exist secured by the courts, there were no further attempts to close the Chinese school, but the policy of segregation was enforced and Chinese students were not permitted to attend public high schools. No formal attempts were made to challenge segregation until 1902, when the father of two American-born Chinese children brought a complaint against the school board in court. The case protested the children's expulsion from a non-Chinese school that they had been attending for over a year. The only grounds for dismissal was their race.[74] The challenge was not successful—the court denied the request, thereby upholding the policy of segregation.

An attempt to gain admittance to secondary schools met with more success three years later, when Chinese parents threatened to boycott elementary schools if the board would not permit Chinese children to attend high schools. Under this pressure, the board reluctantly reversed its policy and opened its high schools to Chinese students.[75]

Throughout most of the nineteenth and early twentieth centuries, then, the Chinese in San Francisco were disfranchised, with local ministers their only consistent allies. This lack of political power was exacerbated by a virulent anti-Chinese sentiment, which became a focal point of political activity. Together these factors made it difficult for Chinese to secure even the minimal schooling that was legally due them. Moreover, these obstacles dampened Chinese interest in public schools—which for a variety of cultural reasons was somewhat ambivalent from the start—and Chinese parents preferred to send their children to private institutions. Public schooling for the Chinese was nominal or nonexistent. After the waning of anti-Chinese activities, Chinese parents began taking advantage of the avenues of power that were open to them—first, the courts in 1884 and 1902, and in 1905 a school boycott. Only in this way were Chinese pupils able to obtain concessions from the school board.

Politics and International Pressures Give Japanese Access to Public Schools

The case of the Japanese in San Francisco contrasts sharply with that of the Chinese. Although the two groups shared many characteristics, two important differences led the Japanese to have considerably more success in pressing their claims on the public school system. Most decisively, the San Francisco Japanese community could exercise political leverage by appealing to Tokyo. The Japanese government took a keen interest in the status of its citizens abroad and as a growing naval power and trade center, Japan had the political and economic capacity to negotiate vigorously with other governments on such issues as the well-being of its nationals. The Japanese also benefited from a more tolerant community attitude toward their presence in San Francisco. The opposition to Japanese immigration was both less widespread and less prolonged than the anti-Chinese agitation. Anti-Japanese activities in San Francisco did become an important part of the Union Labor party's activities at the turn of the century, but neither the Democratic nor the Republican party focused on them. Finally, the small Japanese community residing in San Francisco clearly defined integrated schooling as a high priority, to which they would devote considerable energy and resources.

The tale of the Japanese and public schooling in San Francisco centers on the 1906 "school board incident" in which a school board order requiring the Japanese to attend Oriental School provoked international attention and brought federal intervention in local school politics. Before that time, the few Japanese children—only ninety-three were in attendance in 1906—who lived in San Francisco attended regular public schools.[76] No complaint was ever raised about this until after 1901, when the Union Labor party, a newly formed group that had hoped to become the party of labor, brought the issue to public attention by advocating the segregation of Japanese pupils.[77]

Once in office, the Union Labor party officials did not pursue this issue. The board of education, however, "began to receive letters from the parents of white scholars, complaining of the enforced association of their children with children of Japanese immigrants in the public schools."[78] Most of these protesting letters were concerned that older Japanese boys were attending primary grades where they were in daily association with young white girls and boys.[79] In May 1905 the board of education passed a resolution calling for separate schools for "Japanese pupils, . . . not only for the purpose of relieving the congestion at present prevailing in our schools but also for the higher end that our children should not be placed in any position where their youthful impression may be affected by association with pupils of the Mongolian race."[80]

The resolution appears to have been mostly rhetorical. The Chinese School was too crowded to permit entry of Japanese pupils, and there were not sufficient funds to establish a new segregated school. Nor did the board take any steps to implement its resolution. Later that year the Japanese and Korean Exclusion League, an anti-Japanese organization composed of representatives from local labor unions, took up the issue and began petitioning the board to segregate the Japanese pupils.[81] This deadlock over implementing an exclusionary schooling policy was broken in April 1906 when the San Francisco earthquake and fire decimated the population of the Chinese School, creating room for Japanese pupils. The Japanese and Korean Exclusion League revived its agitation for separate schools in August 1906, launching a propaganda campaign and petitioning the board of education.[82]

The board was not long in responding, and in October 1906 it ordered Japanese pupils to attend the Oriental Public School—as the old Chinese School was now to be called. Japanese parents flatly refused to send their children and held numerous community meetings to develop an organized response. The secretary of the Japanese Association appealed to the board to rescind its decision, threatening legal action. When the board declined to reconsider the issue, the Japanese community publicized it in Japan, where the incident was widely discussed as a grave blow to Japanese national pride. Through its consul in Washington, Tokyo lodged a formal protest with the United States government.

Roosevelt highly valued the amity of the Japanese government, both as a trading partner and as a naval power in the Pacific. Critical of the board's decision, he dispatched an emissary to gather information and in the process to try to convince the board to open its schools to the Japanese. When the board refused, the federal government decided to press legal action. In December, the United States attorney was instructed to prepare a test case against the board. Legal proceedings that had been initiated by the Japanese were withdrawn in favor of the federal government's case, *Aoki v. Deane.*

The reasons the San Francisco board of education gave for excluding Japanese were that they were keeping out white pupils because of their great numbers and that the Japanese pupils were mainly overage men. Much noise was made about Japanese men sitting next to "girls of tender years."[83] A careful study by George Kennan refuted both these claims. In December 1906 he found that of the 28,736 pupils in the San Francisco public schools, 93 were Japanese. Of this number, 28 were girls and 34 were boys under fifteen. Only 6 Japanese males over fifteen years old were in primary schools.[84]

After considerable negotiation, a compromise was finally worked out calling for the board to rescind its decision that Japanese pupils must attend the Oriental School. A provision against overage pupils in the primary grades was retained. Roosevelt, in return, committed himself to negotiate a "gentlemen's agreement" with Japan to end immigration of Japanese laborers to the United States. The legal action was dropped. On 13 March 1907 the segregation order was rescinded. Thereafter Japanese pupils attended the same schools as white pupils.

A few embers left over from the dispute continued to smolder into the next decade. The California legislature tried to pass a bill providing for the resegregation of Japanese in public schools. The attempt failed—but only after a second vote and heavy federal pressure.[85] Some years later, in 1921, a state law was in fact passed ordering the segregation of Japanese pupils. However, San Francisco continued to allow Japanese pupils to attend the city's public schools without complaint. The fire of anti-Japanese sentiment in San Francisco did not outlive the Union Labor party.

Because of their small numbers, the Japanese never posed a serious threat to established social and political relations in San Francisco. In the schools their presence went unnoticed until the Union Labor party raised it as an issue. The party particularly exploited the concern among whites about older Japanese boys in the primary grades. Even though the effort to segregate the Japanese owed its existence primarily to the maneuvers of a political party, and even though no strong anti-Japanese movement developed in San Francisco without access to political power outside the city the Japanese would have had little more than their own group cohesion and commitment with which to fight the segregation order. With a strong government in Tokyo behind them, however, the Japanese successfully challenged the attempt to force their children into segregated schools.

The Emergence of Struggles around De Facto Segregation in Chicago

In Chicago, racial issues held a minor place in school politics throughout most of the nineteenth century. However, as the black population grew in the early 1900s and more black children entered previously all-white schools, friction between the races began to develop. Some whites began to call for formal resegregation of the schools, a move steadfastly resisted by blacks. Nevertheless, the massive wave of black migration to Chicago after World War I, together with the restrictive covenants in housing, created a largely de facto segregated school system by the 1920s. Dissatisfied with both the segregated nature of the schools and the inferior conditions in all-black schools, the black community consistently fought a two-pronged battle to gain entry to white schools and at the same time to upgrade the educational facilities in their own neighborhoods. Although the increased black presence in white schools provoked militant defiance from white parents, Chicago's blacks, in contrast to blacks in Atlanta, held a degree of political power. Chicago's Democratic political machine and its school board appointees responded halfway to demands for better facilities within black neighborhoods but sought to sidestep the politically explosive issue of integration.

Throughout most of the nineteenth century, the relationship of blacks to public education in Chicago was quite similar to that of blacks in San Francisco. As in San Francisco, blacks in Chicago constituted only a tiny fraction of the city's population—1.3 percent in 1900—so that the small number of black children in the public schools helped keep race off the school agenda.[86] Although Chicago schools were integrated from the start, they experienced a brief interlude of segregation in the 1860s. Anxious about increased black migration from the South, members of Chicago's Irish community pressured the city council into passing the "Black School Law" in 1863, requiring all black children to attend segregated schools. This experiment was short-lived, however, since black parents refused to remove their children from the white schools and brought about the law's repeal in 1865.[87]

In the first decade of the twentieth century the issue reemerged, as changes in school boundary lines and pupil transfers occasionally brought black pupils into previously all-white schools, provoking strong and some-times violent reactions from whites.[88] In 1905 a group of white children rioted when they were transferred to a largely black school. Three years later a similar move caused white pupils to boycott schools. In some schools, racial strife was endemic. For instance, the first predominantly black high school was the site of numerous interracial conflicts.[89] Accom-panying these incidents were calls for formal resegregation of the schools. White groups, especially those adjacent to black communities, brought segregation proposals up at school board meetings, and the issue was discussed in the press.[90] The proposals did stir up enough concern among black leaders to induce them to submit a formal protest to the board. In general, however, educational officials did not seriously contemplate reim-posing racial segregation as a formal school policy.[91]

By 1920, demographic trends and restrictive housing policies had worked to produce a practically segregated system. The flood of new black migrants who reached Chicago during and immediately after World War I resulted in a near doubling of its black population.[92] Restrictive covenants signed by property owners caused the black community to be increasingly concentrated in an area known as the "black belt." In the 1930s it was estimated that 90 percent of the city's black population lived in this area.[93]

Apart from producing segregated schools, this extreme residential con-centration also meant that schools in the black neighborhoods were crowded and inferior. According to the Strayer Survey's ratings of elementary school buildings in 1931, 39.2 percent of the black schools were regarded as "so inferior . . . that it is not advisable to expend any consider-able amount of money on them in an effort to make them acceptable plants."[94] The school board's failure to keep pace with the rapid growth of the black community meant that these inferior physical plants were strained beyond capacity. In 1910 there were only 4,160 blacks in the city's school system. By 1930 this number had grown to 33,856.[95] A 1939–40 survey found that ten predominantly black elementary schools enrolled 21,000 pupils though they had a capacity of only 15,000. Thirteen of Chi-cago's fourteen double-shift schools were black, and according to one esti-mate, three-fourths of Chicago's black schoolchildren attended part-time sessions.[96]

Blacks in Chicago, as in San Francisco and Atlanta, placed a high value on education. As Harold Gosnell observed, many blacks "migrated to Chi-cago in order to obtain better school facilities for their children than were available in the South. Education is looked upon . . . as the key to freedom."[97] For blacks, better and integrated schools were a central prior-ity, and they fought tenaciously to achieve that goal.

Unlike their counterparts in Atlanta, Chicago's blacks could vote and in the 1930s were a significant component of the Democratic machine; black demands for better schooling could not be ignored as they were in Atlanta. Nevertheless, Democratic responsiveness to black demands occurred within narrow bounds. When major racial conflicts over schools pitted whites against blacks, the school board attempted to defuse conflict by partially responding to black demands for better schools at the same time as it pursued policies that reinforced the structure of segregation.

Many of the conflicts over integration stemmed from the board's practice of shifting school-district boundaries to conform with the changing racial composition of neighborhoods. The formal opposition of black organizations to this gerrymandering was accompanied by vigorous protests from the black parents and pupils who were directly affected by boundary changes. In most cases, however, the school board was responsive to the wishes of the white community. Thus, despite calls by the Chicago Council of Negro Organizations and the Chicago and Northern District Association of Colored Women for redrawing school boundaries to remove segregation and to allow children to attend the schools nearest their homes, the board retained segregated boundaries in response to pressure from the restrictive covenant groups supported by the Chicago Real Estate Board.[98] Nor was the active mobilization of many black parents and children sufficient to induce the board to reconsider. One boundary change in 1933 particularly enraged the black community. One thousand mothers met to protest the ensuing segregation, and over seven hundred black pupils signed a protest petition. Parents organized the Fifth Ward Civic and Protection Association, whose activities kept the segregation issue alive and eventually succeeded in gaining permission for some black pupils to enter the schools. The board of education did not redraw the boundaries.

A second source of conflict was the board's practice of putting blacks into separate branches of high schools. To promote more efficient use of facilities, school officials could establish branches of overcrowded high schools in elementary school buildings with empty seats. School officials frequently assigned all black students to a single branch school to prevent racial mixing. On one occasion this practice sparked vehement protests from neighborhood residents, the Chicago Urban League, the NAACP, and a state representative. When Mayor Kelly overruled the school board and ordered black freshmen to attend the main high school, whites responded with a massive boycott.[99] Although white students returned after the school superintendent threatened them with loss of course credit, deep racial tension characterized relations in the school for the next two decades.

A third board practice that drew black protests concerned transfers. School authorities permitted white pupils living in predominantly black areas to transfer to schools that were mostly white. Because such transfers were rarely granted to black pupils and were clearly used as tools of segregation, blacks opposed them. School officials made occasional efforts to resolve the transfer problem. In 1933 the superintendent canceled all transfers of high-school students and ordered them to enroll in their home districts. His order was unenforced and ineffective.[100] In 1944 a similar order was followed by citywide protests, after which the board of education overruled the superintendent and modified his order.[101]

As these episodes illustrate, integration of large numbers of blacks was no more politically possible in the North than in the South. Despite the persistent efforts of blacks, the school board rarely responded to protests against segregation. In instances when school officials did take action, the vehement reaction of the white community usually forced them to back down. Blacks were somewhat more successful in implementing a second goal—improving predominantly black schools. This was an issue on which white politicians could attract black votes without driving away white supporters. Even here, however, success required a great deal of persistence. One major struggle over better facilities concerned the construction of a second black high school. By 1930 the single black high school was seriously overcrowded, with 3,400 students packed into a building intended for 1,900.[102] Even though a new high school in the heart of the black belt would intensify segregation, blacks were in this instance more concerned about improving accommodations for their secondary-school students. A new school was finally built, though behind schedule, and when it opened enrollment exceeded capacity by 1,400.[103]

Overcrowding and inferior facilities in elementary schools were also major concerns. In one episode the blacks of Chicago's Lilydale neighborhood staged a drive that secured the construction of an elementary-school building for their children, but only after recourse to picketing and vandalism. The black residents of Lilydale sent their children to a cluster of mobile schoolrooms that one resident described as a "strange looking assortment of packing box structures which might easily be mistaken for one of these abortive hobo villages which occasionally spring up on city dumps."[104] Rather than demanding admittance to the white elementary school, Lilydale's blacks limited their efforts to replacing the mobile units with a new school building.

In 1939 the issue of overcrowding became important in municipal elections for the first time. At the annual board of education budget hearings, thirty-eight speakers complained of the conditions in black schools.[105] During the mayoral campaign that spring, Republican Dwight Green asked black voters if their children were "compelled to attend overcrowded schools in shifts from 8 a.m. to 6 p.m. because by 'unwritten law' the present School Board . . . designates these schools 'colored' when near you are schools with adequate room."[106] In response to Green's campaign, Mayor Kelly attempted to appease black voters by appointing Midian A.

Bousefield, husband of the first black school principal, as the first black member of the board of education.

The black experience in Chicago's schools mirrored blacks' political position within the city. Because they constituted an important voting bloc, blacks could not be totally ignored by the Democratic machine during its period of consolidation. Yet on the issue of schooling, violent opposition by whites to integrated schools constrained the course followed by school officials. The aim of the school board was to alleviate the worst instances of overcrowding while avoiding integration of blacks with students in surrounding white neighborhoods. Although they continued to press for an end to segregated schools, blacks often opted for improvement of black schools at the expense of integrated ones. By the 1950s and 1960s however, the demand for educational equity in the form of school integration would be a central black concern in Chicago, as it was in San Francisco and Atlanta.

Conclusion

The struggle for equal access to public schools dominated the minority experience with the American educational system. For over a century blacks and other minorities tirelessly pressured local school officials to provide decent facilities for nonwhites. Because local political arrangements generally set narrow limits on black political participation, the quest for better schooling called for considerable community mobilization and organization. Concerted and persistent effort, along with strategic use of meager political resources, produced only modest results in the battle to upgrade minority education. Even when demands were tempered so as not to disrupt prevailing social arrangements, benefits were minimal unless minorities could threaten public officials with political sanctions. Local school officials' continued disregard for minority schools eventually led to demands for integration, which now seemed to be the only way to achieve true equality.

The history of Atlanta's black community shows the struggle as a three-stage process: first for the right to attend public schools, second for improvements in minority schools, and finally for integrated classrooms. The timing of these phases differed in the North, where blacks enjoyed more political influence. Yet even though they challenged de jure segregation, northern blacks usually settled for better schools in their own neighborhoods in lieu of desegregation rather than to jeopardize the benefits they could win. In neither the North nor the South did local school boards admit large numbers of blacks to white schools.

The contrasting experiences of the Chinese and the Japanese in San Francisco underscored the indispensability of political leverage on the local level: the two cases also demonstrated the need for resources outside the city when demands for integration faced local opposition. San Francisco's Chinese shared the black experience of exclusion and separation, which they could not successfully challenge. In contrast, the unique situation of the Japanese allowed them to demand and win integration despite the objections of the San Francisco school board. Federal intervention on their behalf made the crucial difference.

The quest by racial minorities for equal educational opportunity displays the widespread popular demand for schooling that existed. Elites did not "compel" nonwhite children to attend school, as some recent scholarship has implied, but instead denied them access or crowded them into poor, inadequate buildings. Ironically, these actions were often taken largely because of the popular demand for education within the white majority. Working-class whites were loath to see scarce public funds used to support black or Oriental education when schools for whites were frequently overcrowded and inadequate. The intensity of interracial conflict over school policy indicates once again that public education was a popular priority.

The differential success of racial minorities in the three cities also emphasizes that political relationships critically shaped the direction taken by public schools. Schools were opened to blacks and Orientals when political pressures dictated such action, not when the labor market needed more servile dark-skinned workers. Changes in school policy followed changes in the political status of racial minorities much more than any changes in their economic place. When blacks lost political status, as they did in Atlanta after 1892, they also lost educational opportunities. When blacks gained political strength, as they did in Chicago in the 1930s, they also won better schools. The correspondence between school policy and private-sector economic change was a good deal more ambiguous.

This does not mean that economic conditions were of no importance to racial issues. Quite clearly, working whites feared market competition from poorly paid, racially differentiated neighbors, and racial tension frequently increased during times of economic stress. Yet what was decisive for resolving these conflicts was the political status that minorities had achieved in American society. As blacks and Orientals gained their political rights, their rights to public education also came to be recognized.

Our analysis of the political forces shaping race relations in education has moved from the nineteenth century into the first decades of the twentieth. In the second part of this book we focus even more decidedly on the growth and change that occurred in urban schools after 1900. In so doing we shall reconsider the much studied, much maligned reforms of American urban education. In the process of looking at these reforms in urban education we shall discover that many of the shibboleths and truisms about school reform cannot be sustained by a careful look at the Atlanta, Chicago, and San Francisco experience. Reform, it now seems to us, has been understood in too narrow a set of categories. Reform was much more—and much less—than a class struggle, and reformers were often much more—and much less—than a class-conscious elite who imposed their interests and values on a resistant working-class majority. Reform was itself as complex, uncertain, and pluralistic as many of the other forces shaping urban schools.

Part Two

Reforming Public Schools

6 Urban Reform without Class Conflict

Though the pressures for change had been building for some time, reform came suddenly to the Atlanta public school system. On 28 May 1897, in a city council meeting ostensibly called to consider some routine matters pertaining to the city's waterworks, Alderman James G. Woodward introduced a resolution that replaced the sitting seventeen-member school board with a new board comprising one member from each of the city's seven wards. Despite a recent escalation in the conflict between the school board and Mayor Charles Collier, the move came as a surprise to virtually everyone in Atlanta, including all the members of the school board.[1] The entire operation took only a few minutes. As the Atlanta *Constitution* observed the next day: "A Texas hanging couldn't have gone off with the precision and nicety of the sudden execution. . . . The ax revolved and the heads were basketed."[2]

The action of the city council raised an immediate public outcry in Atlanta: a mass meeting held the following day denounced the move as "illegal, revolutionary, despotic, and dangerous." The city's newspapers gave the unfolding story front-page coverage and banner headlines for several days.[3] Within a week of the "astounding coup," however, the new board had organized itself and won the endorsement of both city newspapers.[4]

THE CLASS CONFLICT MODEL OF URBAN REFORM

In this chapter we assess the adequacy of the class-conflict model of progressive educational reform for understanding the 1897 reform of the Atlanta schools. Urban reform in general and school reform in particular have frequently been interpreted in bipolar class-conflict categories. According to the model, the forces behind reform drives were social and economic elites who had become disturbed by the rising power of working-class immigrant politicians and organizations. Attacks on corruption and patronage, calls for efficient administration and scientific management, and demands for good government and citizen participation were seen simply as more or less well-disguised campaigns to dismember institutional bastions of working-class power.[5]

Most of these interpretations of urban reform are based upon incomplete research carried out in northern cities. When attention has been paid to the South, the racist twists to populist and reform efforts have received the greatest emphasis. Yet the southern experience with reform requires broader consideration. Demographically, at the turn of the century southern cities differed dramatically from their northern counterparts in a variety of ways. Foreign immigrants represented a negligible fraction of the population in most southern cities, whereas blacks were nearly as numerous as whites. Industrialization was barely under way in the region, and the urban working class was racially divided and politically weak. Economic and political power remained firmly in the grip of the traditional white, "Bourbon" elite.

These differences raise the question whether the divergent political and economic characteristics of northern and southern cities spawned reform movements that differed significantly from one another. Did those differences come either in the political process through which reform was carried out or in the content of the reforms that were implemented? The Atlanta experience with reform is an especially promising test case: Atlanta has always been the southern city most attuned to developments in the North, calling itself the Gate City and the capital of the progressive New South. If the class-conflict model of urban reform is appropriate for analyzing reform movements in any part of the South, it would presumably account for developments in Atlanta.

We show that many of the policies often said to be characteristic of reform were carried out in Atlanta in that year: the school board was reduced in size, the administrative powers of the superintendent were increased, temporary economy measures were implemented, and progressive curricular innovations were introduced. We also show, however, that the political process that led to reform in Atlanta was quite different from the process as defined by proponents of the class-conflict model. While the reformers in Atlanta were members of the middle and upper classes, as the model suggests, the Atlanta school reforms were carried out not over the objections of working-class politicians but rather at the expense of the city's most prestigious civic leaders. In contrast to the efforts of urban elites to "get the schools out of politics," the political connections of Atlanta's reformers were so blatant that their opponents justifiably accused them of introducing politics into the public school system.

On the basis of our findings, we have concluded that class conflict is not a necessary condition for urban reform. The data suggest that at a minimum the class-conflict model inadequately accounts for southern reform politics. Instead, the primary sources of urban school reform are to be found in the new administrative requirements created by increasingly large and multifaceted educational organizations, and in the rising political strength of middle-class professionals who were as suspicious of traditional social elites as they were of working-class politicians.

EDUCATIONAL REFORM IN ATLANTA

At the end of the nineteenth century, Atlanta was relatively small but rapidly growing. The city had barely twenty thousand residents in 1872, when it began its public school system. By 1900 the population had more than quadrupled to nearly ninety thousand, and growth continued apace in the succeeding decade. The black population of Atlanta grew at a slower rate than the white population. At the turn of the century nearly 40 percent of the city's residents were black. The representation of immigrants in Atlanta's population declined from 6.5 percent in 1870 to an insignificant 2.8 percent in 1900. The city's economy was also growing and changing in these years. Between 1880 and 1890 the aggregate product of Atlanta's industries nearly tripled as the locally oriented food processing and construction industries were surpassed by industries producing for regional and national markets. Though aggregate economic growth was slowed by the national depression between 1890 and 1900, technological and organizational changes in this decade greatly increased the productive efficiency of Atlanta's industries, and the amount of value added in the production process by employees grew by more than 60 percent.

The demographic and economic development of Atlanta was reflected in the growth of the city's dual public school system. Table 6.1 shows that grammar-school enrollments more than doubled between 1878 and 1890 and nearly doubled again in the following decade. At the secondary level no schools were provided for black children, but white enrollments increased rapidly if less steadily than at the primary level. Between 1878 and 1900 enrollments in the system as a whole grew by nearly 300 percent, and at the turn of the century more than half the eligible children in the city were enrolled in school. The rapid growth of the city and its public school system set the stage for educational reform in Atlanta in 1897.

The Content of School Reform

In some ways the Atlanta school reform fits rather well with the class-conflict model. The instigators of the reform movement were Mayor Charles Collier and newspaperman Hoke Smith, both well-established members of the city's economic and political elite. Collier was a noted proponent of Henry Grady's New South ideology and an active advocate of Atlanta's economic growth and civic improvement. In this connection he had served as president of the corporation that had staged the Cotton States and International Exposition in Atlanta in 1895, an event intended to

TABLE 6.1 Atlanta Public-School Enrollments, 1878–1910

Year	Black Primary Enrollment	Black Pupils per Teacher	White Primary Enrollment	White Pupils per Teacher	Secondary Enrollment (White)	Secondary Students per Teacher	Total[a] Enrollment	Percentage[b] of Cohort in School
1878	1,269	90.6	2,081	63.1	317	45.3	3,667	
1882	1,111	69.4	2,813	63.9	332	41.5	4,256	
1885	1,533	—	3,659	—	379	42.1	5,571	
1890	2,373	—	5,402	—	638	49.1	8,413	39.2
1895	4,705	117.6	9,042	64.6	901	50.1	14,767	
1896	3,566	89.2	9,330	76.5	860	47.8	13,937	
1897	3,484	87.1	9,558	64.6	941	49.5	14,328	
1900	4,069	92.5	9,047	55.2	922	41.9	14,236	51.4
1905	4,164	74.4	10,066	46.4	810	31.2	15,539	
1910	5,346	75.3	14,146	40.8	1,271	28.2	21,418	50.1

Sources: Atlanta Board of Education, Annual Report, 1878–1910. United States Bureau of the Census, Population, 1890, 1 (part 2): 114; 1900, 1 (part 2): 122; 1910, 1:450.

[a]After 1895, total includes night students, all of whom were white.

[b]School-age cohort, ages five to nineteen.

attract entrepreneurs and northern capital to the Gate City and to open up the city and the region for increased development and industrialization.[6] Smith was the editor of the Atlanta *Journal* and an increasingly important political figure known for his "progressive" sympathies. He had served as Grover Cleveland's secretary of the interior in the early 1890s, and he was to be elected governor of Georgia in 1906. Like Collier, Smith was a vigorous proponent of southern development and industrialization: he maintained a lifelong interest in educational reform and especially vocational education.[7]

The content of the Atlanta school reforms corresponds with the content of reforms described by the class-conflict model in other respects as well. The change in board membership resulted in a shift of administrative power from the school board to the professional staff of the school system. The reduction in school board members from seventeen to seven and in board committees from ten to two limited the extent to which members could involve themselves personally in the day-to-day administration of the system. This shift in power was further encouraged by the addition of a full-time assistant superintendent to the administrative staff and by an extension of the rights and responsibilities of the superintendent. He and his assistant were permitted to participate fully in the meetings of the school board for the first time, and a variety of administrative tasks that had previously been handled by board committees, including the adjudication of disputes between parents and teachers and the ordering of supplies, were placed under his authority.[8] As was often the case in other cities, the Atlanta school reform thus increased the power of the administrative staff at the expense of the school board itself.

A further parallel between the reforms in Atlanta and those in other cities deserves mention. The members of the new board came into office committed to introducing manual training courses into the schools. In his first annual report to the mayor and council, board president Hoke Smith expressed his desire "to see industrial work introduced all through our schools, and the minds of the children so trained as to fit them for the practical utilization of what they learn."[9] He reiterated this wish in the two succeeding years, and in 1900 a director of manual training was employed and a workshop was constructed in Boys' High School. According to Smith, this was "simply the beginning of manual training. We hope to see it gradually develop until manual training for boys and girls will help to prepare the children of our schools for practical work."[10]

In sum, Atlanta's school reform removed the sitting board of education from office, strengthened the superintendent and his staff at the expense of the temporary board, and added manual training courses to the curriculum. The list makes the Atlanta experience sound like the prototypical reform movement, in which a powerful elite seized control of the school

system, centralizing power in the office of the superintendent and rational-
izing procedures throughout the system over the protests of the poor and
working classes. A closer look at school reform in Atlanta, however, shows
that while there are similarities with the class-conflict model, there are
equally important differences. It is to these discrepancies that we now turn.

The Politics of School Reform

Prereform Politics. Politics in Atlanta before the reform of the school
system were hardly working-class politics. Power in the city was virtually
monopolized by elite members of the business, commercial, and professional community. Atlanta's black citizens were not represented in city
government after 1870, and they were deprived of what little political
influence remained to them by the institution of the "white primary" in the
early 1890s.[11] The white working class was significantly underrepresented
in office as well, though the rival factions of Atlanta's elite required the
support of the city's workers for electoral success and therefore competed
for working-class votes.[12]

The preeminence of the city's elites in municipal politics was promoted
by the absence of party competition in Atlanta, where the Democratic party
was the only recognized political organization, and its influence was
reflected in the putative ideological consensus that governed political discourse. The consensus, which precluded the emergence of sharp divisions in
the white electorate, was maintained in large part because of the ostensible
need to keep Atlanta's black citizens out of power.[13] The consequence was a
political system based on the distribution of graft and patronage and
divided along factional lines.[14] As the Atlanta *Journal* explained: "It is
well-known that for several years past there have been two factions in the
council. . . . They have alternated in the control of that body, and the
faction that has a majority for the time being has everything its own way so
completely that the minority might as well not be there so far as the choice
of department officials is concerned."[15]

The two factions were led by J. W. English and W. H. Brotherton.
Brotherton was a prosperous dry-goods merchant with strong ties to the
local branch of the American Protective Association and Atlanta's organized working class, while English was one of the region's leading indus-
trialists and a large-scale employer of leased convict labor, with his political base in the chamber of commerce.[16] Brotherton was the leader of the
powerful Prohibition Club in city politics, whereas English often worked
with Atlanta's liquor interests.[17] At the same time, however, the composition of the two factions was subject to dramatic changes. In the municipal
election of 1896, for example, a dispute between the labor and Prohibition
elements in the Brotherton faction caused the Atlanta Federation of Trades
to break its customary political ties and endorse the English ticket.[18]

Though union and other working-class support was eagerly pursued by the two factions, the split between them marked a division within the civic elite rather than a division along class lines, with the English faction tending to enlist the support of somewhat wealthier and more prestigious citizens and to present the more eminent candidates for office.[19]

An important part in the factional struggle was played by Atlanta's two newspapers, the *Journal* and the *Constitution*. Rivalry between the two was to emerge as the predominant feature of Georgia politics in the 1900s, when the "progressive" faction led by Hoke Smith and the *Journal* vied with the "conservative" faction led by Clark Howell and the *Constitution* for political and economic control of the state. In the 1890s, however, political competition between the two was largely confined to the local arena. The *Journal* most often stood with the several elements of the Brotherton faction, while the *Constitution* allied itself with the traditional elites who dominated the English faction.[20]

A complicating factor in the municipal politics of Atlanta in these years was the persistence of "friends and neighbors" ties, which eroded factional divisions and occasionally transcended them altogether. The political ascendancy of Clark Howell's brother Albert within the Brotherton faction in 1896, for example, caused the *Constitution* to sever whatever ties had traditionally bound it to the English faction and to work vigorously for the election of the Brotherton ticket.[21] This shift in itself would probably have been enough to bring the *Journal* to endorse the English candidate, but the English faction's nomination of C. A. Collier for mayor ensured the new alignment, for Hoke Smith had studied law in Collier's father's law firm, and Collier himself had been a member of the original corporation Smith organized to purchase the *Journal* in the mid-1880s.[22]

The portrait of Atlanta's political system that emerges is thus one in which the principal function of municipal politics was to distribute economic and political favors between competing factions of the city's social and economic elite. Political conflicts were based on disputes not over issues, with the possible exception of Prohibition, but rather over the control of city government and the political advantages that could be reaped from it. Black and white members of the working class played virtually no role in city politics. They were unable to take part in the definition of issues or to contest seriously for office, and their political activities were largely restricted to efforts to trade votes to one faction or the other in return for a share of the favors to be dispensed. Blacks were deprived of even this power after the institution of the white primary, but white workers continued to gain occasional concessions from the factions. Though the factions were in some respects definable entities, their boundaries remained relatively fluid, and dramatic shifts in membership could and did occur. Personal antagonisms were frequently at the root of political rivalries, and "friends and neighbors" relationships frequently determined the alignment of forces.

Thus, in contrast to the picture of urban politics described in the class-conflict model of urban reform, Atlanta politics in this era were not defined by disputes between classes. The city's business and professional leaders were in firm control of the economic and political institutions of the city, and such political dissension as did occur in these years developed within the city's elite.

Elites and Traditional School Politics. The school board in particular was a bastion of power for Atlanta's traditional civic elite. The school board was uniformly composed of members of the city's business and professional elites and included some of Atlanta's wealthiest and most eminent citizens. Among them were men like L. P. Grant, the president of the Atlanta and West Point Railroad; Logan E. Bleckley, Georgia's best-known lawyer and subsequently chief justice of the Georgia supreme court; E. E. Rawson, a pioneer industrialist who had made his fortune in real estate; S. M. Inman, a cotton merchant who was reputedly the wealthiest man in Atlanta; and J. W. English.[23] Most important among the members of the school board, however, was Joseph E. Brown, who served as president of the board until his election to the United States Senate in 1888 and continued to dominate its deliberations until his death in 1894. Brown had served as the Confederate governor of Georgia, and he reigned as a member of the state's "Bourbon triumvirate" after Reconstruction, serving a term as chief justice of the Georgia supreme court. He was also president of the Western and Atlantic Railroad, the Southern Railway and Steamship Company, the Walker Iron and Coal Company, and the Dade Coal Company, which made him one of the wealthiest and most powerful men in the Southeast.[24]

Members of the school board were appointed for seven-year terms, and they were routinely reappointed if they were willing to serve.[25] With the exception of authority over annual appropriations, which was retained by the city council, power over the school system was fully vested in the school board.[26] Exempted from political controversy by the wealth and status of its members, the duration of their tenure, and the nature of its charter, the prereform school board was essentially free to administer the schools according to its own conservative preferences, without regard for the exigencies of local electoral politics. Thus, in contrast to the situation commonly described in educational reform literature, in which prereform school politics are said to have been ward and neighborhood based, under the control of working-class politicians and their allies, in Atlanta the school system was unified under the direction of elite, "citywide" interests from its inception.

Issues in School Politics. The issues that precipitated the reform of the Atlanta schools also differ from those cited in class-conflict literature. In the mid-1890s, public protest arose over the board's policies of textbook selection and the frequency with which new books were assigned in the schools, because of the high costs parents were obliged to bear.[27] Controversy also arose over curricular reform. Many Atlantans, including the mayor and members of the city council, urged such innovations as a departmental organization of the faculties of Boys' and Girls' High Schools and the addition of manual training and vocational subjects to the curriculum of the primary and secondary schools. Although the school board made some slight modifications in response to these demands, efforts to modernize the curriculum proved largely fruitless before 1897.[28]

By far the largest public dispute arose over corporal punishment in the schools. Protests about the thrashing of recalcitrant children increased dramatically after 1890, and demands that corporal punishment be forbidden in the public school system were directed to the school board by middle-class parents, prominent citizens, and members of the city council with increasing frequency and impatience as the decade passed.[29] Atlanta's teachers, however, argued that the hickory switch was essential if they were to maintain order in the city's classrooms. The school board sided with them.

Opposition to the school board found its champion with the inauguration of Mayor Collier in 1897. Collier was quick to protest against the prodigality of the school board in its administration of the public school system, and he joined in the public controversy over other issues as well. From his position as an ex officio member of the board, he tried unsuccessfully to encourage curricular reforms and other changes in the system, and he worked hard for the abolition of corporal punishment. Declaring that no living man or woman would ever whip one of his children, the mayor declared that the retention of corporal punishment in the public system had led him to enroll his own children in private schools.[30] Taking over the leadership of the forces opposing the practice in the city, he circulated a petition among the influential citizens of Atlanta that demanded that teachers in the public schools be prohibited from whipping children. When he had collected over one hundred signatures—from "persons whose names it was believed would have weight with the Board of Education"—he submitted the petition to the board.[31]

The public outcry against corporal punishment was heightened by noisy press coverage of a sensational case involving a student at Boys' High School who had been severely beaten by a teacher after allegedly drawing a knife in the classroom. The controversy between the boy's father and the teacher was heard by a committee of the school board over a period of weeks, and a number of columns appeared in the city's newspapers in which the opinions of prominent citizens on the "all-absorbing topic of the hour" were published.[32] The grievance committee of the school board nevertheless found in favor of the teacher, and a measure introduced by Mayor Collier to abolish corporal punishment throughout the school system was defeated by a board vote of twelve to four.[33] Speaking for the majority, D. A. Beattie asserted: "This movement is all nonsense. They don't do half enough whipping in the schools now, and it's foolish to talk about stopping it altogether."[34] The day after the vote was taken, the city council voted to abolish the school board. Among the first actions of the newly appointed board were the prohibition of corporal punishment in Boys' High School and the introduction of strict regulations governing its application in the city's elementary schools.

The Political Consequences of Reform. In further contrast with the class-conflict model of educational reform, the restructuring of the Atlanta school board was engineered not by a civic elite intent upon seizing control of the public school system from the working class and its political allies, but rather by a coalition of groups within the civic elite, including Mayor Collier, who sought to reform the educational system and by the Brotherton faction, which sought greater political control over the schools. The effect that school reform in Atlanta had was to shift power over the educational system out of the hands of the traditional civic elite and into the hands of somewhat less prestigious men, including lawyers and other middle-class professionals, small businessmen, and men with political ties to the local labor movement.

The public response to the change in boards reflected its political character. The Atlanta *Journal*, formally allied with the English faction in city politics, greeted the change with equanimity despite the key role played by the Brotherton faction. The editor's "progressive" sympathies and his ties with Mayor Collier, who had instigated the reform movement, offset concern about the introduction of politics into the public school system. In contrast, the Atlanta *Constitution* expressed outrage at the council's action, despite its recent affiliation with the Brotherton faction, because its editors had traditionally had close ties with the conservative elites who predominated on the "exterminated" board. The *Constitution* devoted considerable attention to a mass meeting held on Saturday, 29 May, which denounced the council's "illegal, revolutionary, despotic, and dangerous" action and attacked "the ring controlling our city government."

In response to the public uproar, three of the new board members, who had especially close ties to the old board and the city's traditional elite, declined to serve, but replacements were quickly elected by the city council.[35] After a meeting with Mayor Collier the following Monday, the members of the new board were duly sworn in, and they held their first

meeting that afternoon. To quiet apprehensions about political interference in the city's public school system, Mayor Collier successfully proposed
an amendment to the city charter that forbade future city councils from
removing school-board members from office before the expiration of their
terms.[36]

Although the initial members of the reformed board differed little from
their immediate predecessors, a longer view shows that the 1897 reform
ushered in a new era in Atlanta school politics. After the change the school
board was no longer controlled by the city's traditional social and economic elites but was run by men of substantially lesser prestige, as can be
seen in table 6.2. Members were appointed to shorter terms, and they
remained on the board for shorter periods than their predecessors. The
average term of board members before 1897 was nearly eight years; after
1897 the average term was just over four years. In addition, members were
appointed by wards after 1897, and they were chosen more for their political connections and sensitivity to ward concerns than for their prominence
in the city as a whole, as had been the case earlier. Whereas the old school
board had been dominated by members of the civic elite, the new board was
dominated by lawyers and minor politicians and had representatives from
a variety of interest groups, including organized labor.[37] Thus the political
changes that accompanied reform removed Atlanta's traditional "downtown" elite from power and replaced them with men with more particularistic, ward-based concerns, thereby increasing the political responsiveness
of the educational system.

TABLE 6.2 Social Composition of Atlanta School Board, 1872–1918

Occupation	1872–97		1897–1918	
	Mem-bers	Board-Years	Mem-bers	Board-Years
Bank and corporation presidents	20%	31%	—	—
Lawyers	29	24	36%	43%
Other professionals	16	15	7	7
Other bank and corporation officials	11	6	18	18
Realtors and insurance men	5	5	20	16
Proprietors	18	20	13	11
Employees	—	—	4	5
Unknown	—	—	2	1
Number	44	347	45	184

Source: Atlanta City Directories, 1872–1918.

Note: Percentage totals may not sum to 100 because of rounding.

The Causes of Educational Reform in Atlanta

Although speculation as to the causes of the council's "astounding coup" was rampant in the midst of the controversy, two major viewpoints quickly emerged. Mayor Collier, as spokesman for the "combine" that had carried out the reform, asserted that the council had acted only to make the administration of the schools more efficient: "There is no significance to the movement except that the board was too large and we thought to cut it down. None of the old members were re-elected because we did not want to offend half of them by leaving them off."[38] This explanation satisfied the Atlanta *Journal*, though the paper also reminded its readers of the recent disputes over teacher salaries and corporal punishment and even suggested that "the entire school system of the city may be revolutionized by this change of boards."[39] Whereas the mayor and his allies explained the changes largely in terms of improving the efficiency and accountability of Atlanta's schools, the *Constitution* took a more political view, asserting that the restructuring marked an end to the political independence of the public school system: "The most vicious feature connected with it . . . is the fact that it throws our entire public school system into the very center of the whirlpool of political agitation. . . . At any hour of the day or night—especially night—it may become the victim of some political combination and suffer the deadliest results of secret deals, jobs, and manipulations."[40]

The competing explanations of the Atlanta school reform offered by the participants in the dispute were both partially correct. The political causes were the conflicts that had arisen between the city council and the school board in the mid-1890s. These were brought on by the unwillingness of the school board to abolish corporal punishment, adopt curricular innovations, or modernize school administration, despite the demands of the mayor and other politically influential citizens.

But if immediate political conflicts triggered the change, broader pressures for efficiency and modernization in education provided the context within which particular political circumstances could engender large-scale organizational consequences. Mayor Collier and other members of the "combine" that engineered the reform of the school system—especially Hoke Smith—were self-conscious advocates of a modern, industrialized, and prosperous New South, with Atlanta as its regional capital, and they worked throughout their lives to bring their vision into reality. They were cognizant of contemporaneous reform movements in other cities and aware of the ideas of educational experts and reformers elsewhere. Dedicated to modernizing their region, they were alive to the contributions a modern, reformed school system could make, and they chafed at the obstacle to development posed by the traditional, inefficient organization of the public school system and the domination of the system by the city's older civic elite. Recognizing the political opportunity presented by the conflict between the school board and the city council, the mayor acted in 1897 to implement administrative and organizational changes that made the public school system more responsive to the changing economic and political circumstances of Atlanta and the South.

The Fiscal Consequences of Reform

There remains the question of the effect of reform on school expenditures in Atlanta, for in contrast to San Francisco during this same period (see chap. 2), reform meant not just organizational and administrative modernization, but severe cutbacks in the school services provided to the children of the city. If other school reforms embodied no obvious class bias, it is more difficult to see how drastic budgetary cuts were anything other than hostile to the increasingly widespread, popular demand for public schooling, which expressed itself in overcrowded classrooms and, in the black community, in continuous, organized efforts to gain better facilities. Was the reformers' concern with efficiency indeed a disguise for a business-oriented concern with the rising costs of a labor-intensive public service?

Shortly after his inauguration, Collier persuaded the school board to pass a 9 percent pay cut for all the city's teachers. In addition, he pushed an ordinance through the city council that prohibited the school board from purchasing any supplies for the schools without the express authorization of the mayor and the council.[41] These efforts to enforce economy in the public school system were resisted both by the old school board and by Atlanta's teachers. In his annual report to the mayor and council, the board president asserted the rights of the school board against those of the city's elected leaders: "I ask for the schools the best financial support that the condition of the treasury will admit of, and that the Board be permitted to exercise its judgement not only as to what shall be taught and who shall teach, but also what shall be paid, keeping within such appropriation as you shall make for the schools."[42] Though the board partially acquiesced to the mayor and modestly reduced teacher salaries, its president chose to resign rather than submit to all of Collier's demands.[43] Understandably concerned about the effects the mayor's economy measures would have on their standard of living, Atlanta's teachers supported the school board in its resistance. A petition signed by every teacher in the school system asked the board president to withdraw his resignation and return to office.[44]

The drive for economy in the administration of the school system intensified after the abolition of the original school board. The newly appointed board responded to the mayor's demands for reduced expenditures by firing several teachers (and a number of principals), cutting the length of the school year by a week, and imposing additional salary cuts on the teachers in 1897 and 1898.[45] The approach of the new board was summed up by its president, Hoke Smith: "As a rule the teachers are doing good work.

The Board found it necessary to give up the services of some, and it may be necessary to give up the services of others."[46]

As table 6.3 makes clear, the economy measures implemented by Mayor Collier and the new board of education had a profound impact on the public school system of Atlanta. Instructional expenditures were reduced absolutely in 1897, and they remained below the level reached in 1896 until after the turn of the century. The level of total expenditures, including building and other capital expenses, was affected even more dramatically. Total expenditures were reduced more than 25 percent between 1896 and 1897, and in constant dollars they did not regain their former level until 1905. These reductions in the level of appropriations to the school system occurred at a time when the population of Atlanta was increasing rapidly, and they resulted in increased class sizes plus the exclusion of substantial numbers of would-be pupils. Per-pupil expenditures were reduced about 10 percent from 1896 to 1897.

The answer to what effect reform had on school finances lies more in the economic situation of the times than in a philosophy of penuriousness, supposedly a concomitant of reform. At the time of the reform Atlanta, like most other American cities, was in the midst of a nationwide depression, which forced service reductions and economy measures in all sectors of society, both public and private. Collier reduced the level of city services generally, as well as the salaries of all municipal employees,[47] and he was quick to demand that the school system be operated more economically and efficiently. When he met resistance, the mayor observed: "I have been

TABLE 6.3 Atlanta School Expenditures, 1878–1910

Year	Instructional Expenditures ($000s)		Total Expenditures ($000s)		Instructional Expenditures per Pupil	
	Current Dollars	Constant Dollars[a]	Current Dollars	Constant Dollars[a]	Current Dollars	Constant Dollars[a]
1878	38.1	47.6	38.1	47.6	10.39	12.98
1882	44.8	52.1	55.3	64.3	10.52	12.23
1885	57.6	75.8	76.3	100.4	10.35	13.61
1890	89.3	114.5	137.5	176.3	10.62	13.60
1895	136.2	186.5	138.6	189.8	9.22	12.63
1896	151.8	205.2	198.7	268.6	10.89	14.72
1897	142.0	189.3	142.0	189.3	9.91	13.58
1900	144.0	180.0	168.7	210.9	10.11	12.64
1905	215.3	247.5	249.0	286.2	14.02	16.11
1910	343.7	358.0	475.8	495.6	16.05	16.72

Source: Atlanta Board of Education, Superintendent's Reports, 1878–1910.
[a]1913 = 100. Federal Reserve Bank of New York Cost of Living Index.

surprised and mortified to find that this department was the only one disposed to hamper us in our efforts to put the city government on a business basis."[48] To be sure, the depression may have created the occasion that forced reformers to cut public spending. Yet in subsequent years of reform rule, as prosperity returned to the city and the nation, Atlanta's school expenditures regained and then surpassed previous levels.[49] Tables 6.1 and 6.3 show that for white students, at least, and to a lesser extent for blacks, reform resulted in reduced class sizes and increased expenditure per pupil after the turn of the century. The pecuniary consequences of reform thus proved to be among its least enduring features.

CONCLUSION

In this chapter we have shown that the politics of Atlanta school reform differ from those described by a bipolar, class-conflict model of urban reform. If there were parallels between many of the innovations in Atlanta and those made in other cities, in Atlanta the changes were not carried out against the opposition of a locally oriented working class. Instead, they were brought about by a younger faction of the city's elite that was dominated by professional men and concerned with the modernization and development of the city and the region, and the reforms were carried out at the expense of traditional economic and political elites. As opposed to the shift in power from ward politicians to citywide elites, the Atlanta reforms transferred power from the city's traditional civic elite to men of lesser status who were better attuned to the demands of ward and patronage politics. Although in Atlanta the working class was not a visible participant in the reform movement, either in support or in opposition, the faction ordinarily supported by the city's labor movement was the one engineering the reform.

That practically identical reforms were successful in Atlanta and in a number of northern cities, despite dramatic differences in the political contexts, is an anomaly that the class-conflict model cannot explain. As we have noted, the model describes conflicting interests generating political controversy between two social classes, with the dominant class securing a policy outcome favorable to its interests. But if similar policy consequences occur in *all* cities, whether reform is opposed by conservative elites or by organized workers, then in what sense can the policy reforms in any context be attributed to class-based political conflict? If progressive educational reform came about as a result of the victory of economic and social elites over working-class groups and organizations, then why did reform occur where no such class struggle was visible?

There are two complementary responses to these questions. The first suggests that the political processes through which reform occurred in particular cities were essentially epiphenomenal. The changes in school organization in the late nineteenth century were required by contemporaneous socioeconomic changes in American society. The explosive growth of urban populations, the rapid expansion and diversification of urban economies, and the increasing complexity of urban social relationships, common to all regions at the turn of the century, imposed rapidly rising enrollments and a broader range of social responsibilities upon big-city school systems. As these systems grew larger and undertook to provide a new and diverse array of services, their management became increasingly complex. Organizations that once had been directed by a small group of part-time lay board members now required the full-time attention of a highly trained professional staff. Urban school systems thus came to resemble one another not so much because of the particular political circumstances that shaped them as because of the attributes of function, complexity, and size that they had in common.

Although this functional argument is persuasive in many ways, it is theoretically problematic to identify the "causes" of a structural arrangement with its functions or "consequences." No matter how beneficent a social institution may be, the desirable consequences of its presence cannot constitute an explanation for the structure's coming into being.[50] Thus the functional explanation becomes plausible only when linked to a second response to the queries posed. This explanation, like that provided by a bipolar class-conflict model, identifies a strong social group, an emerging professional class, with an interest in urban educational reform. Because it identifies a more complex pattern of social interactions than that suggested by the bipolarities of class conflict, however, it can resolve the apparent contradiction between the political process of reform in Atlanta and those in the cities of the industrialized North.

The difficulty with a simple class-conflict model is that it reduces complex, multiparty political contests to simple two-sided disputes. Even in northern cities, debates over urban reform involved Protestants, Catholics, teachers, administrators, professionals, and politicians as well as workers and capitalists. Especially important was the emerging autonomous role in both northern and southern cities of middle-class professionals, who supported urban educational reform for their own distinctive reasons. In class-conflict models the interests of middle-class professionals are treated as almost synonymous with those of the business community, yet campaigns for urban reform pitted middle-class professional groups against business elites as often as they divided the middle class from labor unions and other working-class organizations.

As urbanization and industrialization progressed in the late nineteenth century, there was an increasing demand for a wide variety of professional services, including those provided by lawyers, doctors, social scientists, journalists, social workers, teachers, and public administrators. Professional associations represented the interests of these and many other emerging occupations with increasing effectiveness. In addition, many professionals felt confident enough of their growing social esteem to argue that public policy was an arena for professional expertise, scientific administration, and the exercise of high levels of technical proficiency. Although those offering class-conflict interpretations of urban reform have emphasized the differences between these middle-class values and interests and those of working-class immigrant groups, few have appreciated the simultaneous challenge these professionals offered to businessmen skeptical of any claim to expertise that was not market tested and wary of the costs of a new array of professionally administered public services. The more politically sophisticated leaders of the emerging professional class understood their role to be midway between the interests of capital and labor. If they felt unions were often too self-interested, they were at least equally alarmed at the increasing concentration of power in the business community. Their efforts to reduce politics to administration were inspired in part by a desire to rationalize and subject to scientific scrutiny what had previously been decided by campaign rhetoric and political muscle. While the understanding of the reformers was in some ways myopic—in their public rhetoric, for example, they seldom mentioned the new jobs for professionals their plans would require—they nevertheless correctly understood that opposition to their proposals came as often from business as from labor.

7 Compromise Reform

Reform in Atlanta meant the triumph of an emerging class of professionals over a traditional conservative elite. But because the city lacked strong unions, an active political machine, and a large immigrant population, it is difficult to claim from the Atlanta story alone that the class-conflict model presents a distorted vision of school reform in urban America more generally. To elaborate our argument that reform was produced by a broader set of forces and that reformers were as often in alliance with labor and teachers as in opposition to their interests, it is important to examine the processes of reform in Chicago, a rapidly growing industrial city where class conflicts regularly erupted in school affairs. In that city the most important legislative effort to reform the schools was promulgated prior to World War II. This was the Otis Law, passed by the Illinois legislature in 1917, the year the United States entered World War I.

The Otis Law, with provisions that changed power relations among teachers, superintendents and the school board, was in many ways a classic school-reform law. The office of the superintendent was strengthened by extending the term from one to four years, by giving the superintendent power to hire and fire teachers, and by more clearly defining responsibilities for the day-to-day administration of the system. The school board gained more independence from the city council, including both the power of eminent domain and the authority to buy and sell school lands. In addition, the board was given the power to borrow funds up to 75 percent of the taxes to be collected the following fiscal year. For the teachers there was more job security. They were to be granted tenure after three years of service, with dismissal only for cause and upon written charges. Teachers who were fired had recourse to a board investigation.

In spite of its scope and its importance for the internal administrative reorganization of Chicago's schools, the Otis Law was not a "triumph" for school reformers. Rather, it was a compromise law—a settlement reached after business leaders, working with machine politicians, failed to pass the more conservative Baldwin bill in the face of opposition from middle-class school reformers who had been working with teachers and labor groups on behalf of more sweeping reforms. As in all compromises, parties to the dispute settled for what was most important to them. For the teachers that meant legally established tenure; to Mayor William "Big Bill" Thompson it meant continued control of the schools through an appointed board; and to the middle-class school reformers it meant increased responsibilities for the superintendent, from whom they expected improved administration.

Compromise on the school law was necessitated by political events in Chicago during the preceding two years. Thompson had been elected mayor in 1915, and his two-year reign was a period when "the spoils system swept over the city like a noxious blight, and the city hall became a symbol for corruption and incompetence."[1] A solid faction of aldermen had begun to oppose every measure bearing the stamp of city hall, among them Charles Merriam from the University of Chicago's political science department and Robert Buck, a former labor reporter for the Chicago *Tribune* and the *Daily News*. When the council, under the leadership of Buck, began an investigation into relations between Thompson's administration and the school system, Thompson vowed to defeat Buck, Merriam, and the other aldermen who opposed him in the 1917 municipal election. The campaign became vitriolic, keeping supporters and opponents of school reform fighting for their political lives at home in Chicago. Both the reformers and the Thompson machine suffered enormous losses, with the regular Democrats emerging as the clear victors. With matters in Springfield not being attended to, and with America's involvement in the war softening passions on domestic issues, a compromise—the Otis bill—was passed by the legislature.

PREREFORM POLITICS

On Mayor Thompson's first inauguration day in April 1915, Fred Lundin, the mayor's campaign director and behind-the-scenes brain of his rise in politics, staged a massive Prosperity Day parade in Thompson's honor. Education was depicted as an important part of the new administration by a little red schoolhouse surrounded by children and by a float with several girls holding a banner that read, "The Chicago Schools—We Teach the 3R's to 331,567 children."[2] In fact, under Big Bill's rule, education was to have a prominent place, but probably not the sort anticipated by the fanfare of the Prosperity Day parade. During Thompson's years in office, Chicago witnessed a period when two boards of education vied for authority, when board members were convicted of embezzling funds, when a superintendent was locked out of his office by the board, and when Thompson absurdly accused a superintendent of letting the king of England take over the Chicago schools.[3]

Thompson's political history had not been particularly noteworthy before his accession to the mayoralty in 1915. He had served one term in the city council, had been elected county commissioner in 1902, and had lost a bid in the primary of 1911 for a seat on the Cook County Board of Review. During these years Thompson had also developed close ties to Republican boss William Lorimer, a United States senator who was voted out of office in 1912 for allegedly bribing his colleagues. It was through his connection with Lorimer that Thompson became acquainted with Fred Lundin, who had served as a state senator and United States congressman and who had since become a financial and political power in city politics. Well before the 1915 campaign Lundin was privately telling friends that "Big Bill" Thompson would be the next mayor of Chicago, a man he could "mold and guide and control."[4]

To secure victory, Thompson, with Lundin's help, had to defeat Judge Harry Olson in the Republican primary and then Robert Sweitzer, the challenger who would overcome the incumbent mayor Carter Harrison in the Democratic primary. In both campaigns Thompson was the candidate reformers feared most. Although Thompson assured the public "that I would not, if nominated and elected, use the power of the mayor's office to build up political machines," reform leaders knew better, and in the primary Merriam, Buck, and Jane Addams all backed Judge Olson, railing at Thompson's record on the city council. But the reformers were better at decrying corruption than at corralling votes, and Thompson overwhelmed Olson in the primary and then Sweitzer in the general election.

Thompson lived up to the worst fears of Chicago's reformers. He handed Lundin the city payroll and told him to "play with it," and both the city cabinet and the city payroll were taken over by Thompson's and Lundin's loyal troops. Within four months of the election, nearly ten thousand temporary but renewable appointments were made, circumventing civil-service requirements. The two politicians also used the device of eliminating a specific job and its incumbent only to create a newly titled position for a more loyal jobholder. Commenting on the new appointments, the city papers denounced Thompson as having "a low sense of responsibility," as "betraying the public trust," and as having "reverted to his previous self."[5]

Apart from the newspapers, Thompson's chief opposition came from the reform-minded aldermen. They concentrated their attack on Thompson by calling to the public's attention his attempt to use the schools for patronage purposes. The reformers seemed to believe that even if the public accepted patronage and corruption in most quarters, there was at least a chance they would rebel at the thought that their children's welfare was being jeopardized for political purposes. Their first attack on Thompson thus focused on his nominees to the board of education, who were criticized for not having the necessary educational and residential qualifications. So successful was this tactic that they were able to get all but one of Thompson's initial nominees disqualified.[6]

But the conflict over nominees to the school board was only the beginning of the battle between Thompson and the reformers over the Chicago schools. In the ensuing two years the school board would fire union activists; the reformers, in alliance with teachers and labor leaders, would call for sweeping governance reforms; the machine-backed mayor and his business allies would counterattack with their own so-called reforms; and the Otis compromise would become law.

REFORMERS RESPOND TO THE UNION-BUSTING TACTICS OF THE CHICAGO SCHOOL BOARD

Although Buck and his allies resisted Thompson's initial appointees to the school board, eventually the mayor prevailed and Chicago witnessed a full-scale, direct attack on public-school unionism. The board of education began its campaign in January 1916 by announcing that an impending school deficit could be avoided only by cutting teacher salaries 7.5 percent. When the Chicago Teachers' Federation (CTF) mounted its own effort to safeguard salaries, the board countered by challenging the educational commitments of the union, claiming teachers were putting their salaries ahead of the welfare of the schools. A state senate committee, chaired by Perceval Baldwin, undertook an investigation of the Chicago public schools, apparently at the behest of the Thompson organization, and the committee's attorney found that the CTF's ideals were "salaries first, increases second and the schools very last."[7]

Inspired by these senate committee findings, Jacob Loeb, chairman of the school board's committee on rules, presented a resolution forbidding teachers to hold membership in organizations affiliated with labor unions. The board of education adopted the rule by an eleven to nine vote. The policy, known as the Loeb rule, was aimed at the CTF, although the Principals Club and other groups were also affected. Loeb, however, went out of his way to say publicly that he did not mean the Principals Club, and that the CTF was his target.[8] It was his claim that "a union in the public schools was intolerable."[9]

Response to passage of the rule was vociferous, but in spite of this public outcry and court injunctions temporarily restraining the Loeb rule, matters worsened for the teachers. Jacob Loeb was elected school board president. He now promoted the passage of rules that permitted him to dismiss teachers he opposed. In place of the standard policy of granting tenure to teachers after an examination, a four-month trial, and a three-year probationary period, which had for years been the board's practice, Loeb instituted another rule that made all teaching positions elective by the board at the end of each year. Loeb's intentions became obvious to all when he presented the board with a list of teachers to be dropped; thirty-eight out of the sixty-eight eventually dismissed were CTF members, including nearly every officer of the CTF. Since all of them had been graded good or excellent by their superiors,[10] it was clear that the board's decision was an antiunion policy.

Those who supported the Loeb rules spoke of the need for efficiency in operation of the schools and expressed antiunion sentiments. A group of Methodist ministers, for example, said that the "old rule made it possible for inefficiency to become entrenched," and a businessmen's magazine argued that the Loeb activity was designed "to save the schools from the labor politicians, by discharging teachers who held labor union team work of more importance than public school class work.[11] Indeed, a group of leading businessmen from the Illinois Manufacturers' Association, who supported the Loeb rules, organized the Public School League (PSL) in the fall of 1917 with the understanding that "any efforts to improve materially the conditions now existing in the public schools of Chicago must be based on the elimination of the CTF and its politico-labor activists."[12]

Meanwhile, reformers around the country criticized the Loeb rules. The *American School*, a journal for educational administrators, claimed the rules were improper because the discharge of the teachers was done by a businessman, not a schoolman. The *New Republic* attacked Loeb for making himself the spokesman for "the least enlightened and least intelligent section of the manufacturing and commercial class in the country which makes the destruction of unionism its chief aim and glory." Assistant Superintendent William McAndrews of New York, who would later become Chicago's superintendent, called the act "tragic" and "stupid."[13] In Chicago, reform groups including the City Club, Women's Club, Chicago Federation of Labor, Hull House, PTAs, and others were aroused to action. A large group of these reformers came together at a mass meeting in June to form the Public Education Association (PEA). At this mass gathering, one of the principal speakers was Alderman Buck, who reminded the audience of four thousand that the board of education had a direct connection to the visible government of Chicago and that the purpose behind the rules was "to make the jobs of the teachers political spoils, to crack the whip over the teachers and tell them which way they shall jump politically in order to save their jobs."[14]

This was neither the first nor the last time Alderman Buck and his reform allies would rush to the defense of the teachers. When the 7.5 percent salary cut had been proposed, Buck had demanded full access to the books of the board of education in order to determine how the board's management of money had caused the crisis. Not surprisingly, the board rejected the demand,[15] but Buck then instituted court proceedings to force the board to open its records. Throughout this controversy the City Club, the Chicago Federation of Labor (CFL), and the Chicago Women's Club joined Buck in pressing the teachers' case.[16]

As the issue ripened and the salary dispute turned into an ugly antiunion drive, Buck took stronger measures. As chairman of a subcommittee of the city council—the Committee on Schools, Fire, Police and Civil Service—Buck was in a position to carry out his own investigation. In Buck's words, "not even the peril of political death" would prevent him from getting to the bottom of the ousting of the teachers.[17] The work of the council committee was supported by the CTF, the CFL, and a variety of other reform groups including the PEA. University of Chicago professors George Mead and Charles Judd, both PEA members, would eventually assist Buck in selecting experts to appear before the committee. The committee heard from past and present board members including Jacob Loeb, plus education experts from around the country who included Superintendents William H. Maxwell of New York City, Ben Blewitt of Saint Louis, Frank Spaulding of Minneapolis, and Charles E. Chadsey of Detroit, as well as Leonard Ayres of the Russell Sage Foundation.[18] Others included President Charles Eliot of Harvard, Ella Flagg Young, John Dewey, and Ellwood Cubberley of Stanford.[19]

The Buck subcommittee was so clearly the major vehicle for educational reformers that it encountered the stiffest possible resistance from the mayor and his machine allies. Under the leadership of President Loeb, who argued that the council subcommittee had no right to investigate school matters, the board of education voted to deny it access to board records and passed a motion appointing a committee of its own to consider undertaking its own educational survey. Four of this committee's five members were Loeb supporters who had favored the dismissal of the sixty-eight teachers.

The mayor himself was silent during the early weeks of the controversy. According to one source, he was not about to comment openly because such overt activity had hurt previous mayors.[20] Yet there can be little doubt that Thompson backed Loeb's efforts. For one thing, one of his close supporters, now the statistician for the schools, was said to be urging the dismissal of all CTF, Catholic, and anti-Thompson teachers.[21]

When the Buck report finally came out, it was clearly a statement of the goals and objectives of the Chicago school reformers. It listed twelve findings concerning the operation of the public schools, concluding with recommendations for reorganization. Not surprisingly, many of the recommendations were directed at removing the influence of the mayor and other city politicians from schools, enhancing teacher rights and status, and putting checks on the conduct of the board. The committee recommended an elected, salaried school board, which would end direct mayoral influence. The number of board members was to be reduced from twenty-one to seven, to be elected on a nonpartisan basis for six-year terms. Teachers were to be initially appointed for three one-year terms as a probationary period, after which they could be removed only for cause. Dismissal could occur only after notice had been given, the teacher had had an opportunity to improve, and a full hearing had been held. The committee also recommended teacher councils, a standard salary schedule, and some means of measuring teacher efficiency. The superintendent, who was to assume complete authority (under the board) over the entire system, was to have the power to appoint teachers. Finally the board, whose powers were specifically enumerated, was urged to spend more time on general policy and less on details. All powers of the board were to be exercised at public meetings, and records of the system were to be made public. It was suggested that standing committees (where Loeb had conducted much of his activity) be abolished. The report concluded with the proposal that any bill or bills submitted to the city council for its approval should provide for a referendum by the people of Chicago.[22] On 21 February 1917 a bill encompassing all these recommendations was introduced into the Illinois house of representatives.[23]

THE CONTENT OF THE SCHOOL REFORM BILLS

The Buck committee investigation so agitated Chicago school politics that the legislative recommendations based on its investigation could not simply be ignored. The Thompson forces thus countered with their own version of reform known as the Baldwin bill. Senator Baldwin had chaired the senate committee that investigated the CTF. Working with the business-backed Public School League, Baldwin proposed to change the governing arrangements to give the board more financial autonomy. This he did by providing the board with the power to sell school property. However, in all other key respects the Baldwin bill kept existing arrangements intact.

A third bill, the one that eventually became law, was sponsored by Ralph Otis of the school board. As befits a framer of compromise legislation, Otis was not strongly identified with either side in the dispute, nor did he play an active role in any of the public debates or forums. He had originally been an ally of Jacob Loeb but broke with the Loeb faction when the board passed the law requiring annual review of teachers, which culminated in the removal of the sixty-eight teachers. In Otis's view, Loeb, Thompson, and the antiunion forces had simply gone too far: "It makes it possible, if not everybody connected with the board is honest, to remove teachers without notice."[24]

It is worth comparing the Otis bill, which passed the legislature, with the Buck bill, which had strong reform backing. As can be seen in table 7.1, both pieces of legislation reduced the size of the board, both gave the superintendent an increased role in teacher recruitment, both extended the length of the superintendent's contract, and both limited the board's power to dismiss teachers. However, the Otis Law did not give the superintendent authority over the school system's business manager, omitted many procedural safeguards for teachers, left the final power of teacher appointment in the hands of the school board, and continued the tradition of a board appointed by the mayor. Moreover, it gave the board authority to sell school lands and to borrow money in anticipation of taxes to be paid, changes sought by Thompson and his machine allies. In short, the Otis Law was both less supportive of a professional superintendency and less firm on teacher rights than was the reform-backed Buck bill. On the other hand, it did give the teachers procedural safeguards against political dismissals. To that extent at least, reformers preferred the Otis Law to nothing at all.

THE POLITICS OF SCHOOL-REFORM LEGISLATION

The prospects for passage of the Otis bill in the spring of 1917 were not very great. When three highly contrasting pieces of legislation pertaining to only one city are introduced in a state legislature, the elected representatives usually throw all three into a committee until a basis for compromise is found. But in this case compromise was far from the minds of any of the three sides to the contest. Initially, the backers of the Baldwin bill seemed to have the upper hand. With the power of the Thompson machine behind him, Baldwin pushed his bill through the state senate in February, almost before the Otis bill had even arrived in Springfield. Meanwhile, Jacob Loeb, the Public School League, and the Chicago *Tribune* joined in attacking the Buck bill, arguing that it would give the CTF control of Chicago schools.[25] While he saved his most severe criticism for the Buck bill, Loeb attacked the Otis bill too, emphasizing its reform features. On the other hand, the Otis bill had the increasingly effective support of several members of the school board and the board attorney, and in the end the support of key figures with responsibility for the Chicago schools would prove decisive.

The Weakening Reform-Labor Alliance

The Otis compromise probably would not have passed, however, except for a peculiar set of circumstances that combined to weaken both the CTF and its reform allies, on the one side, and Mayor Thompson, Jacob Loeb, and the machine-business alliance on the other. Fundamentally, the dismissal of the CTF members from the schools had taken a severe toll on the organization, since the CTF felt it had no choice but to pay its members their salaries while the board's actions were being challenged in court. These salaries, together with the court costs of the union's legal action, were rapidly absorbing all its funds. Moreover, the CTF lost membership steadily in 1915 and 1916, since the union was constantly under attack by daily newspapers and leading community groups and individuals. Nor could the CTF be confident that the legal suit would restore its financial losses. Nothing in a teacher's contract guaranteed anything more than a year's tenure, and though malice was apparent it was difficult to show that the board of

TABLE 7.1 Selected Comparison of Education Bills before Illinois Legislature, 1917

Provisions	Present Law	Buck Bill	Baldwin Bill	Otis Bill
Board of education	Twenty-one members—appointed by mayor	Seven members—elected, $5,000 annual salary	Twenty-one members—appointed by mayor	Eleven members—appointed by mayor, unpaid
Recall of board members	—	Petition of 5% of votes cast in last election	—	—
Taxes	Council levies and collects	Council levies and collects; no tax anticipation borrowing	Council levies and collects; no tax anticipation borrowing	Council levies and collects; board could borrow 75% tax anticipation
Sale of property	Consent of council	Section 16 lands subject to referendum on petition of 3% of votes cast in last board election	Vote of three-fourths of members of the board; council approval not required	Vote of three-fourths members of board; right of eminent domain; council approval not required
Teachers	Appointed by board; no definite term	Appointed by superintendent each year; after three years, tenure; board approval	Appointed by board; no definite term; no tenure	Appointed by board on recommendation of superintendent; tenure after three years

Examinations for teachers	—	Board to make provisions	—	Create special examining board
Teacher dismissal	—	Only for cause, inefficiency or neglect of duty on written charges; requires due notice and hearing; legal counsel permitted	—	Only for cause; written charges; teachers may request a board investigation, and board's decision is final
Educational councils	Optional with board	To advise superintendent on textbooks, courses of study, questions of policy; may initiate questions of policy; these duties and powers statutory	Optional with board	Optional with board
Superintendent	One-year term	Four-year term	Optional with board	Four-year term; no authority over business manager or attorney

Source: *Public Education Association Bulletin*, no. 2 3 March 1917.

education had acted illegally. As it turned out, the Illinois supreme court, in a decision made shortly after passage of the Otis Law, ruled that the board's actions had been legal, making it unnecessary to restore the salaries of the sixty-eight teachers. As Jacob Loeb rejoiced—"there isn't a happier man in Chicago than I am today,"[26] the CTF was broken by the decision. In a month Loeb forced it to withdraw its affiliation with the Chicago Federation of Labor, and though it remained the dominant teachers' organization for another decade, its power and influence steadily waned.

The CTF's reform allies on the city council were hardly in better shape in the early months of 1917. City primary elections scheduled for 17 February pitted Buck, Merriam, and four other reform aldermen against the Thompson juggernaut. Buck was especially vulnerable to political reprisals, for he was only a one-term alderman, and his chief opponent lived in the ward Buck represented. Charles Merriam seemed better situated, since he represented a reform-minded area near the University of Chicago and had a long, prestigious council career.

School issues were prominent in the campaign. Indeed, they were a critical basis for the evaluation of candidates by the Municipal Voters' League (MVL), the city's most politically active reform organization, which remained unalterably opposed to Thompson's machine-style politics. Among the criteria used to rate aldermen was whether "they stood with Alderman Buck in the fight to place the school board under the investigating jurisdiction of the city." In their fight for cleaner schools Buck, Merriam, and the other reformers won not only the praises of the MVL but also the backing of the Women's City Club, whose leadership included such well-known reformers as Jane Addams, Grace Nicholes, and Sophonisba Breckinridge.[27] In their supporting comments the reformers emphasized the opposition of the Thompson forces: in Victor Olander's words, "the same old gang" was opposing reform once again.

The tactic Thompson used against Merriam and Buck was to charge them with aiding labor domination of the schools. Because of his high visibility during the school controversy and council investigation, it was easy to connect Buck to the teachers and to labor, and Merriam, too, had voted with Buck in the council on all the school-related issues, though he was not as outspoken in his support. Merriam had also antagonized business leaders when he refused to head a movement in the city council to place businessmen in control of the school system.

The campaign developed into the kind of contest on which the Thompson regime thrived. City hall politicians, businessmen, board members, and the Chicago *Tribune* campaigned aggressively against the aldermen, forcing Buck, Merriam, and their supporters to respond defensively. Loeb actively campaigned against both Buck and Merriam, calling Buck a tool for Margaret Haley, the outspoken leader of the CTF, and Merriam a "high-brow hypocrite" who was the "foe, the enemy of the Chicago public school system."[28] The chief investigator for the Baldwin Commission claimed that Buck and Merriam were allied with forces operating in Chicago "to undermine American democracy and the public schools."[29] The Chicago *Tribune* came out strongly against the aldermen,[30] calling Buck's legislation vicious and tying him to Haley, and the Public School League charged that Buck and Merriam were part of a plot to give the CTF control of the schools.[31] Given all these allegations, Buck and Merriam were forced to devote considerable time to defending themselves. Buck, vainly attempting to show how the real issues were being ignored, explained: "The grafters and sportsmen . . . have used the school issue to divert attention from the real issues. . . . They don't tell you whether they are for breaking down civil service, white washing paving funds, stuffing payrolls and such things."[32] Similarly, Merriam denounced the city hall leaders for using "the sacred cow of public education as a mask for political grand larceny."[33] But Buck still lost by a landslide and Merriam, after several recounts, was declared the loser by five votes. Along with Merriam and Buck, two other reform aldermen were also defeated.

The *Daily News* editorialized that the outcome of the primary clearly demonstrated that support of the teachers was not a popular campaign position. The Buck bill never got out of the legislative committee to which it had been referred.[34] Senators and representatives, spotting the most obvious of losing causes, quickly dissociated themselves from this piece of unpopular educational reform. Labor and its well-meaning but politically ineffective reform allies had seldom been so badly routed. School politics, supposedly the "Achilles' heel" of the machine, proved to be its area of great success.

The Thompson Machine Weakens

After such an overwhelming victory over the reform aldermen in the Republican primary of February 1917, it is surprising that the Thompson forces did not simply force the Baldwin bill through the Illinois legislature in the ensuing months. But victory over fellow Republicans in the primary did not guarantee a Thompson success in the general municipal elections in April. Indeed, Thompson was so pressed by the political campaign that legislative matters such as the Otis bill were simply put to one side.

Although Merriam and Buck had been eliminated from the race, they did work against city hall candidates and stump for Democrats, making a special effort in Buck's ward.[35] In the end they succeeded, as the Democrats swept the city, defeating most Thompson-backed candidates. The mayor remarked that the reduction of Republicans on the city council was due to the "guerrilla warfare" that had been waged against him.[36]

Thompson's defeat was also brought about by the changing political climate produced by America's increasingly close alliance with Great Britain. Thompson was one of the country's most enthusiastic pacifists, and he expressed well the German, Italian, and Irish sentiment that neither side in the European conflagration deserved United States support. While this position had undoubtedly won votes for Thompson in 1915, by spring 1917 pacifism was giving way to war fever as German submarines roamed the Atlantic, threatening to sink ships carrying food and munitions to Britain. When Congress voted formally to declare war on Germany and the other Axis powers on 4 April 1917, the event could not help but affect the Chicago general election, which occurred shortly thereafter. The Chicago Democrats, flying high the patriotic banner, overran Thompson and the remnants of pacifism in the city. Even Thompson's own supporters turned against him. School-board president Jacob Loeb broke with Thompson and began his own anti-German campaign, eliminating German-language instruction from the schools and searching for German sympathizers among the staff. Although the reformers had been routed in the primaries, the Thompson machine collided with Wilsonian Democracy in the general election.

War smothered the school conflagration in still another way. For months the battles between Haley and Loeb, Buck and Thompson had figured prominently in the local press. Now the only news reported was war news. Indeed, domestic disputes were seen as unpatriotic, a sapping of national energy at a time when unified effort was needed. If the world was to be saved for democracy, business and labor would have to work cooperatively at home, and political machines and urban reformers would have to put their petty disputes aside. War abroad brought peace at home. Waving the white flag of reconciliation, Ralph Otis's moderate compromise seemed increasingly attractive.

Compromise Legislation

Since the senate had already approved Baldwin's bill, the Otis compromise was first considered in the house of representatives. So strong were the currents of domestic compromise that even before the general election or the formal congressional declaration of war, the house overwhelmingly approved the first major restructuring of the Chicago school board in decades.

On 5 April, one day after war was declared, the bill arrived on the senate floor, the arena where Thompson forces had previously been dominant. Thompson's corporation counsel Senator Samuel Ettelson, made one last effort to ditch the Otis bill. He tried to have it sent back to committee on the quite reasonable grounds that the Otis compromise was so different from the Baldwin bill that it needed committee consideration before a floor vote could be taken. Ettelson noted that even such a fervent supporter of the CTF as the Chicago *Daily News* objected to portions of the bill, saying that the triple-headed executive (superintendent, business manager, board attorney) was an inefficient type of administration. He complained further that the senate was about to act without hearing from Jacob Loeb, the board president, and he argued once again that the Otis bill would lead to union control of the schools.

Ettelson's protests failed to convince his colleagues. They insisted that the bill had been debated for five or six weeks in the house, where interested parties had had plenty of opportunities to make their views known. Why had not Loeb made his objections at that time?[37] That Loeb, Ettelson, and other Thompson supporters had been fighting for the machine's political life in the Chicago elections was not a persuasive enough reason for senators now convinced that Thompson's influence was on the wane and that Loeb's unionbusting had gone too far. In a spirit of compromise and moderation, the senate approved the Otis bill with only Ettelson dissenting.

As is the nature of compromise legislation, no one was entirely satisfied, but all the groups secured what they wanted most. The teachers won a degree of job security, which to union leaders justified their bitter struggle. The Thompson machine kept the power of board appointments in the hands of the mayor and won for the school board the power to sell school lands and to borrow money in anticipation of taxes, measures that in the short run would ease fiscal crises. Even the reformers could take a degree of satisfaction from the outcome. The Otis Law reduced the size of the school board and gave the school superintendent somewhat more control of school affairs. Although the teachers would have preferred more procedural safeguards, the Thompson machine disliked the reduction of patronage opportunities, and the reformers saw only marginal progress toward a professional, autonomous public school system, it can hardly be said that anyone lost, and many could claim at least a partial victory.

In historical perspective the longer-range consequences of the Otis Law are a good deal more ambiguous than the immediate participants could have envisioned. If the Thompson machine won new borrowing rights for the school board, these would be most extensively used by reform superintendent William McAndrew, who spent the school system almost to bankruptcy. But if the borrowing authority of the school system proved a mixed blessing for the machine politicians, neither did the CTF's troubles come to an end. Jacob Loeb remained on the Chicago school board; the CTF lost its court suit, disaffiliated from the Chicago Federation of Labor, and after fighting new battles for one more decade collapsed altogether. Only when teachers regrouped within an entirely new trade union, the Chicago Teachers Union, would they win the rights and prerogatives they had long demanded. Finally, the reformers had to wait until after World War II to see their cherished ideals firmly in place. Although the Otis Law enhanced the power of the school superintendent, the conduct of the job very much depended upon the personality and goals of the officeholder as well as on the superintendent's relationship to the board and to city hall. From the reformers' perspective, even though the Otis Law was the highwater mark of legislative reform in Chicago, there was still room for improvement. Allen Pond, head of the Progressive Education Association, best summed up the effects of the Otis Law when he urged its amendment in the next legislative session: "The bill carries," he said, "a perpetuation of the present unfortunate administration."[38]

CONCLUSION

Whatever the consequences of the Otis Law, careful analysis of the politics of its passage surely lays to rest the often repeated but seldom demonstrated claim that reformers were invariably close allies of business elites. The conflict in Chicago was exactly the opposite of what many have come to accept as the typical pattern. Instead of establishing links to the business community, Chicago reformers, including Buck, Merriam, the Municipal Voters' League, the women's clubs, and parent-teacher associations, were firmly allied with the Chicago Teachers' Federation and the Chicago Federation of Labor. They opposed cuts in teachers' salaries, sought to protect the CTF from the union-busting tactics of the board, and pushed for passage of the Buck bill, which provided extensive protection for teachers. Reform support for labor objectives was not undertaken for any mere tactical political advantage. On the contrary, Buck and Merriam sacrificed their political careers by backing the teachers to such an extent that they were placed on the defensive by the Thompson machine in the 1917 Republican primaries and lost to the machine candidates.

Similarly, events reveal that though the Thompson machine exploited ethnic issues to its political advantage, it was hardly a challenge to the business elite of Chicago. On the contrary, Thompson gave full support to Jacob Loeb's union-busting campaign, and he worked closely with the Public Service League, a businessmen's organization formed by the Illinois Manufacturers' Association, campaigning openly against the CTF. The school board Thompson appointed was as business dominated as any board could be. In the decade between 1910 and 1919, of the seventy-one persons who served on the board, it was possible to identify the occupations of fifty-eight. All but three of these were corporate officials, proprietors, lawyers, physicians, or other professionals. Only three were nonmanagerial employees or labor union officials.[39]

Finally, in the Otis Law struggle, reformers revealed their commitment to improved school efficiency, more protection for teachers as professionals, and greater direct citizen involvement in policymaking. They proposed a strengthened superintendent and a board further removed from personnel decisions and other day-to-day matters, hoping thereby to eliminate patronage and corruption from school practice. They favored teacher-tenure legislation in part for the same reason and in part to allow teachers to act as professionals. And they favored an elected school board, recall provisions, and a referendum on the sale of school lands in order to distance the schools from city hall and direct mayoral involvement. Together these provisions of the Buck bill stated the reformers' faith that science, expertise, and professionalism could be put to the service of the democracy and that voters would respect that service.

From another era we can wonder at the naiveté of that faith. Would not a professional superintendent's office turn into a self-aggrandizing bureaucracy? Would not the teachers use their union power to protect the ineffective as well as the dedicated among their ranks? Would the voters always be able to appreciate dedicated public service even when professional reformers provided it? But if the reformers' political realism is open to question, in the Otis Law controversy at least they can hardly be accused of acting as "front men and women" for Chicago's business elite.

One of the dimensions of the conflict was, of course, the fight between business and labor interests with respect to public-sector unionism. The Chicago Federation of Labor backed its teachers' union, and the Illinois Manufacturers' Association responded with the Public Service League. The reformers, middle-class professionals that they were, preferred to stand somewhat to one side of this direct clash of interests, calling for facts and expertise to resolve the conflict. Yet in the end, when businessmen attempted to crush unionism in the schools the reformers rushed to the teachers' defense, even at great political sacrifice.

It might be said that not too much should be drawn from this one incident in a long struggle for political power in Chicago. Even though the Otis Law was the only legislative reform enacted for Chicago's schools before World War II, the schools had flirted with reform on other occasions. If the reformers were aligned with the union movement at the time of the Otis Law, it does not mean that such an alliance was invariant. As middle-class professionals, reformers sought to enhance the autonomous status of the school system in a world of competing values and interests. If they were at times the proponents of labor's cause, at other times they felt that business concern for public efficiency was equally worth espousing. In the next chapter we shall see how four strong-minded superintendents and one school-board president gave quite distinct meanings to the term reform.

8 Reform and the Professional Administrator

The Progressive Era was marked by various attempts to reform educational administration. In Chicago, the Harper bill of 1898 first tackled the ticklish problem of school governance by seeking to restructure through legislation the relationships among school boards, superintendents, and teachers. This zeal for reform culminated in the Otis Law of 1917, which gave the superintendent more authority over staff hiring and firing and the day-to-day decisions involved in running a school system. Similarly, in San Francisco the Claxton amendment of 1920 attempted to clearly define the duties of the superintendent, as did a 1921 city charter amendment in Atlanta.

The powers given to superintendents through reform legislation have been seen as attempts to bureaucratize education, taking the reins from the people and placing them in the hands of professional school administrators. Rather than responding to the ethnic diversity of big cities, "administrative" reformers are said to have helped create cultural homogeneity by centralizing power in the school administration. Rather than involving the teachers in educational decision making, reformers supposedly sought to establish a hierarchical set of administrative procedures, thus keeping the teachers at the bottom of the educational pecking order. Rather than emulating educational leaders like Horace Mann and John Dewey, reformers are said to have admired prominent businessmen. As in a corporation, power would flow from the top down, with all important decisions made by the superintendent.[1] This then, was, in Tyack's words, the "one best system" sought by schoolmen, a system of centralized power with the ability to make decisions free from political influence.[2]

However, reformers cannot so easily be characterized. Leaders of the progressive education movement, which began as a "many-sided effort to use the schools to improve the lives of individuals,"[3] wished not only to improve the administration of growing school systems but also to enhance the role of the teaching professional with respect to pedagogical philosophy and classroom management. The administrations of Progressive Era superintendents, moreover, were not as "closed" or as powerful as a revisionist interpretation would have us believe.[4]

As diverse and ambiguous as progressive educational reform certainly was, two major themes appear with such regularity that they must be considered central components or virtually inevitable concomitants of this political movement. First, reform meant educational expansion—more for the schools to do and more resources to carry out the expected tasks. From a purely organizational perspective, therefore, reform was good for the schools. Second, school reformers encouraged the professionalization of the educational enterprise, a goal that at times forced them to choose between two not altogether compatible programmatic objectives. On the one side, reformers demanded more efficient administration; they preferred a strong superintendent with responsibility for the entire system, coupled with a well-delineated, and perhaps limited, role for school boards. On the other side, reformers encouraged teachers to think of themselves as professionals who had a distinctive body of knowledge to apply to pedagogical processes. When teachers and administrators joined together against external political influences, reformers generally backed them both with unqualified support. Reformers had more difficulty when asked to choose between teachers and their administrative superiors, because they never did directly confront the question of the appropriate organizational role of the professional. From the point of view of organizational efficiency, the judgments of the professional educator must be subordinated to the expectations of the superintendent and his or her aides. But from the point of view of professional autonomy, teachers had to be given the discretion, the support, and the independence to apply the skills they were learning in teachers colleges.

The difficulties reformers had in resolving these questions are evident in the experiences of five strong administrators: Robert Guinn, president of the Atlanta school board from 1914 to 1918, Superintendent Joseph Marr Gwinn of San Francisco (1920–33), and Chicago superintendents Edwin G. Cooley (1901–9), Ella Flagg Young (1909–15), and William McAndrew (1924–27). In this chapter we shall see how these administrators expanded the resource base for public education, introduced a set of curricular innovations, fought a variety of opponents including conservative elites, machine politicians, and business leaders as well as trade unionists and school employees, developed stronger administrative capacities, and encountered, more often than not, intense teacher opposition. Reform superintendents were neither heroes nor devils, but they had an agenda that placed them at odds with a diversity of opponents that changed according to the issue at stake and the political context in which it was raised.

REFORM ADMINISTRATORS SUPPORT FISCAL EXPANSION

The twentieth century opened with the demand for places in public schools unabated. Average daily attendance in Chicago grew by over 177,000 pupils from the turn of the century up until 1925, while in San Francisco attendance nearly doubled from 37,000 in 1910 to 64,000 by 1926. Total enrollment figures for Atlanta show a phenomenal increase from 14,000 in 1900 to slightly over 56,000 by 1925. Yet schools had been decentralized, being governed by large, special-interest-oriented boards, and were totally unable to keep up with demand. Administrators thus established rules designed to keep children out of schools, not in them. For example, one finds from the public schools of Atlanta a list of Rules for Scholars that includes the following:

> Should you break with the school ere the
> School year is out,
> Your right to re-enter may come into doubt
> With candidates new for the coveted seat,
> On equal conditions, you'll have to compete.[5]

The pressure on facilities, plus the requests for new subjects, especially those related to vocational training, together with the severe budget restrictions imposed on the schools, led to widespread demand for greater fiscal support. It is sometimes argued that reform-minded superintendents resisted such pressure in the name of efficiency, but in San Francisco and Chicago the pattern was quite the opposite. In San Francisco, for example, Joseph Gwinn, the first superintendent appointed after the reform of the city charter in 1920, restored the school's fiscal health. Whereas total expenditures per pupil before the reform charter had fallen steadily in constant dollars from $225 per pupil in 1910 to $97 in 1920, by 1924 they were rising steadily, and by 1926 they had surpassed the 1910 figure (see table 8.1).

TABLE 8.1 Average Daily Attendance and Expenditures per Pupil, San Francisco Public Schools, 1910–26

Year	Number of Teachers	Total Average Daily Attendance	Average Daily Attendance per Teacher	Expenditures per Pupil	
				Current Dollars	Constant Dollars[a]
1910	1,198	36,774	30.7	90	225
1916	1,521	47,526	31.2	64	137
1920	1,928	50,458	26.0	83	97
1924	2,218	57,098	27.8	126	173
1926	2,543	63,989	25.0	175	231

Sources: San Francisco Superintendent of Public Instruction, *Annual Reports*, selected years.

[a]1947–49 = 100.

In Chicago downward trends were reversed after 1905 when Dunne, the reform mayor, appointed a new school board. This allowed for expansion in the later years of Cooley's superintendency and opened the door for Ella Flagg Young's administration, a time when the Chicago schools enjoyed one of their more sustained periods of reform. Between 1910 and 1915, the pupil/teacher ratio dropped back almost to its 1900 level and expenditures per pupil in constant dollars climbed by 11 percent (see table 8.2). Under Young's leadership, the years 1910–15 showed a growth in staffing that kept pace with enrollment expansion. Expenditures per pupil also continuously climbed.

After William Thompson drove Young from office, Chicago's expenditures on education failed to keep pace with the city's growth. Between 1915 and 1920 school expenditures in constant dollars declined by nearly 10 percent. But when William McAndrew assumed the office of superintendent in 1924, the system underwent an expansionary phase once again (see table 8.3). Indeed, the story of Chicago school finances under McAndrew is at such variance with so much that has been written about this reform superintendent that the tale is worth telling in some detail.

Appointed by reform mayor William Dever, McAndrew was at first welcomed by teachers, reformers, and the business community alike. As a charter member of the Public Education Association, he had considerable standing in progressive education circles around the country. As a former teacher and principal in Chicago schools, the teachers thought he would support their interests. As an appointee of the reform mayor, the Civic

TABLE 8.2 Average Daily Attendance and Expenditures per Pupil, Chicago Public Schools, 1890–1925

Year	Number of Teachers	Total Average Daily Attendance	Average Daily Attendance per Teacher	Expenditures per Pupil	
				Current Dollars	Constant Dollars[a]
1900	5,701	208,841	36.6	42	118
1905	5,514	223,203	40.5	35	91
1910	6,101	229,997	37.7	44	110
1915	7,272	273,845	37.7	53	122
1920	8,447	300,349	35.6	94	110
1925	11,672	386,810	33.1	113	151

Sources: Average daily attendance (ADA) and number of teachers from Board of Education, *Proceedings.* Expenditures per pupil computed using ADA and data from the Department of Finance, *Annual Statement of the Finances of the City of Chicago,* 1890, 1895, 1900; and *Comptroller's Annual Report: Finances of the City of Chicago,* 1905–25.

[a]1947–49 = 100.

Federation supported him, as did faculty at the University of Chicago School of Education. Because he was known as a successful administrator in the difficult New York public school system, the business community supported him. Many reform groups were impressed by his evident commitment to educational expansion as well as to better management practices, and few could deny that the schools enjoyed a great organizational impetus during his term of office.

Although the tales of the McAndrew school wars, including the battles over teachers' councils, the platoon system, and the junior high school, have been recounted on several occasions,[6] the fiscal story of his superintendency, perhaps the single most significant development, has been overlooked. In part this is due to the difficulty of ferreting out fiscal details; in part it is because the political battles of the time focused on quite other matters. But whatever the reasons, few have realized that McAndrew exploited the public purse on the school system's behalf with such abandon that at the conclusion of his administration he left the Chicago schools on the edge of fiscal disaster. The great irony of the McAndrew reign lies in the extent to which this reformer seduced leading businessmen into giving him their fervent support at a time when his own financial policies can be described as nothing short of profligate. McAndrew talked the "efficiency" game with campaigns for platoon systems, junior high schools, and more businesslike administration. But while these slogans won business support and infuriated teachers and labor groups, McAndrew was in fact making resources available to teachers and pupils to an extent unprecedented in the city.

Consider first the sheer expansion of the public schools during the 1920s as depicted in table 8.3. In that decade elementary enrollment increased by 60,000 pupils, and the high schools grew from 160,000 to nearly 230,000 students. The percentage of the school-age population enrolled in the public schools jumped from 51 percent to 59.4 percent, the largest increment in any single decade since the very beginning of their establishment. The percentage of the fourteen- to seventeen-year-old population in school increased from 21.7 to 34.2 percent. Quite clearly, it was during the McAndrew administration that secondary education came of age. No wonder he was forced to address problems of managing a large, complex organization and that he proposed devices such as the junior high school and the platoon system to accommodate the large numbers of newcomers attending the schools.

Even with these efficiencies and even in the face of exploding enrollments, table 8.2 shows that the pupil/teacher ratio fell (from 35.6 to 33.1 between 1920 and 1925) and per-pupil expenditures increased in both current and constant dollars. The increment in expenditures per pupil in constant dollars was no less than 37.3 percent, an extraordinary increase in

TABLE 8.3 Average Daily Attendance of School-Age Population, Chicago, 1890–1930

| Year | Elementary School[a] | | High School[b] | | Average Daily Attendance of Total School-Age Population (%) | School-Age Population as Percentage of Total City Population |
	Average Daily Attendance (%)	Age Cohort (N)	Average Daily Attendance (%)	Age Cohort (N)		
1890	46.6	214,470	3.7	100,472	32.9	28.6
1900	57.4	347,745	6.3	146,860	42.2	29.1
1910	63.8	338,800	9.7	157,470	46.6	22.7
1920	61.7	440,296	21.7	160,201	51.0	22.2
1930	70.9	500,594	34.2	229,543	59.4	21.6

Source: United States Bureau of the Census, *Population,* 1890, part 2, 117; 1900, 2 (part 2): 126; 1910, 1 (part 1): 439; 1920, 2:291; 1930, 2:743.

[a]School age is five to thirteen for 1910 to 1930 and five to fourteen for 1890 to 1900.

[b]School age is fourteen to seventeen for 1910 to 1930 and fifteen to nineteen for 1890 to 1900.

light of the equally extraordinary enrollment expansion occurring simultaneously.

In pursuing these fiscal policies, McAndrew had certain advantages that Young had not enjoyed fifteen years earlier. For one thing, the Otis Law of 1917 gave the board of education (and its superintendent) much more authority over the appointment and promotion of teachers, the purchase of textbooks and equipment, the selection of school sites, and the construction of buildings. More important, the law permitted a school budget based on an estimate of taxes collectible instead of on taxes already collected from the previous fiscal year, which before the Otis Law had prevented Cooley, Young, or any other superintendent from borrowing funds in anticipation of new tax revenues.[7]

The school board had begun raising revenues by means of tax-anticipation warrants immediately after the passage of the Loeb rule, but McAndrew took advantage of the new arrangement to an unprecedented degree. In 1925 he included in his school budget both the funds from the 1924 tax levy, collectible in 1925, and the 1925 levy, collectible in 1926.[8] Although this innovative practice allowed the superintendent to report a budgetary surplus, in reality the school system was falling into debt. Before long McAndrew himself reported the consequences of this policy:

> It is no exaggeration to say that the financial system is nearing the breaking point.... On the basis of present revenue the schools cannot complete the year 1927 without exceeding legal borrowing power and unless additional revenues are provided at once, the schools cannot go through the year 1927 without omitting some of the regular session, or cutting teachers' salaries, or eliminating present activities, or taking other drastic steps.[9]

By 1926 the board had shifted from using cash in hand to obtaining credit by the sale of tax warrants, and in doing so it used up almost eleven years of tax income in ten years' time.[10]

Of the five strong school leaders, only one did not campaign for an expansionary school system, and this superintendent, Edwin G. Cooley, can hardly be labeled a reformer (even though some revisionist historians have posthumously awarded him such a designation). In his own day Cooley and his policies were continually, and often successfully, challenged by Chicago's own reform movement. The City Club opposed his plans for vocational education, the school board appointed by a reform mayor rejected his "merit" plan for the advancement of teachers, and the teachers who criticized him had many close ties to Chicago's reformers. In short, it is difficult to see in what war Superintendent Cooley earned his reform stripes.

When his fiscal policies are compared with those of superintendents who did have close ties with reform groups, one can see that Cooley failed to expand the city schools at the rate necessary to keep pace with the growth of the school population. During the early years of his superintendency (1900–1905), the number of teachers in the system declined even while students in average daily attendance increased by 6.4 percent (see table 8.2). As a result the pupil/teacher ratio in the schools increased from 36.6 to 40.5, and per-pupil expenditures in current dollars fell by nearly 17 percent. In constant dollars the drop was even greater—nearly 23 percent. All this was occurring in a decade of national expansion and prosperity. Cooley was constrained by a variety of external factors, to be sure. Deficit spending was absolutely prohibited by state law, and Chicago was unable to obtain more funding from the state legislature. Yet it may be of more than passing significance that these downward trends were reversed after 1905 when Dunne, the reform mayor, appointed the board that selected the first Chicago superintendent strongly supported by reformers—Ella Flagg Young.

REFORM ADMINISTRATORS EXPAND SERVICES AND CURRICULUM

School administrators used some of the increased resources at their disposal to expand the services available to students. They improved facilities, reduced class sizes, introduced vocational education, and in one case even explored the possibility of teaching sex hygiene. Not all the innovations they proposed were popular, but neither did opposition come consistently from any one class or group.

In Atlanta Robert Guinn, a progressive school-board president, led that city's attempts to "catch up" with northern schools. In 1914 Guinn's primary concern was with such basics as severe crowding and a hopelessly inadequate physical plant. Guinn was successful in persuading the board to commission a survey of the schools that would identify problem areas. The survey, which was conducted by a state supervisor of education, found inadequate lighting, heating, ventilation, fire protection, grounds, equipment, instruction, space, and courses of study.[11] Guinn encouraged the board to address the criticisms the survey raised. Elective subjects were instituted for the high school, the course of study was revised and carefully graduated from year to year, and grading practices were altered. The board also initiated summer schools to allow children who had failed a year to catch up and remain with their peers.[12]

Guinn's multifaceted campaign for reform eventually faltered, and he finally resigned in 1918. But, significantly, it was opposition from some of the city's most entrenched and conservative interests, not the clamor of working-class populists, that brought Guinn's reform drive to an end. Guinn had initially disturbed the city's leading citizens when he removed from office the conservative, lackluster, but nonetheless well liked superintendent of schools. But it was his attempted merger of the sex-segregated white high schools that embittered Atlanta old-timers. Alumni of Boys' High School were so upset that the school's principal was emboldened to attack the school-board president publicly. In an interview with the Atlanta *Constitution* that precipitated Guinn's resignation, the principal averred that he had gone more than the extra mile: "I am making this statement because I have been forced to swallow the Prussianized system inaugurated by Major Guinn . . . until it has reached the point where I must give up or fight."[13] Atlanta's mayor was extremely disturbed by this public expression of distress (which must have been only the tip of an iceberg of resentment) and immediately opened an investigation. It had hardly begun when Major Robert Guinn resigned.

Although reform administrators like Guinn were expanding curricula and constantly attempting to bring new ideas into public education, Edwin Cooley, who has sometimes been mistaken for a reformer, was not expanding public schools but was doing his best to establish a competing system— one of vocational education that would be administered not by the public schools, but by business. With the aid of the Commercial Club, Cooley pushed for passage in the state legislature of a bill to provide a dual educational system with two high schools, one providing a "classical" education and one specializing in vocational education.

The bill was totally unacceptable to a large number of Chicagoans, however, including labor and most reformers. While they recognized that many teenagers had left school and were unemployed, and while they knew the nation needed some trade instruction and continuation schooling and that such instruction should be funded with public money, they were nevertheless adamant that vocational education should remain part of the public school system. Their distrust of the business community surfaced in accusations that business was motivated by the desire to have a well-trained pool of cheap, submissive labor.

In 1914 the Illinois State Federation of Labor (ISFL) published, through its committee on vocational education, a report strongly opposed to radical differentiation of education. Although it declared that the "dual system of administration is a menace," it reported that "workers [still] desire vocational and technical training." The committee's report concluded: "We believe that vocational school courses should at all times be under the guidance and control of the school authorities having the direction of general education as the best system adapted properly to educate our children."[14]

Others were aware of the need for vocational education and responded by drafting bills to be presented to the legislature. Among them was the City Club, a quintessential reform organization with a large number of professional people, including 164 educators active in its education committee. In 1912 this group published a report on issues involved in proposed legislation for vocational education in Illinois. Written by George H. Mead, Frank Leavitt, and Earnest Wreidt, all academics from the University of Chicago, it contained a "suggestive draft" of a bill for vocational education. Offering the draft as a compromise substitute for the Cooley bill, the City Club proposal kept the administration of vocational schools under the auspices of the public schools.[15]

Professional educators joined reformers in their fight against the Cooley bill. They claimed that a dual system of education was administratively wasteful and inefficient and that it contradicted the democratic value of general education by creating a segregation of social classes. Young, Cooley's reform-minded successor, used all her influence against it, claiming it would train youth to accept a lower status.[16] John Dewey opposed it: "Its right development will do more to make public education truly democratic than any other one agency now under consideration. Its wrong treatment will as surely accentuate all undemocratic tendencies in our present situation, by fostering and strengthening class divisions in school and out."[17] Not only did a separate school system seem undemocratic to the educators who opposed Cooley, in addition, it was apparent that a dual system of education would attract many students away from the public education system, a development educational professionals could scarcely applaud.[18] With the alliance between organized labor, school reformers, and professional educators cemented, the Cooley bill stood little chance of passing the state legislature either during the 1915 session or again during the 1917 session. By 1917, however, Congress had passed the Smith-Hughes Act along much the same lines as the City Club had proposed, and vocational education programs were established within public schools throughout the country.

REFORM ADMINISTRATORS AND THE PROFESSIONALIZATION OF EDUCATION
Centralizing Power in the Superintendent's Office

Progressive Era administrators were, without question, committed to growth in the number of responsibilities and rights that defined the office of superintendent. At the same time, they were interested in divesting themselves of day-to-day obligations that were merely time consuming and hardly status enhancing. McAndrew expressed this common philosophy in the colorful language that characterized his controversial administration:

> Other school systems suffer from the tradition that every teacher with a special idea or complaint, every principal, every inventor of a new device, or author of a new book, every friend of an applicant for promotion should properly take the case to the "head man."... A system directly touching a total of 545,929

pupils and paid members must work clumsily on the old village
conception of a one man affair. It must adopt the motto of other
big businesses; "organize, deputize, supervise."[19]

Chicago's Cooley and Young, San Francisco's Joseph Gwinn, and Atlanta's
Robert Guinn had had similar inclinations before him, and the quest for
power and autonomy led them all into conflicts with groups that felt their
interests were threatened.

Joseph Marr Gwinn of San Francisco found his opponents to be members
of the board itself, all of whom were jealous of the prerogatives they enjoyed
and reluctant to give up their bases of power. In addition, he faced considerable antagonism from those groups outside the school department who had
not supported the Claxton amendment of 1920. Upon his appointment in
1923, Gwinn had established new departments of business, personnel, and
educational research and service.[20] He also attempted to introduce new
courses into the curriculum, including gym classes and practically oriented
classes such as "how to set the table."[21] His decision to implement the
progressive curriculum angered the anti-Claxton groups, and they began a
drive to modify the electoral arrangement once again by launching support
for an elective board of education. According to one of the sponsors of the
proposed amendment, the president of the Northern Federation of Civic
Organizations, the move was supported by seventeen civic organizations,
including the Building Trades Council and, in a reversal of its position a
decade earlier, the Labor Council. The amendment was defeated, but by
working with factions of the board who opposed Gwinn, the group was able
to force Gwinn's resignation.

The issues that surfaced in Gwinn's firing were largely administrative.
His competence as a business manager was called into question: in testimony before a grand jury it was charged that Gwinn had been responsible
for illegal ratings, causing some four hundred teachers to be misclassified
too high and consequently overpaid for a few years;[22] he had gone with four
of his staff members to a National Education Association meeting at the
city's expense; and mismanagement was supposedly uncovered in the
school cafeteria and in book-purchasing procedures. Gwinn's reputation
suffered, and he was forced to resign in 1933.

Gwinn himself traced his firing to the animosity between those who
wanted an elective board and those who had backed the reforms proposed
in the Claxton report. Gwinn publicly implied that "his dismissal had been
motivated by parochial, patronage and religious feelings."[23] There is evidence that labor resented the fact that Gwinn came from outside San
Francisco and had brought other outsiders into the school department,
taking jobs away from locals. The "labor" representative on the board of
education, Daniel Murphy, charged that "inexperienced, out-of-towners

are getting city jobs because they know someone."[24] Murphy strongly insisted that higher positions should be filled "from the ranks."[25]

The outcome of Gwinn's firing was an increase in the power of the board at the expense of the superintendent. The board moved to institutionalize its power by establishing the position of a comptroller who would have full power of audit, take charge of all departmental employees with the exception of the superintendent and his immediate staff, and keep all records including teacher rating files. This innovation removed all business matters from the hands of the superintendent and set up a competing center of administrative and executive authority responsive to the board. Thus, San Francisco departed from the strong superintendent system that had been adopted following the Claxton recommendations, and reformers effectively abandoned the new structures they had embraced ten years earlier.

Ella Flagg Young of Chicago had a clear notion of her role vis-à-vis both the school board and the teachers. She supported lengthening the term of office of the board and the superintendent from three to five years. This, she felt, would somewhat remedy the problems brought about because of frequent changes in the personnel of the board. She also urged "a definite statement both of the duties of the superintendent as the educational executive of the Board and of the authority delegated for the purpose of meeting these duties."[26] Similarly, Young, who strongly supported the Chicago teachers, believed, nevertheless, that if "the superintendent upon the receipt of the report [from the Teachers Council] believes the majority of teachers and principals mistaken, there should be no further effort made to secure the adoption of his views by a vote of the councils. He should act in accordance with his own judgment and be held responsible for the outcome."[27]

For Young's first two and one half years as superintendent her relations with the board went smoothly. However, as the terms of the reform board members who had hired her expired and they were replaced with business-oriented appointments made by a new mayor, Young found that many decisions she felt were essentially administrative were made by others. She complained that salaries had been set without her approval and that three of her recommendations for principalships had been turned down. Later that year the board took the course of study out of Young's hands, claiming there were too many "fads and frills" in the elementary curriculum.[28] She resigned, but her resignation resulted in a protest march on the mayor's office, a rally led by reformers and school people, and her reinstatement by Mayor Harrison. Young remained superintendent until 1915, when William "Big Bill" Thompson was elected mayor. At that point, with anti–Teachers' Federation board member Jacob Loeb dominating the board and Thompson publicly supporting him, Young gave up the struggle and resigned.

Reform Administrators and the Professional Teacher

Reformers were committed to a strong superintendency. They supported Edwin Cooley's admnistrative innovations even while objecting to his vocational schemes. They backed Gwinn until he could no longer promise the honesty and efficiency that was the reform hallmark. Even Young, the teachers' friend, believed in an independent, assertive administrative entity. Yet it was precisely this relationship between a strong, professional superintendency and a professional teaching force that proved to be reform's pedagogically least well defined and politically most contentious position. Reformers were not antilabor, anti–working class, or antiethnic, but they were unable to spell out exactly how the independent professional teacher was to work with or respond to the strong leadership of the professional administrator.

In *The Search for Order*, Robert Wiebe describes how it was to be a nineteenth-century schoolteacher. "Ridiculed . . . as Ichabod Cranes and fussy schoolmarms, teachers embodied the apparent paradox of exceptionally low prestige in a land that acclaimed universal education."[29] Few could afford to live "on the teacher's starvation salary, few saw opportunities for advancement and therefore very few—often the Ichabod Cranes and futile old maids—devoted a life to it." Teaching became a way station for men in search of administrative careers and young ladies in search of husbands.[30] Salaries were dismal, averaging $650 a year for a woman elementary school teacher in 1905, half what a male earned in the same position.[31] Classes were large and many children could not speak English. Teachers were hired by school boards on the basis of personal knowledge and political connections. There were no provisions for job security, and teachers could be and frequently were dismissed for political reasons at the end of the school year, replaced with someone having better connections.

Along with the lack of standards for working conditions came the lack of standards for teaching as a profession. Institutions training teachers for their jobs were scarce. Between 1877 and 1902 no such institution existed in Chicago, lending fuel to scathing indictments like those of Joseph Rice, written in 1893: "In the public schools of Chicago I found the instruction, in general, so unscientific that in judging them by the minimum requirement I should regard their standard as very low. Some of the teaching was by far the most absurd I have ever witnessed."[32]

By 1905 things had begun to change as teachers became interested in upgrading their profession, and by 1910 Ella Flagg Young had become president of the National Education Association, a position traditionally held by male school administrators. Teachers became active members of professional associations, which supported their gaining specific academic training by attending colleges and by earning graduate degrees. This quest for professionalization led to conflicts with school boards and superintendents over salaries, performance rating, and educational policymaking, for just as teachers were becoming professionalized, so the field of educational administration was becoming increasingly self-conscious and internally disciplined as well. Both administrators and teachers constantly attempted to accrue power and influence, and both fought the others' attempts to impose restrictions or judgments. Reformers were supportive when school people were united against the rest of the community, but they found it harder to decide between administrators and teachers, when each group used professionalism as a justification for its claims.

One of the most noteworthy instances of the conflict caused by the professionalization of educators occurred in Chicago while Edwin G. Cooley was superintendent. In this case, reformers came down firmly on the side of the teachers. Upon taking office in 1900, Cooley addressed the issue of poorly trained teachers. Believing that a large part of the problem was the way teachers obtained their jobs—that patronage appointments did not always go to the best-qualified candidates—he secured from the board the right to appoint and promote teachers. His next move was to institute the merit system, under which teachers' salaries would be determined by tests and ratings from administrators, which would be kept secret from the teachers. The system proved extremely unpopular with the teachers, who complained to board members appointed by the new reform mayor. These new reform-oriented appointees inquired into the secret ratings, claiming to find that if one held experience and grade level constant there were no differences between the marks of those who passed the examination and those who did not. Subsequently they abolished the secret marking plan, asking administrators to share their evaluations with the teachers, who were to be marked either "efficient" or "inefficient."[33] In 1907, under the influence of this same board, the previously secret ratings were made public, revealing that virtually all the teachers had been rated at 80 percent sometime or another during their careers. Consequently, twenty-six hundred teachers were advanced on the salary scale,[34] and the Cooley "merit plan" was modified so that teachers could substitute five courses of thirty-six hours each for the examination. Further, the reform board prepared a plan for a ten-year schedule without promotion tests, which was never put into effect because reformer Dunne lost the 1907 mayoral election to Fred Busse.[35]

In Atlanta, "Major" Robert Guinn had already angered the city's elite by firing a popular superintendent and by trying to merge the traditional sex-segregated high schools into one. Thus, when the principal of Boys' High School decided to attack Guinn publicly, he found the teacher issue effective in winning broad support: "Teachers everywhere are dissatisfied and disturbed. . . . The plan of paying the teachers in twelve monthly installments instead of ten, as formerly, is apparently for the purpose of making an effort to keep the schools running twelve months . . . without paying the teachers any more money.''[36]

This was but one of several political miscalculations Guinn made, and in its investigation of the allegations against him, the board concluded: "During the progress of the investigation, it developed that much of the constructive work now in the schools is the result of his efforts. At the same time it also developed that there was a lack of harmony between the president of the Board and the teachers.''[37] The Guinn incident had a very concrete effect. Teachers, labor, and a section of the city's elite worked in concert to amend the city charter and provide for a smaller, elected school board lest another Major Guinn attain power. Teachers steadily gained influence in the system throughout the 1920s and 1930s, and by 1943 they were able to elect one of their own, Ira Jarrell, as superintendent.

Ella Flagg Young, elected in 1909, had been a longtime teacher and administrator within the Chicago public schools, and when she assumed the responsibilities of the superintendency she kept those ties. Throughout her administration, she was consistently supported by the teachers and by school reformers. Her greatest contribution was the effort she made to bring teachers into educational decision making by encouraging the growth of teachers' councils, formed to give administrators advice on educational matters. By 1913 the teachers and principals had been organized into sixty-four councils, which met regularly to discuss changes in the course of study.[38]

Young has not been treated as one of the great school reformers. She was not male, she did not have strong business support, and she emerged out of the Chicago public school system rather than marching in from afar. Yet her reform credentials were solid. She was the favorite of the reform bloc on the school board that had dumped Cooley, and even though her appointment as superintendent came after Dunne's reform mayoralty had ended, she owed it directly to the votes of board members he had appointed. As superintendent she expanded school operations, raised per-pupil expenditures, fought for higher teacher salaries, attempted to limit the influence of the school board and end patronage practices, and created the councils that became so popular among teachers. Throughout her superintendency she had cordial relations with labor and received unwavering, enthusiastic support from the established middle-class reform groups of the city. Finally ousted by an economy-minded, business-dominated school board placed in office by William Thompson, one of Chicago's most notorious machine mayors, Young was no less subject to changing political tides than were other reformers. But she demonstrated beyond question that reform goals did not always coincide with antilabor policies or probusiness attitudes.

The teachers' councils she established continued to operate with varying degrees of effectiveness until William McAndrew assumed the Chicago superintendency in 1924. McAndrew was not a supporter of the councils. He did not think that the principals should be excluded from them, and he did not think council meetings should be held on school time. Teachers responded to the first criticism by pointing out that many teachers would not feel free to say what they really thought with principals present. As to the second, it was pointed out that only four teachers' council meetings, two local and two group sessions were scheduled each semester. Members of the city council, groups of citizens, and several newspapers supported the teachers' right to hold their meetings. McAndrew appeared to be weakening under public pressure, but in September 1924 he issued a bulletin to the principals: "No dismissals of pupils from their classes during regular school hours shall be made for the purpose of meetings of councils, either high school or elementary."[39] This event brought McAndrew into a prolonged, sustained conflict with the teachers that manifested itself when he attempted to introduce a variety of organizational innovations, of which the two best known were the platoon system and the junior high school. By far the largest number of objections came from the teachers, although organized labor was also antagonistic toward the platoon plan.

The platoon plan or Gary system, as it was sometimes called, was an administrative arrangement that moved children from class to class and onto the playground for supervised recreation when other children were using the available rooms. It had first been used in Gary, Indiana, and had been supported by United States Steel, a vociferous critic of organized labor. McAndrew thought it would be a good way to give children more hours in school than the present half-day sessions allowed.[40] The Chicago *Tribune* lauded the idea that the schools would take over "not only the scholastic training of the child but the supervision of his play."[41] The Teachers' Federation gave no quarter in its fight against the plan. It sent nine members to a number of cities where the platoon system had been tried, and they came back with negative reactions to the idea. They opposed it on the grounds that children, especially shy ones, should not have to establish relationships with so many teachers, that it was best for both children and teachers to get to know each other well. They also claimed that the plan would mean more preparation time, more students, and more hours of teaching time for the teachers. Labor's criticisms of the platoon plan included the belief that its proponents wished to cut school expenditures—more children per teacher and more children per plant. They also suspected the plan of being a way to rush children through the lower grades "at a faster speed than is considered wise under the present methods."[42]

The other innovation that caused considerable controversy was the junior high school. Chicago had seriously considered junior highs even before McAndrew's arrival, following the recommendation of Charles Judd, a professor of education at the University of Chicago. Junior highs were suspected by the elementary teachers in particular, who foresaw a threat to their status in the new system. A large body of junior-high teachers with different needs and better salaries would threaten the dominant position of the Elementary Teachers Council. That indeed happened, with the younger teachers who took the examination for the new positions becoming enthusiastic about new approaches to teaching adolescents and resenting the federation's blanket opposition to the junior highs.[43]

Through all these controversies McAndrew received loyal backing from the business community and reformers—including the City Club and Mayor Dever. Only with Dever's defeat by William Thompson was McAndrew removed from office. Unlike Cooley, who had business backing but was opposed on most issues by reformers, and unlike Young, who was supported throughout her tenure by reformers and labor alike, McAndrew's administration divided the teachers and school reformers, because reformers saw him extending the size and scope of the public schools while they perceived teacher opposition as parochial and self-interested.

CONCLUSION

The Progressive Era in education was a response to problems created by the increasing size and complexity of urban school systems, which led many to believe, as William McAndrew did, that the old village conception of education as a one-person affair was sadly out of date. New, progressive educational administration attempted to develop clearly defined responsibilities and prerogatives for the superintendent as distinct from the board, more autonomy in running the system, and less personal involvement in day-to-day maintenance decisions. In addition to this new idea of professionalism for administrators, the Progressive Era spawned an interest in professionalized teaching as well. There was a need for uniform standards or qualifications for newly hired teachers, teacher training should be upgraded, and the level of instruction was to be raised.

Expansion was another of the keystones of Progressive Era administrations. Modern times required a new curriculum, and vocational education was added, as were other courses such as Young's "Chicago course" and sex hygiene and Gwinn's gym classes. In addition to expanding the curriculum, progressive superintendents were willing to spend more on the schools, thereby raising expenditures per pupil and lowering the pupil/teacher ratio, even during a time of unprecedented enrollments in the schools.

In attempting to carry out these objectives, reform-minded superintendents found themselves in conflict with other interests—sometimes teachers, sometimes middle-class reformers, sometimes labor, and sometimes business. In fact, what marked the Progressive Era was not an imposition of reform from the top down, but an unprecedented pluralistic give and take, which explains why it was the reform superintendents' relationship with the teachers that proved to be their most enduring political problem. It was hard for teachers to accept the fact that it was not only the administration of big-city school systems that needed an overhaul by 1900—that the actual instruction needed reexamination as well. All reform superintendents attempted to address the issue of poorly trained teachers, albeit in different ways. On nearly every occasion the teachers resisted change, whether the policy was junior high schools, the platoon system, or merit pay. Only Ella Flagg Young seemed able to assert strong leadership and at the same time maintain the warm support of her staff.

That Young, a woman, was the most successful superintendent in this regard was probably not coincidence. Beneath all the policy disputes, an underlying issue smoldered, and from its embers came the sparks that ignited particular conflagrations. The teaching force was primarily female, but the administrative force was disproportionately male. Even positions at lower levels of the school administration were likely to be staffed by males. As late as 1894, nearly half of all Chicago's principals were men (at a time when a male elementary school teacher was a rarity). Moreover, they held the highest-paid positions. As can be seen in table 8.4, 17 percent of the male principals in 1894 earned more than two thousand dollars a year, while only 8 percent of female principals did. Fifty-seven percent of the women received less than sixteen hundred dollars a year, while only 18 percent of the men were so poorly paid. Better paid and in positions of authority, male administrators were thus suspected of looking out for their own interests at the expense of the many female elementary school teachers, whose jobs were neither as well paid nor as secure as the teachers would have liked. Further, women were in the midst of a national campaign

TABLE 8.4 Salaries of Principals, by Sex, Chicago, 1867–93

| | School Year | | | | | |
| | 1867–68 | | 1882–83 | | 1893–94 | |
Salary Level	% Male	% Female	% Male	% Female	% Male	% Female
Low ($1,000 to $1,599)	—	100	11	71	18	57
Middle ($1,600 to $2,199)	95	—	89	28	64	36
High ($2,000 to $2,699)	5	—	—	—	17	8
Number	19	5	27	32	48	51
Not available	—	—	—	—	3	3

Sources: Chicago Board of Education, Annual Reports, for the relevant years.
Note: Percentage totals may not sum to 100 because of rounding.

to secure the vote, and the Chicago Teachers' Federation was very active in the suffrage movement. Indeed, it was the open political climate of the Progressive Era that enabled female teachers to speak out against this discrimination.

Although Progressive Era reform laws such as the Otis Law and the Claxton amendment raised the status of educational administration as well as instruction, they did not guarantee reform control of the schools. By the late 1920s, when hard times hit the country, public schools were again under attack, accused of being too costly and overextended in services. It is to the role of reform in a time of extreme financial difficulty that we now turn.

9 Finance and Reform: Issues of the Thirties

Any picture of the social forces shaping urban education must include the bad times as well as the good. When adverse economic conditions overtook the country in the early 1930s, the school systems of Chicago, Atlanta, and San Francisco found themselves in exposed positions, primarily because of their enormous growth and the increased services they were offering, including kindergartens, vocational education programs, junior highs, extended sports and music activities, and junior colleges. In addition, a drop-off in the depression era birthrate caused school attendance to decline, and schools became overcommitted, with too many teachers and too many capital expenditures.

The varied recovery the three systems were able to make is largely explained by the financial structures that supported them. Chicago suffered greatly, because it was exceptionally dependent on local sources of taxation, and many businesses were unable or unwilling to pay their taxes during the depression. San Francisco fared better, because an amendment to the state constitution, passed in 1933, charged the state with responsibility for school funding. Three taxes—a new state sales tax, a state use tax, and an income tax—provided the resources needed to finance these increased responsibilities. Since the state was required to allocate an additional thirty dollars per elementary-school pupil based on average daily attendance and sixty dollars for each high-school student, funds available to the city greatly increased. As a result, San Francisco was able to avoid the cutbacks in school expenditures that Chicago was forced to make. Although Atlanta schools did not grow during the depression era, neither did they experience the severe budget cutbacks suffered by Chicago schools. Atlanta was guaranteed an annual appropriation by the city council, and though numerous attempts were made to abolish this arrangement by reforming the city charter, at least the white schools had financial stability, albeit at a subsistence level, during this period (see table 9.1).

At the same time that the depression era forced a reappraisal of education's appropriate role in view of its budgetary needs, it also caused a shift in local political coalitions. Groups that had been able to work together in a

TABLE 9.1 School Expenditures per Pupil in San Francisco, Chicago, and Atlanta, 1930–40

| | San Francisco | | Chicago | | Atlanta | | | |
| | | | | | White | | Black | |
Year Ending	Current Dollars	Constant Dollars[a]	Current Dollars	Constant Dollars[a]	Current Dollars	Constant Dollars[a]	Current Dollars	Constant Dollars[a]
1930	152	213	166	225	116[b]	83[b]	116[b]	83[b]
1935	157	267	197	336	119	70	41	24
1940	173	289	143	239	180	108	67	40

Source: Yearly Statistical Reports of the Atlanta Public Schools. Annual Statistical Reports of the San Francisco Public Schools. Monthly Reports of School Statistics, Proceedings, Chicago Board of Education.

Note: Per-pupil expenditures computed using current expenditures plus debt servicing. Pupils are those enrolled in high school, elementary, kindergarten, trade, vocational, opportunity, continuation, and special schools. Evening and adult schools and city colleges are excluded.
[a]1947–49 = 100.
[b]Breakdown by race not available for 1930.

decade of optimism now had to reexamine their individual interests under more pressing economic conditions. In Chicago of the 1930s, school men and women found themselves isolated from all the major centers of power, business became primarily concerned with budget deficits and high taxes, labor sacrificed broad social goals for the most immediate interests of its staunchest members, and politicans discovered that teachers "delivered" very few votes. In Atlanta the business community and the city council proposed one charter reform after another, subjecting the school board to pressures of all sorts in order to reduce the annual appropriation and the board's independent decision-making status. School people initially found their friends in the labor movement and among a reform group of citizens from Atlanta's prosperous Northside. But teachers eventually separated themselves from labor in Atlanta, forming an alliance with the business community instead. In San Francisco, labor was a strong contender with business for power and influence in municipal government, and the thirteen-year administration of Mayor Angelo Rossi, with its accommodation style of politics, gave various groups access to decision making; as a result, teachers and labor found many mutually compatible goals. In the school department, internecine struggles for patronage power within the board, between the board and the superintendent, and between the board and the city administration took the place of substantive policy debates occurring elsewhere.

The role of labor in public education was also altered by the events of the thirties. But even in this worst of times, school reform did not preclude labor from participating in policymaking: in Chicago, it was labor that enjoyed machine-bestowed benefits and that sacrificed school reformers on the altar of patronage and jobs; in San Francisco, reformers were responsible for the development of a governance structure that allowed labor, with the aid of a sympathetic mayor, to have considerable influence in school affairs; in Atlanta, southern traditions and racial antagonism, not reform, kept labor from creating its own agenda.

CHICAGO: THE ISOLATION OF REFORMERS

Chicago was not the typical depressed city; its condition was far worse. During the decades preceding the 1930s it had grown at a breakneck pace, becoming an important national and international center of commerce. Large numbers of immigrants coming to the city caused the population to mushroom; from 1900 to 1930 the average increase per decade in the population had been 26.1 percent.[1]

The depression brought an end to this industrial boom, and by 1930 only 54.8 percent of the total Chicago work force still had jobs.[2] Those who succeeded in keeping their jobs saw their wages drop precipitously. Whereas in 1929 the average weekly earnings had attained an all-time high of $31.15, four years later they had dropped 38 percent to a low of $19.38. Many Chicagoans lost their life savings as 177 of the city's 228 banks closed their doors.³ Thousands were evicted from their homes for failing to pay their rent. During the first years of the depression, relief was woefully inadequate, and local agencies were not capable of dealing with the devastation. As of October 1932 Illinois had received one-half of all federal relief loans.⁴

Chicago was also the city in which the school system was the most severely affected by financial constraints. Unlike the situation in San Francisco, little help for schools was forthcoming from the state. The board received a sixteen-dollar grant per pupil, as did every other school district in Illinois.⁵ And Chicago schools, unlike those in Atlanta, did not receive an annual guaranteed appropriation from the city council. Instead, the school system was primarily dependent on the property tax, and the dramatic fall in assessed property values put the schools in a very precarious situation. Added to this were the problems brought about by the board's deficit financing, a method to which the board had resorted to finance tremendous growth from 1920 to 1930. With the advent of the depression, local property taxes became a matter of great controversy in local politics.

All the major participants in the great battle over school finances— business, labor, teachers, and politicians—were also contestants in the debate over the local real-estate tax, a debate that had become heated by 1927. Business, labor, and the teachers alike were unhappy with the existing local tax-assessment machinery. The five members of the board of assessors had each carved out an independent fiefdom, and each had made assessments in his territory independent of the standards and procedures of the others. Their work was overseen by a three-man board of review, whose duty it was to equalize assessments and hear appeals. The only people happy with these arrangements were the politicians involved, for the complexities of the system allowed many opportunities for responding to particular claims and special requests, which could be granted in response to political contributions of one kind or another. But while this practice had long been accepted as a constituent of Chicago politics, tax-assessment policy in the late twenties was also criticized for dramatically underassessing property in general. At a time when economic prosperity was forcing rapid increases in property values, a tax-assessment machinery based on tradition and connections was unlikely to respond rapidly to steep increments in real market value. Teachers complained that schools lacked proper fiscal support, labor claimed that vested interests were holding tax assessments in check, and business leaders became concerned that government policy was not sufficiently rationalized.

Under the leadership of county board president Anton Cermak, who saw tax reform as one of the issues that would help him win the next mayoral election, a Joint Commission on Real Valuation was appointed to assist the county assessors in making the 1927 quadrennial assessment of county property values. The commission, which consisted of "prominent business-men and citizens," hired a professional director who lacked the usual political connections and was committed to assessing property "by eco-nomic value, not political value."[6] Teachers, other school leaders, and the ranks of organized labor were cheered by the prospect of a systematic review of real estate that would focus on real economic value; school finances, which had grown increasingly precarious, seemed on the verge of restoration.

When the results of the commission's work became public, however, labor and the teachers saw nothing short of a disaster in store for Chicago's schools. In the first place, the commission's very existence delegitimized the existing tax machinery, causing short-term financial havoc for local governments. When the county board of assessors ignored the work of the commission in its ensuing assessment, a wave of public protest greeted its findings, and amid charges and countercharges a revised assessment was not completed and released in full until April 1930.[7] During the interim no tax bills were issued by the county treasurer, leaving local governing agencies without any property-tax revenues for two years.

With no taxes being collected, the commission attempted to rescue the schools and other local agencies by appealing to business and civic groups. In response to these appeals, a citizens' committee led by businessman Silas H. Strawn raised $74 million for the purchase of tax anticipation warrants to help carry over local government agencies. But though this provided some short-term relief, a second blow fell. When the revised assessment finally emerged in 1930, it greatly reduced the tax base for the city. In light of the depression, this devaluation was necessary, it was said, to "equalize" valuations between the city and the rest of Cook County and between Cook County and the rest of the state.[8] Even so, many taxpayers reasoned that their tax bills were too high, given the general decline in property values. Of the one million assessments for the county area, ap-proximately 450,000 were challenged in court. By 1933 over $200 million in back taxes was owed by the "tax strikers."[9]

By the time the tax assessment was finally published in 1930, the city's debt was enormous. Even though no taxes had been collected for two years, municipal expenditures had increased from $77 million in 1929 to over $109 million in 1930.[10] At the same time, the deficit of expenditures over revenues grew from $7 million to $45 million.[11] Most of the gap between tax revenues and expenditures was made up by issuing tax anticipation war-rants.

Business and the Political Machine

The city's growing financial problems were especially disturbing to business interests, since Chicago banks owned most of the increasingly shaky bonds and tax anticipation warrants. In addition, many businesses contended they could not afford to pay the same tax rate during the depression as during times of normal prosperity, and they demanded that municipal expenditures be reduced. In 1931 the business community, along with many other groups in the city, deserted the Thompson camp, turning instead to Anton Cermak, whose mayoral victory signaled the beginning of particularly close ties between business and the Democratic machine.[12] Since business support for Cermak was coupled with overwhelming support from the city's ethnic communities, he defeated Thompson by nearly two hundred thousand votes, carrying forty-five of fifty wards. With his victory in 1931 and the Democratic gubernatorial and presidential victories in 1932, virtually all sources of patronage came under Democratic control.

After Cermak's election, business turned with more vigor to cutting government costs. Under the leadership of Fred. W. Sargent, a committee on public expenditures was formed that exercised enormous influence, forcing the school board to cut its budget dramatically. As Sargent later wrote: "They [the banks] have shown that they positively will not lend money for any municipal function that does not have our active support. This has been a powerful lever in dealing with the really small number of recalcitrants in public office who still cling to faith in Santa Claus."[13] However, although the committee did obtain a reduction in educational expenditures in return for a promise to help the board meet its financial obligations, the committee members did not dictate the specific programs to be cut. Instead, Sargent wrote, "we have tried to indicate the size of the economies which must be achieved and left it to the responsible authorities to work out their own plans of economy."[14]

The committee's close ties to the city's Democratic politicians persisted when Edward J. Kelly succeeded Cermak in the mayor's office. Kelly made five new appointments to the school board, and although none of these appointees were major leaders of the business community (two were coal company presidents, one was a realtor, another was president of a neighborhood bank, and one was Charles Fry, head of the Machinists Union), all advocated further economies in the school budget. On the very same day that the appointments were made, Kelly announced that downtown bankers had "practically agreed" to purchase nearly thirteen million dollars worth of 1932 school tax anticipation warrants.[15]

In July 1933 the board announced its new economy program for the schools. It included the termination of a number of educational services and the attenuation of many others. All the city's junior high schools, the

Parental School for delinquents, the Crane Junior College, and all but one of the city's continuation schools were permanently closed; house arts and manual training were discontinued in the elementary grades; all swimming pools were closed, and the activities of athletic teams, bands, and orchestras were terminated. Kindergartens were cut by 50 percent; all elementary physical education teachers and 50 percent of the gym teachers were discharged. The teaching load of high-school teachers was increased to seven classes a day, and the visiting teacher service was discontinued. In all, some fourteen hundred teachers lost their jobs. Cutbacks were also made in administration; the bureaus of vocational guidance, curriculum, and special education were abolished, and there were dramatic reductions in the bureaus of compulsory attendance and child study.[16] Warming to his responsibilities, the school-board president even asserted, "these are permanent cuts . . . in my opinion, the schools will really serve their purpose better as a result of this program.[17]

The Labor/Teacher Split

The teachers, whose salaries had been cut 23.5 percent between 1931 and 1933, were among those feeling the effects of the financial crunch most severely. Between March 1930 and September 1934, only eight paydays were on time, and for several of those they were issued paper "scrip" instead of money.[18] Part of the problem was the teachers' lack of political muscle in a city where political muscle was everything. Since 1915 the Chicago Teachers' Federation, headed by capable Margaret Haley, had been the strongest of the teacher organizations. However, Haley and the CTF had been heavily involved in the drive for a new assessment of property in the city in 1927. When that drive produced such disastrous results, Haley and her organization lost face, and as the economics of the city worsened they found themselves increasingly at odds with other teacher organizations.

During the course of the next few years, the board's actions frequently incited the teachers to action, much of it seemingly spontaneous. There were parades, mass rallies, meetings in Grant Park to protest payment of salaries in scrip, and marches on the mayor's office. Considering the large number of activities with which teachers promoted their cause, the amount of publicity accorded them by the labor press, the *Federation News*, was extremely limited. Historically, organized labor's position on public education had been clear and consistent. Although not supportive of all educational reforms, they nevertheless pushed for curricular expansion, increased public financial support for the schools, and better working conditions for teachers. They had firmly aligned themselves with those who opposed the school board's economy moves. Fifteen years earlier, the relationship between teachers and labor had been so strong that when board member Loeb told Haley to disaffiliate the CTF from organized labor, labor chief John Fitzpatrick is said to have not seen a problem. The two groups had so much in common they could continue to work together without being formally affiliated.[19]

Just a couple of years before the great fiscal crisis, the *Federation News* had printed an editorial stating that "as organized labor was the major instrumentality in establishing the free, tax-supported public school, it continues to be the protector of our free public school system from all forms of exploitation."[20] Like the teachers, the Chicago Federation of Labor (CFL) felt that the solution to the school system's financial problems lay not in the economy measures that businessmen advised, but in increasing the revenues available to the schools. It had supported the drive for reassessment of the 1927 property revaluation, in which the CTF had played such an active role. The *Federation News* asserted: "Honest reevaluation of the property is the remedy that will provide the schools of Chicago with the needed funds, end the crippling of the school system, allow for a fair compensation for teachers, and terminate the unsanitary and perilous crowding of the schools."[21]

A number of changes had taken place in the fifteen years since 1915, however, that explain labor's increasingly weak support for and eventual desertion of its public-school allies. First, in the early thirties the unionized teachers represented only a miniscule portion of the total CFL membership and, at that, were divided into several distinct groups. Further, the teachers were divided into several organizations, all based on different salary schedules and statuses attributed to groups within the teaching force. There was a Substitute Teachers Union, an Elementary School Teachers Union, a Junior High Teachers Association, a High School Teachers Association, a Principals Club, and so on. With the 1933 announcement of the board's economy measures, talk of consolidating the teachers' organizations increased, but progress was uneven until 1936 when John Fewkes, a physical education teacher, campaigned for the presidency of the Men Teachers Union on a platform of immediate amalgamation of all teachers' organizations. By October 1937 the Chicago Teachers Union (CTU) was formally chartered as Local One of the American Federation of Teachers with a membership of 6,461—43 percent of the city's elementary-school teachers and 62 percent of the high-school teachers. A year later its membership stood at 60 percent of the city's teachers. Superintendent William H. Johnson and the board of education viewed the CTU with hostility. Johnson declared it was not a teachers' organization and banned its activities from school premises.[22] As time passed, the superintendent's resistance to meeting with CTU representatives diminished, but throughout the thirties the union was still unable to gain recognition as an agent of collective bargaining.

Another reason that helps explain the limited attention given to the teachers' plight by the CFL is the general unemployment of the period. The onset of the 1929 depression had knocked the bottom out of the construction industry in the city, and members of the building trades unions were suffering from the consequent slowdown in new construction starts. Other locals were also having contract difficulties and were involved in strikes, so the teachers' problems constituted only a small fraction of the many facing the CFL.

While both of these factors were responsible for the tension between organized labor and the teachers, it was the political tactics of the machine that dealt the final blow to the relationship. This it did by rewarding labor leaders with political perquisites and by extending its patronage to the more powerful arms of the CFL at the expense of the weak Teachers Union. When Mayor Kelly appointed seven new board members, one of them was Charles W. Fry, president of the Machinists Union. To the surprise of labor activists, Fry participated in drafting the drastic cutbacks announced in July of 1933.[23]

The general body of the CFL vehemently denounced the cutbacks, passing a resolution addressed to the board of education.[24] Several days later, CFL president John Fitzpatrick protested the economy measure in a speech before a mass meeting in the Chicago Stadium sponsored by the various teachers organizations and the Citizens' Save Our Schools Committee.[25] In spite of its vociferous denouncement of the economy program, there was evidence of ambivalence in labor's response, which first became apparent in the CFL's treatment of Fry. A motion to have the school-board member called before the executive committee of the CFL to explain his role in formulating the economy program was withdrawn, and another motion condemning Fry was defeated. The machine was able to use group pride to divert labor's attention from the substantive issues raised by the school cutbacks.

The machine also used its patronage weapon to disrupt the traditional labor-teacher alliance, giving jobs and high salaries to school maintenance workers, who were members of the Building Trades and Services Union. These workers had maintained close ties with city politicians since at least the early twenties. Although ward committeemen had long seen to it that political favorites were appointed to jobs in the school system, patronage in the custodial ranks of the schools exploded after 1927.[26] Ruling on a suit brought by the firemen responsible for the heating plants alleging contract abuses on the part of the janitors who hired them, the appellate court ruled that school maintenance workers had to be placed under the provisions of the civil service act.[27] The consequences were new contracts with the board, which now had to be negotiated with separate unions for engineering-custodians, firemen, janitors, and women janitors instead of allocating a lump sum for the engineer-custodians. The numbers of custodial assistants "needed" for maintaining the plants burgeoned, and when necessary the civil service provisions were circumvented by making temporary rather than permanent appointments.[28]

An indication of the consequence of these changes can be seen in table 9.2. The proportion of the wages of maintenance workers in the engineer-custodian category to the total wages of elementary teachers jumped from 10.5 percent in 1927, the year of the appellate court's ruling, to 16.8 percent by the very next year. The same thing happened in the high schools, where funds designated for engineer-custodians' salaries changed from 7.6 percent to 9.8 percent of expenditures on high-school teachers' salaries. The percentage grew steadily throughout the 1930s and 1940s, and by 1947 engineer-custodians' salaries as a proportion of the amount spent on

TABLE 9.2 Expenditures on Engineer-Custodian Wages as a Percentage of Expenditures on Teacher Salaries, Chicago, 1925–47

Year	Elementary School	High School	Total
1925	9.7%	7.0%	9.3%
1926	9.9	7.2	9.2
1927	10.5	7.6	9.7
1928	16.8	9.8	14.4
1929	18.8	10.1	16.3
1930	NA	NA	NA
1931	16.7	8.5	14.2
1932	18.1	8.6	15.2
1933	18.6	8.5	15.4
1934	20.3	9.2	15.9
1935	19.2	9.9	15.5
1936	19.6	10.1	15.8
1937	19.6	10.1	15.7
1938	18.8	9.7	15.0
1939	18.9	NA	NA
1940	20.4	10.0	15.8
1941	20.5	10.2	15.9
1942	20.9	10.1	16.1
1943	21.4	10.0	16.4
1944	22.1	10.8	17.2
1945	22.8	11.7	18.1
1946	22.9	12.2	18.4
1947	22.2	12.7	18.5

Source: Annual reports of receipts and expenditures in Chicago Board of Education, Proceedings.

elementary and high-school teachers' salaries was 18.5 percent. Clearly, the economy measures taken during the 1930s did not affect custodial workers in the same way they affected teachers.

One early controversy was a harbinger of the pattern that prevailed throughout the decade. At a mass rally in July 1933 the school superinten-dent proposed a series of measures designed to reduce school expenditures without curtailing instruction. Prominent among these measures was a plan to reduce the wages of engineer-custodians and janitors. The *Federa-tion News* was highly critical of this proposal, declaring that the engineer-custodians and janitors had already made great sacrifices.[29] Since they belonged to one of its unions, the CFL defended the Building Service Trades people whether or not their numbers and salaries were inflated by political patronage. Although the CFL opposed the 1933 economy program, it did not strenuously oppose even deeper cuts in teacher salaries, a decision that alienated the teachers and the reform-minded Citizens' Schools Committee and caused organized labor to become increasingly isolated from the advo-cates of school reform.

The Citizens' Schools Committee

Anxious to develop a strong base from which to attack the economy mea-sures of the board, representatives of various teachers' organizations met with interested civic groups to found the Citzens' Schools Committee (CSC) in 1933. Teachers provided much of the impetus for the CSC in its early period: one of the earliest membership reports records that 4,545 out of the total membership of 5,159 were schoolteachers.[30] The group was, in effect, a "major front organization" for the teachers,[31] but it also had substantial support among the prestigious and traditionally reform-minded civic clubs of the city.

The CSC contended that economy in the school system was possible, but that cutbacks should be made in operations and administrative costs rather than in instructional costs. Pinpointing the political machine as the reason for inefficiency and waste in the schools as well as throughout city govern-ment, it drew upon data published by the United States Office of Education that seemed to show that expenditures for operation and maintenance of school plants were unusually high in Chicago relative to other cities. According to the 1936 report, the average percentage of total school expend-itures for the maintenance plants was 12.7 percent in seventy-three major cities during 1934–35. In Chicago it was 18 percent. Of the ten largest cities in the United States, Chicago had the highest per-pupil administrative costs and the lowest per-pupil instructional costs.[32] The CSC found itself quite alone in its battle against maintenance costs, however, since orga-nized labor continued to support the janitors.

The CSC did succeed in making the schools an important issue in local politics throughout the 1930s and 1940s. It actively supported the restoration of school services, the teachers' demands for higher salaries, and efforts to increase state aid to local schools. Beginning with its attempt to establish ward councils, it also was active in local politics. But until after the war the group had few political successes. One of the explanations for the organization's inability to develop a viable political presence was the difficulty it experienced in buiding coalitions with other groups. Since the CSC necessarily attacked the business community and its part in the economies forced on the schools, it was unable to attract prominent businessmen to its membership and consequently had limited financial resources.[33] The committee was equally unsuccessful in attracting members of Chicago's ethnic communities, even though appeals were made in many of the city's foreign newspapers.[34] Attempts were made to establish ward councils, small discussion groups in each ward through which citizens would be able to express personal opinions.[35] Even though by 1936 there were ward councils in forty wards, this drive had to be abandoned the following year because of public apathy, lack of funds, and political bickering.[36] Cut off from powerful political allies, the CSC eventually evolved into a watchdog organization, criticizing political influence in the schools.[37]

SAN FRANCISCO: THE DISMANTLING OF REFORM

Whereas Chicago reformers were isolated in the thirties, in San Francisco politicians and reform-minded board members shared power. Since the Riley-Stewart amendment to the state constitution guaranteed an annual amount per child based on average daily attendance, the schools were on a more secure footing. As a result, taxation controversies of the magnitude of those in Chicago did not occur. Since finance was not the focus of the conflict in San Francisco, and since San Francisco was not governed by a powerful machine, uneasy shifts in the balance of power between machine and reform-oriented board members defined school politics. Ironically, the two sides worked together to undo the reform structures that had seemed so firmly established.

The Reform of San Francisco's Schools

The reform amendment approved by the voters in 1920 was known as amendment thirty-seven, or the Claxton amendment, after United States commissioner of education Philander Claxton, who surveyed the city's schools and made the recommendations on which it was based. It called for a board of education composed of seven nonsalaried directors to be appointed by the mayor. Teachers were to be excluded from serving on the board, with the idea that it should represent "that part of the community on whose behalf educators are employed.[38] The superintendent was no longer to be elected, but was to be appointed by the board. The hydra-headed school system, with both an elected superintendent and an elected board, had come to an end.

The Claxton reform had been rejected by voters in 1918, in large part because of the opposition of teachers' organizations, whose members were to be excluded from serving on the school board. Since the teachers had the support of labor organizations and a variety of neighborhood groups, who had backed the idea of an elected superintendent, the amendment had been defeated two to one. Two years later, however, the amendment was passed, primarily because of the support of the San Francisco Labor Council, which reversed its position. During the administration of progressive governor Hiram Johnson, the State Federation of Labor had been trading its support on progressive issues for the enactment of prolabor measures.[39] In the case of the Claxton amendment, the Labor Council appears also to have lent its support in hopes of obtaining influence over such educational issues as vocational education, an objective it attained during the decade following passage of the amendment.

For thirteen years the political rules established by the Claxton amendment governed San Francisco's schools. The superintendent was Joseph Gwinn, who provided strong, reform-minded leadership. Yet Gwinn, too, became susceptible to the charges of malfeasance and corruption that had always been a staple of politics in this frontier town. In the aftermath of his resignation the school board vowed "never" again (at least for a decade, anyway) to allow a superintendent to exercise the independence and autonomy Gwinn had enjoyed. Instead, they returned to a new version of the hydra-headed form of government the city had experienced before the Claxton reforms.

The Undoing of Reform

The undoing of this administrative reform was gradual, the result of a series of small steps and decisions that had none of the drama of the passage of the Claxton amendment, but nonetheless reshaped the character of school governance in ways Claxton would never have thought possible.

The first step toward reform's undoing was taken internally. The board increased its power relative to that of the superintendent by establishing the new position of board secretary. The secretary had full power of audit and was in charge of personnel policies for all departments, except for the superintendent and his immediate staff; he was also responsible for keeping all records, including the teacher rating files. The effect of this innovation was to remove all business matters from the hands of the superintendent and to set up a competing center of administrative and executive authority that was responsible to the board.

With the dismissal of Superintendent Gwinn and the appointment of J. A. Ormond as board secretary, San Francisco departed from the superintendent-centered system it had adopted following the Claxton recommendations.[40] Because of their mistrust of superintendents with full executive authority, reformers now effectively abandoned the new structures they had embraced ten years earlier. As the new arrangements developed and separate domains of power were established, it became apparent that the objective of "efficient administration" had been undercut by the division of administrative authority.

The second factor contributing to reform's demise was the strategy pursued by Mayor Angelo Rossi. As the result of his predilection for appointing a diverse group of board members, three centers of power emerged. The first was the superintendent, who sought to increase his institutional power in the system by challenging the prerogatives of the board, particularly those of Ormond. Board secretary Ormond, and the minority faction of the board that aligned itself with him, constituted a second center of power. This minority faction consisted of three members, the leader of which was Philip Lee Bush, representative of the "world of finance and commerce."[41] Bush derived much of his power on the board from his close association with Ormond and his perennial chairmanship of the strategic finance committee. The two other board members, who generally sided with Bush, were also drawn from the upper stratum of San Francisco society. The third center of power consisted of the majority bloc on the school board, including a number of professionals and the "labor" representative; several members of this group were Catholics, active in church affairs.

Throughout Mayor Rossi's tenure the board exhibited this consistent four-to-three split, with the majority closely aligned to Rossi. Although there is no direct evidence that his pattern of appointments was a deliberate strategy to control school politics, one analyst has noted that "some of the more critical political observers have insisted that personalities on the board were deliberately chosen with a view toward attaining 'evenness' of split over policy matters.[42]

Why did this internecine bickering over questions of governance and authority dominate San Francisco school politics of the 1930s? There were three reasons. In the first place, there were no overwhelming educational issues that attracted the attention of the wider public and served to polarize it in any powerful way. The Riley-Steward amendment, passed in 1933, meant that by 1935 the state was providing the San Francisco schools with funds for 57.7 percent of their operating expenses:[43] therefore school finances were not the contentious public issue they were in Chicago. Second, the various board members, though selected to be "representative of particular groups," were only loosely tied to their "constituencies." Over time, school directors tended to grow out of touch with the changing interests of the groups from which they were drawn as they carved out areas of expertise that brought them power within the school board. Third, the majority coalition on the board was too heterogeneous to speak consistently for any one set of interests. Newspaper criticisms of the board during this period do not charge a lack of responsiveness but rather allege that individuals on the board used its programs (its building program, for example) as a "sop" to "sectional voters."[44]

The Board and the Teachers

Board diversity, together with fairly adequate fiscal support from the state, also kept conflict over teachers salaries to a minimum. In part the board was fortunate that the teachers themselves were divided. What one teacher had noted in 1906 still seemed to be true in 1936: "teachers are . . . united in the common cause of earning their money [but] . . . divided in the effectual means of obtaining it."[45] The moderates were represented by the Teachers Association, which included most administrators as well as female elementary-school teachers in its membership. The association maintained such close relations with the school board that its three-term president, Joseph Nourse, was chosen superintendent for seven years. The more militant teachers' organization, the Federation of Teachers, consisted of three union-oriented groups that often took a more adversarial role, assuming leadership in many of the struggles to protect teachers' salaries. Male high-school teachers had founded the first teachers' union in 1919, and now in the thirties they continued to be disproportionately active in its leadership.[46]

Organized labor supported the salary demands of the more militant teachers, in line with its general policy of minimizing the impact of the depression on city workers. A citizens committee formed by the school board in 1928, in response to teachers' demands to raise salaries, which throughout the 1920s had been "inexcusably low,"[47] was chaired by the editor of the *Labor Clarion*, James W. Mullen.[48] The committee recommended a schedule that would encourage teachers to obtain more training by using it as a gauge for progression on the salary schedule. Members also agreed that the merit principle should be recognized through "periodic appraisal of the teacher's work."[49]

Consistent with this responsiveness to group concerns, the board adopted the salary schedule soon after the committee recommended it. But the board discontinued salary increments in 1932, and the following year San Francisco voters approved a 3–20 percent salary cut for all city employees.[50] Three years later, in response to organized teacher action, the board restored annual increments to all except probationary teachers.[51]

In summary, San Francisco's reform movement, which triumphed in 1920, provided for a smaller school board appointed by the mayor. For over a decade this structural arrangement had allowed a professional superintendent to provide strong leadership. But the appointed board also proved compatible with a markedly different political style, which emerged in 1931 with the election of Angelo Rossi as mayor, and teachers as well as the labor movement more generally had a steadily increasing role in forming school policy. In addition, the availability of state funds under the Riley-Stewart amendment allowed a more generous response to teacher demands than in Chicago.

School politics of the thirties, like the politics of the city as a whole, thus were characterized by a patronage system that allowed both business and labor some influence but eschewed controversial policy decisions in favor of the distribution of particularistic benefits. This, plus the re-creation of the hydra-headed school administration caused by the new position of board secretary, substantially increased the school board's powers. Primarily because of ambiguity in authority, the tenures of superintendents after Gwinn were relatively short, except for the seven years served by well-connected insider Joseph Nourse. Not until after World War II, when Harold Spears arrived in San Francisco to command the school system's most vigorous reform era, would the city again see the political and administrative style that Claxton had recommended.

ATLANTA: THE DISAPPEARANCE OF REFORM

In Atlanta fiscal politics dominated questions of reform in both the twenties and the thirties. As in San Francisco, the worst of the financial crisis was averted because the schools, by state law, were guaranteed an annual appropriation from the city council. As in Chicago, a number of political leaders attempted to force budget cuts on the school department and the teachers at the time of the depression. There were, however, important differences between Atlanta and both these cities. In Atlanta a strange coalition of conservative, middle-class elites, trade unionists, and teachers fought the politicians who controlled city hall. Concerned about maintaining basic educational programs, this coalition, formed in 1919 at the time the city charter amendment was passed, continued until the Second World War, when its success in electing a friendly mayor, plus the emergence of a newly assertive black community, proved its undoing. But one cannot understand the durability of this alliance apart from an examination of the perennial school board/city council controversies over school finances.

Conflict between School Board and City Council

Persistent conflict between the school board and the city council, which had long been a characteristic of Atlanta school politics, continued throughout the period between the two world wars. The basis for the conflict was structural: the city council levied the taxes and allocated the funds, and the school board managed school programs. Each entity could recognize the importance of its own responsibilities more readily than it could appreciate those of the other. Council members were sensitive to the demands of taxpayers, while board members understood the cost of mounting a quality educational program.

Throughout the twenties the battles between board and council led to a series of changes and reversals that together yield a story line not unlike that of a Gilbert and Sullivan operetta. In the wake of reformer Robert Guinn's board presidency (see chap. 8), a teacher-labor-Northside coalition succeeded in convincing the state legislature that Atlanta's school board should be elected at large and that 22 percent of the city council's budget should be automatically designated for school purposes. But as soon as the city charger was amended, city council members and their taxpaying constituents fought back. Arguing that a board elected at large did not represent all parts of the city, they won voter support for the election of board members from within the same ward boundaries that were the basis for electing council members. They also partially withstood the school alliance's demands for a 30 percent automatic allocation of city revenues to the schools. Instead, a compromise increase from 22 to 26 percent was reached.

Within two years of this amendment the issue was reopened. This time the city council proposed a council-appointed school board and refused to appropriate funds even when the schools seemed on the verge of bankruptcy. A committee of bankers and businessmen was formed to investigate school profligacy. Nor did the story end here. In fact, council members continued to make budget cuts and structural reform proposals every year or so throughout the decade. Yet the school board, though always under pressure, succeeded in defending the quasi-autonomy it had achieved in 1919. In fact, school supporters even managed in 1933 to win passage by the state legislature of still one more charter amendment that finally gave them a guaranteed 30 percent of the city's annual revenues.

In retrospect one can see that council members had been fighting a rearguard action. The state of Georgia had finally established (in 1920) compulsory education and obliged school systems to provide free textbooks, and since secondary schools continued to grow in size and complexity, the school board's fiscal requirements were steadily increasing. Atlanta's mayor could insist "that these schools . . . be run on business principles just as the other forty-nine departments of the city should be run," but even though it often appeared to him that "the schools . . . are not being run that way," the underlying pressures for expansion could only be slowed, not held back altogether.[52] A committee of bankers and businessmen could demand the abolition of kindergartens, of free textbooks, and of a teachers' salary schedule, but the board was prepared to risk bankruptcy rather than concede demands so out of touch with broader social and political trends.

But however inevitable the outcome appears in retrospect, it did not seem so to participants at the time. Instead, the acrimonious debate between school board and city council over school finances unified the educational community. The disputes between business and labor, superintendents and teachers, and school board and staff that marked depression-era politics in Chicago were simply not visible in Atlanta. Apart from ever-present tensions, educators in Atlanta spoke with one voice against "the politicians."

The Teachers' Union

The core of the coalition was the Atlanta Public School Teachers Association (APSTA)—for the South, a surprisingly strong and cohesive local chapter of the American Federation of Teachers (itself a member of the American Federation of Labor). Since as many as 90 percent were claimed as members of the union, Atlanta's teachers spoke with a single union-affiliated voice that had not yet been heard in either San Francisco or Chicago. However, the teachers' union was decidedly not antiadministration; on the contrary, its leadership, which included a large number of school principals, worked closely with the school superintendent and the board of education. All parties saw themselves as engaged in a common struggle on behalf of the schools. This cooperative relationship resulted in the appointment of a union president as superintendent of schools, a development symbolizing both the beginning and the culmination of the relationship we are now describing.

The Voice of Organized Labor

With the teachers' union a key, unified component of an otherwise rather weak trade-union movement, the teachers won faithful, continuous backing from the Atlanta Federation of Trades (AFT). Pledging allegiance to the "twin pillars of democracy"—labor unions and public schools—the AFT, through its *Journal of Labor*, opposed all attempts to reduce either the budget or the curriculum of the school system during the depression years and sought to expand and improve the system in the years of economic recovery. As part of its participation in the pro-school coalition, the *Journal of Labor* restricted its editorial remarks on educational questions to expressions of support for the mayor, the board, and the superintendent of schools. The paper reiterated its strong support for expansion and diversification in the programs of vocational education, career guidance and placement, and educational research carried on by the school system, particularly after the school superintendent asked the Atlanta Federation of Trades to help organize and direct the programs.[53]

By the late twenties Atlanta's labor movement was at the peak of influence within the school system, working in concert with the directors of the schools to accomplish its goals for the system: "free schools, free books, and compulsory education to the age of twenty," in addition to better salaries for teachers and a broad program of vocational education.[54] This spirit of cooperation and harmony between the labor movement, the teachers' union, the superintendent, and the board of education attained a pinnacle of sorts when the APSTA president was elected in 1943 to the superintendency by the board of education. The *Journal of Labor* was duly pleased: "Rarely if ever has the labor movement received such an honor as the elevation of Miss Ira Jarrell to the Superintendency of the Schools of Atlanta."[55]

Atlanta School Improvement Associations

The teachers' union, even with the backing of the labor movement more generally, could not have sustained the school board in its budgetary and jurisdictional fights with the city council had it not had the backing of members of Atlanta's professional and business community as well. The exact role of Atlanta's middle class is difficult to document, but enough data remain in the historical record to suggest that some of the city's most conservative citizens found themselves allied with the teachers and the trade-union movement on school issues.

The evidence is clearest when the pro–school board, anticity council faction was first put together during the campaign for an elected school board in 1919. At that time, a number of women from prominent families living on Atlanta's Northside formed the Atlanta School Improvement Association (ASIA). ASIA called for board president Robert Guinn's ouster, circulated petitions on behalf of the superintendent whom Guinn had removed from office, and called for an elected school board. It is somewhat speculative to guess what motivated the leaders of ASIA to attack Guinn with such vigor; after all, Guinn, like ASIA, favored a more adequate level of educational provision than the city council was willing to fund. Undoubtedly, some were simply expressing their support for the former school superintendent, who was well-known to many of the city's oldest families. But the threat Guinn posed to Boys' and Girls' High Schools, as separate entities, mobilized support among Atlanta's more prosperous citizens. Few things can cut more deeply than the threatened demise of one's alma mater or the reorganization of the school one's children are happily attending. Quite clearly, one of the leaders of the anti-Guinn campaign was the principal of Boys' High.[56] Significantly, ASIA was so successful in protecting its interests in this area that it was not until after World War II that the sex-segregated high schools were finally amalgamated.

The charter amendment that established an elected school board gave ASIA a position from which they could influence school policy. ASIA nominated school-board members, most of whom ran unopposed. In the words of one analyst of school-board recruitment: "At-Large voting for the school board meant that the board was to be dominated, though not tightly controlled, by middle-class members from the fringes of the city. . . . Except for the Federation of Trades, middle-class Atlantans were the voters most actively concerned with education. They worked for the nomination of their candidates and then voted for them, while other citizens did not."[57]

Throughout the twenties and thirties Atlanta's schools were thus sustained by a tripartite alliance. As with most coalitions, the members shared some objectives and could accommodate special concerns. The coalition's overriding objective was to save public education from the seemingly relentless attacks of "city hall" politicians and taxpayer interests. Each group needed the help of the others, even though they all had their own priorities. The teachers wanted to maintain a standardized salary schedule and resisted merit pay. The labor unions wanted full educational programming including vocational education. ASIA wanted to maintain quality secondary schools within the traditional framework if possible. They all backed a higher percentage of city revenues for the schools. Thus, some of the city's most conservative and most liberal groups found themselves working together on educational policy.

The Coalition Begins to Disintegrate

As we have seen, the coalition was quite successful. It repeatedly defeated the city council's efforts to replace an elected board with an appointed one. It gradually expanded the city's commitment to education from 22 to 30 percent of its annual revenues. It preserved the traditional high schools but expanded and modernized the curriculum in other areas, including vocational education. By 1933 it was so powerful that even the man who would be elected mayor of Atlanta, James Key, campaigned on a platform that committed him to supporting the 30 percent allocation. When he reneged on this promise, saying that salaries of other city employees would have to be cut if he were to meet the school coalition's demands, the group gained support from local legislators and forced the bill through the Georgia state legislature anyway. Riding high on these victories, the coalition saw this mayor defeated in the next election by William Hartsfield, who not only was one of Atlanta's most popular mayors but also gave untiring support to the public schools, finally putting to rest the decades of incessant school board/city council struggle over school finance.

Ironically, at the very moment when the coalition seemed completely in command, it began to disintegrate. In part it was the victim of its own success. Without a common enemy, internal unity became more difficult to maintain. But more important, the increasing restlessness of Atlanta's black citizens raised new issues that simply could not be accommodated within the old institutional structures. Out of the struggles of the thirties a new business-dominated political regime emerged. Labor then found itself isolated from the teachers, politically active blacks, and the center of political power more generally.

Black teachers' demands for equal pay helped drive these changes. The suit for equalization of teachers' salaries, which succeeded in 1943 (see chap. 5), executed the coup de grace to the bloc that had been formed in the wake of the charter amendment of 1919. Already that faction had been weakened by Hartsfield's election as mayor in 1936. With this victory, teachers' salaries and educational budgets steadily increased. But as long as a strong mayor gave the schools the support they needed, the teachers did not need a close alliance with the trade-union movement. Ira Jarrell, the teachers' union president who was chosen school superintendent the year after the second equal-pay suit was filed, gradually pulled the teachers' organization away from active involvement with the Atlanta Federation of Trades.

In this context black demands had an unanticipated effect on power relations within the white community. Although black teachers' insistence on equal pay served in the short run to unify and strengthen the Atlanta Public School Teachers Association in its opposition to the demands of its black counterpart, in the longer term the conflict between white and black teachers led the APSTA to abandon its most significant and highly valued accomplishment—the salary schedule—and ultimately resulted in the demise of the union. Facing a call for salary equalization, the APSTA consented to a merit-based salary schedule for the Atlanta public school system, thereby finally giving in on the issue that had "made" the union in the campaign against school board president Guinn two decades earlier.

While the teachers were pulling away from the trade-union movement, business leaders were discovering that by making modest concessions to moderate elements in the black community they could provide more stable political leadership than Atlanta had typically enjoyed. They could more effectively control the petty bickering and minor scandals that had previously characterized city politics. Under Hartsfield leadership the "black-Northside" alliance was institutionalized. After 1946, when blacks were once again enfranchised, black voters, coupled with white business money and leadership, governed Atlanta for over two decades. Not until blacks had sufficient political power to assume direct control themselves would the alliance be disturbed. In the meantime the trade-union movement, whose members for the most part rejected political alliances with blacks, were pushed firmly to the sidelines.

CONCLUSION

In periods of economic adversity, the success enjoyed by groups supporting school reform varied according to the soundness of the schools' finances. In Chicago, where the schools were supported by a tenuous and changing property tax, reform was isolated and school services were cut dramatically. Here the Democrats, under Anton Cermak, formed an alliance with business leaders previously associated with the Republican party. Under the pressures of the depression, the Democrats responded to the business community's request for a policy with broad social implications—the demand for economy within the schools. Not only were economic issues in the forefront, but the business community in Chicago controlled access to credit that was vital to the maintenance of school and municipal revenues. The machine then co-opted labor, offering jobs and board appointments. A newly appointed labor representative on the school board voted for the drastic budget cuts of 1933, but he was not publicly chastised in any way by the labor newspapers or leaders, in spite of pressure from the Citizens' Schools Committee (CSC) and the teachers, and in spite of past decades of labor support for public education in Chicago.

The CSC's failure to organize the immigrant communities in some ways seems to fit the claims of those who suggest that schools were never intended to meet the needs of the working class or the poor and that reformers never really cared about community access to schools.[58] Yet the activities of this reform group, when understood in the context of depression politics, point to a quite different understanding of the role of reformers in urban school life. Although the CSC was certainly a middle-class organization, it acted in direct opposition to, rather than in a coalition with, the business community. Its members criticized the educational bureaucracy, they called for decentralization and a return of power to individual wards, and by soliciting the participation of Chicago's immigrant communities, they affirmed a belief in the ability of the general public to determine school policy. Yet neither labor nor ethnic groups would join this movement for reform of Chicago's schools. In the 1930s labor had worked out a cooperative relationship with the machine that provided patronage and political rewards to its leaders, and as a result labor's support of teacher demands was at best lukewarm. In addition it must be recognized that the Catholic church in Chicago had a vast network of its own schools that over one-fourth of the school-age population attended. Concerned with its own fiscal problems, the church was not an active supporter of the public schools, and indeed it backed many cuts in the public-education budget, hoping to provide tax relief for its parishioners.

Within this context, then, machine politics grew. Appealing to the occupational and religious cleavages of the diverse immigrant groups, the machine was able to amass large amounts of power. In these circumstances the appeal of the reformers left the immigrant communities unmoved. Neighborhood patronage was understood; broadly based movements proclaiming loosely defined issues in which the immigrants had a less direct stake were not.

In San Francisco, a guaranteed amount from the state per pupil based on average daily attendance kept finances from being the contentious issue they were in Chicago. Here conflict centered instead on governance and power. With Angelo Rossi in city hall, labor and school reformers vied with business for power on the school board. Here labor and reformers first worked to establish a powerful superintendency and an appointed school board which they felt they could control by their electoral hold over city hall; then they worked in concert to destroy the autonomy of the superintendent when he attempted to usurp the board's traditional powers. This they did by bringing in a board secretary who was responsible for the financial transactions of the schools and who formed another center of power. Thus the schools swung full circle, returning to the decentralized decision making that was characteristic of the prereform era.

Atlanta schools were never funded at a luxurious level, but the efforts of the Atlanta School Improvement Association (ASIA), the closest thing Atlanta had to a reform coalition, at least succeeded in establishing, and eventually increasing, an annual guaranteed amount from the city council for school operating expenses. In this racially sensitive city, the word "reform" acquired a highly specialized meaning. Although the Guinn board attempted to introduce a number of organizational modernizations in 1915, its efforts were defeated by strongly defended southern traditions, which unified whites of all classes in efforts to keep Atlanta's black citizens from gaining political power. "Reforms" basically became efforts to keep the city council from passing charter amendments designed to allow it to control the school board and to reduce expenditures on schools.

ASIA was most powerful in the early 1940s, at which time it succeeded in electing Ira Jarrell superintendent. However, once in power and with no common enemy such as the city council to fight, the coalition began to dissipate. Jarrell, who felt the schools needed business support, led the teachers away from the labor movement. When the 1940s business-black coalition surfaced and the federal government became involved in local issues of black-white equality, trade-union influence in local politics, which had never been strong without the support of middle-class groups, disappeared together with the school-reform movement.

10 Reform and Expansion: Some Conclusions

Americans have long believed that education and democracy are inextricably linked. Schools train citizens both by giving them the capacity to choose able rather than foolish leaders and, by giving them the sense that with education, they will have as good a chance to "get ahead" as do any of their countrymen. But at the same time that schools have helped secure the political foundations of the republic, the give and take of politics has changed and shaped public education. Educators have continually claimed more for their schools, and except in depressed times or when either political machines or conservative elites felt they could ignore popular wishes, they have had political success. Schools, in fact, became the sacred cow of local politics. Candidates gained little political mileage by running against education and though some questioned what they saw as excessive fiscal expenditures, most pledged their commitment to public education's growth and expansion. As time passed, schools became the single most expensive service-delivery system paid for by local taxes, typically consuming over a third of a local government's revenue.

POPULAR SUPPORT FOR PUBLIC EDUCATION

The extraordinarily rapid growth of public education in the United States owes much to the early institutionalization of popular suffrage. Well before the Civil War, and before the historical frame of this book, those white males who had become citizens either by birth or by naturalization were voting members of the urban population. In Chicago and San Francisco, the vast in-migration of new groups of foreign-born voters and the sheer increase in the size of the electorate meant that nineteenth-century politics was in constant disarray. Power shifted among competing factions within the two major parties, third-party movements occurred regularly and were at times successful, and reformers challenged the patronage-style practices of the machine politicians. In these circumstances, public leaders could not safely ignore issues and institutions that were of substantial concern to voters. To refuse support to the public school would have been political suicide.

School people did not receive everything they wanted, of course. Even in a generally favorable climate any special interest will demand more from the local treasury than the tax revenues can allow. In all three cities, school boards repeatedly insisted that city councils and state legislatures provide more revenue, and the revenue-raising bodies of the city and state regularly gave less than requested. Even when board members and council members came from the same social background, their different spheres of responsibility placed them in conflict with one another. School boards felt a special obligation to pay teachers at least minimal salaries and to provide at least an acceptable physical plant. City council members and state legislators, who were called upon to satisfy the requests of various agencies as well as listen to taxpayer complaints, were less likely to be sensitive to educational needs. Conflict over school finance was thus an institutionalized part of local politics.

In these debates, signs of popular discontent with public-school expenditures are notably absent. Ethnic organizations and trade unions generally supported attempts to extend the schools' fiscal base. Unions, which were also attempting to eliminate child labor practices, were especially supportive of compulsory education and viable school systems. The only serious sign of working-class opposition came from the Catholic church, and that must be attributed basically to the church's organizational concern for its parochial schools. Indeed, Catholics gave every indication that in return for state aid to their schools they would endorse fiscally sound public schools.

Articulate opposition to a growing system of public education also came from others who had more to lose and less to gain—the city's business interests. Businessmen did not always seek to reduce the financial base of the public schools, but when depressions occurred or when they felt that schools had indulged in too many "fads and frills," business leaders were willing to use the budgetary ax. Perhaps it was business uncertainty about the value of public education that gave rise to educators' assiduous efforts to court business favor. Businessmen were sometimes told that schools would yield a more productive labor force, a more compliant group of employees, and a more complacent citizenry. But while some businessmen, who were being asked to pay for the education of other people's children, may have agreed with these arguments, other business leaders were aware that education could alert the populace to new possibilities and promise more than the society could deliver without major social change. Schools hardly guaranteed social peace, even though some of their enthusiastic supporters might have claimed this when enlisting what often was grudging business support.

Campaigns for public schools were continual, in part because schools were the most expensive of local government services and in part because schoolmen were concerned about the expansion of rival institutions. Among the most important competitors that threatened the place of public education were the private day and boarding schools that had proliferated from the East across the Midwest and throughout the South. In return for tuition these schools typically offered a classical, academically oriented curriculum that prepared students either for the university or for entry into one of the country's burgeoning professions. Nothing could have developed more easily than a public elementary-school system that served the less fortunate, along with a private secondary system limited to those who could pay tuition. This pattern was, in fact, becoming deeply entrenched in virtually all the European countries during the very same decades that saw the rise of the American high school.

One should not romanticize the social and political motives of those educators who created public high schools in Chicago, San Francisco, Atlanta, and elsewhere. It is unlikely that they were moved primarily by a concern for equalizing opportunities for all children, though this is what they often claimed. In practice, Atlanta's school board provided secondary education for white boys and girls only, and San Francisco's sex-segregated high schools had a basically middle-class clientele. Quite probably, nineteenth-century boards and superintendents spent scarce funds on secondary schools in large part because such institutions lent prestige to the entire public-education enterprise. If public-school children could demonstrate proficiency in the classics, could prepare for the university, could enter business and the professions, then the public schools could clearly establish themselves as something other than charity institutions expected only to instruct the children of the poor.

But even though educators' emphasis on secondary education may have been motivated less by egalitarianism than by organizational prudence, the consequences of their actions cannot be understood apart from the political ideology of nineteenth-century America. Secondary schools were opened almost simultaneously with the creation of the elementary-school system in Atlanta, San Francisco, and elsewhere, because in a society operating according to democratic ideals one could not successfully argue against an educational ladder that led from kindergarten to the university. One could limit the size of the secondary-school offerings on grounds of cost, and one could restrict the types of pupils admitted. But whatever reservations taxpayers and city councils might have had, educators, drawing upon the democratic creed and the reality of widespread popular participation in nineteenth-century municipal politics, captured the high ground when they pronounced the need for advanced opportunities for the more able pupils.

The rhetoric of equal opportunity had its consequences for high-school practices as well. Whatever middle class-bias these institutions had, access to them by sons and daughters of the working class could not be foreclosed altogether. Public schools were in theory open to all, and the procedures of selection and admission had to be, on their face, consistent with these principles. To the extent that it was feasible, all students who wished to pursue their studies at the secondary level had to be given a chance. Quite unexpectedly, the conditions were thus set for an extraordinary expansion of the American high school, one that far surpassed anything in Europe and that by the 1930s would set the stage for the unimagined explosion of college enrollments after World War II.

The coincidence of organizational interests and popular aspirations helped propel this expansion. The schools were eager to extend themselves, especially in a direction that would enhance their prestige, public image, and sense of social worth. A growing secondary-school system meant new and more interesting jobs for educators, provided a more complex, challenging task for school administrators, and gave school-board members the satisfaction of directing an increasingly valuable public institution. But however badly educators wanted to move in this direction, they could not do so without interested students and fiscal support. Trade-union-sponsored child-labor laws helped supply the first of these. Denied access to good jobs, young adults had few options other than continued schooling. Besides, many believed that a high-school education could guarantee better jobs. As the numbers attending secondary school increased, this "guarantee" declined in value, but in the crucial years when high schools initially gained a popular clientele, expectations were high.

Fiscal resources for secondary schooling, though strongly supported by trade unions and reform groups, came less easily, especially in periods of economic crisis. But even in the worst of times few, if any, ventured the opinion that secondary education should be limited to those who could pay tuition. Over the decades, Protestant and nonsectarian fee-paying schools dwindled in number and significance so that by World War II their potential for challenging the public school's dominant role in providing secondary education had all but disappeared.

Public-school people achieved this success in part because they had secured for their institution a preeminent role in vocational education. In the late nineteenth century, apprenticeship training and informal on-the-job instructions were giving way to privately organized programs of industrial education directly supported by leading businessmen. As the demand for vocational education increased at about the turn of the century, a number of business leaders proposed that a separate, publicly funded set of institutions be established for the sole purpose of training workers needed for the new industrial empire. Here on a second occasion one discerns social forces pressing for a secondary education quite different in structure from the comprehensive high school that became so distinctive a part of Amer-

ican society. But business leaders were no more successful than the day-
and boarding-school providers had been decades earlier. Instead of a vocational system developing parallel to the regular academic high school, the
two were integrated under the aegis of public-school administrators.

The vehemence with which public-school officials attacked the proposals for a separate vocational system should not be attributed to excessively
altruistic concerns, though once again democratic symbols were often
invoked in the course of the discussions. Schools had at stake compelling
organizational interests of a concrete and material nature. Had vocational
education been split from the public-school enterprise, private day schools
might have revived to assume an important role in providing academic
instruction, and the public school system might have remained limited to
the elementary level.

If the motives of public-school leaders are understandable, they do not
by themselves account for their ability to defeat strong, well-conceived,
business-backed proposals. That can be explained only by the extraordinary popularity that schools enjoyed among the public at large, together
with the unqualified backing they received from the trade-union movement. Public schools quickly established manual-training programs as
early as the 1880s, when private efforts in this area were only beginning. By
the time the vocational-education movement appeared in full flower, public schools had become so entrenched a part of local political institutions
that they could count on strong working-class and trade-union support for
their claims to a preeminent role in this new area of responsibility.

Racial Conflict and the Critique of the Public School

Several decades later—in the 1960s—public schools would not be so well
placed, and a rival system of vocational education separate from the public
schools would come into being. Although these new industrial education
programs would be named in ways that deemphasized their educative
purposes, the manpower training programs, neighborhood youth corps, job
corps, comprehensive employment and training centers, and community
action programs that were so integral a part of Great Society programming
were close to what Edwin G. Cooley and his business supporters had
proposed before World War I. These programs were administered in
Washington by the Department of Labor, not the Department of Education.
Responsibility at the local level was lodged with municipal government,
not the public schools. The formal authoritative role of the "private industrial councils" grew steadily so that training programs could be closely
related to the needs of local industry. Participation in these programs was
limited to those from poverty backgrounds who, it was felt, were especially
in need of, and appropriate for, training in programs that prepare students
for skilled and semiskilled jobs. Cooley had not proposed a poverty require-

ment on students entering vocational education, but in other respects the manpower programs begun in the sixties had come close to fulfilling his expectations.

Public schools failed to achieve an exclusive role in vocational education in the sixties, though this had been achieved in 1917, in part for religious reasons. The church/state controversy in education precluded federal aid to public schools at the time when manpower development programs were initiated. But in the early 1960s other social forces were also at work, the most important of which was the sense that public schools had not well served low-income members of racial minorities. Whereas in 1917 public schools were seen as the solution to almost any social problem, by 1962 they were defined as part of the problem to be solved. Head Start, Follow Through, Job Corps, and compensatory education were all designed either to change the schools or to found new institutions to pursue what schools had not done.

Schools were vulnerable to such an intrusion on their territory because, as organizations, they had failed to address the needs of racial minorities in the way they had responded to European immigrants. Whereas Chicago's public schools acquiesced to Germans' demands that their native tongue be taught, the Chinese of San Francisco had difficulty getting inside the schoolroom door, much less finding instruction in their own language. Whereas per-pupil expenditures and pupil/teacher ratios in both Chicago and San Francisco were as favorable in predominantly immigrant schools as they were in those serving native-born Americans, the blacks of Atlanta were crowded into dilapidated buildings and taught by a less well compensated staff. Whereas leaders of immigrant groups regularly served on boards of education in Chicago and other northern cities, (see table 10.1),

TABLE 10.1 Percentage of Member-Years on the Chicago School Board, by Ethnic Group, 1870–1928

Ethnic Group	1874–79	1880–89	1890–99	1900–1909	1910–19	1920–28
Anglo	58.4%	39.5%	52.2%	54.2%	29.9%	29.0%
German	26.6	34.2	24.3	24.2	30.9	34.6
Swedish	0.6	5.9	2.7	2.1	11.3	5.6
Irish	11.0	12.5	4.9	11.6	1.27	6.5
Eastern European	1.3	2.6	7.0	5.8	11.8	24.3
Other	1.9	3.9	3.7	2.1	3.4	0.0
Unknown	0.0	1.3	1.1	0.0	0.0	0.0
Number	154	152	185	190	204	107

Sources: Smith 1973; Dellquest 1938; Withcombe 1977; Chicago Board of Education, *Annual Reports*, 1870–1928.

Note: Percentage totals may not sum to 100 because of rounding.

blacks and Asians were frozen out of positions of authority and responsibility in Atlanta, San Francisco, and elsewhere. Whereas secondary education provided a channel of social mobility for European immigrants even before 1920, it hardly existed for blacks in the South until after World War II. Whereas Irish and German teachers populated the schools of the North, earning salaries and gaining principalships at a rate approaching that of native-born Americans, it took a federal suit by the black teachers of Atlanta in 1944 to win equal pay for equal work.

The differences in the treatment of southern blacks and West Coast Asians, on the one hand, and European immigrants in big northern cities, on the other, are best explained by the Europeans' greater political strength. Even though all immigrants entered pretty much at the bottom of the social order and experienced little but economic misery in the beginning, European ethnics soon obtained the vote and eventually became a local political force. Public institutions serving the community usually did not treat these immigrants with open hostility because this would have alienated their support in future elections. Under these political pressures, elected officials gradually incorporated European immigrants into the schools, first as recipients of the services and later as providers. Such was not the case with minorities of other races. Without the vote, these groups had no political base and could make only weak claims on the public schools.

Once racial minorities did become politically active, the schools as institutions were subject to challenge. When the civil rights drive of the 1960s made the educational concerns of racial minorities a central issue in American politics, political leaders not only tried to reform schools but also searched for educational institutions that were alternatives to the public schools. Manpower training programs were handed over to community organizations, other city agencies, and even private firms. In addition, critics generalized from the schooling experience of racial minorities to the nature of public education more generally. Schools do not teach, it was said, they only give credentials. They discriminate, they subjugate, and they perpetuate the status quo. Their historical development began to be selectively described. The people who had once been treated as the heroes of American education now became the villains.

No political movement has been treated more harshly in this recasting of educational history than the campaign for school reform. At worst reformers are characterized as agents of monopoly capitalism who eagerly structured public schools to serve the needs of the corporate-controlled marketplace. At best they are portrayed as innocents whose hopes that schools could soften and ameliorate class conflicts were inevitably dashed by the realities of economic life. From either perspective it is argued that, just as society is fundamentally shaped by economic forces, so those who shaped the schools acted on behalf of dominant economic interests.

THE PLURAL SOURCES OF REFORM

A political analysis of the historical development of urban schools reveals the simplistic, one-sided nature of such a portrait. Like all social movements, school reform was a complex, pluralistic, multifaceted undertaking. Its sources of support, though basically rooted in a growing professional class, were diverse. Its alliances were subtle, numerous, and subject to change, and its objective varied with time and circumstances. The composition of the opposition depended on the issue at stake. Reformers' policies were as often rejected as approved. When adopted, they were frequently amended; when promulgated, they were not always implemented. Oh how well reformers would have fared had they been as unified, as powerful, and as far-seeing in their vision as some now would have us remember them!

As diverse as reform was, its contributions to educational politics and policy permit two broad generalizations. First, whatever their talk of efficiency, school reformers were educational expansionists. When they came to power, the schools generally spent more, expanded their services, and paid teachers higher salaries. When one calculates per-pupil expenditures in constant dollars, one finds that the San Francisco schools did best in nineteenth-century politics when reformers were in power. Chicago schools flourished briefly when Chicago's first reform mayor, George Dunne, appointed a strong reform majority to the city's board of education in 1906. This experience repeated itself when Mayor Dever appointed a reform board that recruited an aggressive, reform-minded superintendent in 1924. Whatever else Superintendent William McAndrew did, he pushed school finances to new highs; indeed, when he resigned he left the schools on the verge of bankruptcy.

The penny-pinchers in school politics were not reformers but machine-connected politicians or traditional, conservative elites. Atlanta's schools labored under a school board governed by conservative elites until reformers in 1897 paved the way for a more expansionary policy once the depression had receded. San Francisco's expenditures reached their nadir in 1885 when Boss Buckley's machine was at the zenith of its power. When business and machine interests were solidly in control of Chicago schools in the early 1900s, school expenditures fell. And Chicago's harsh treatment of public schools during the 1930s depression came at the hands of a strong, disciplined political organization working in close cooperation with the city's leading businessmen.

Machine reluctance to support urban schools generously is understandable for several reasons. First, machine politicians traditionally took a minimalist view of the role of government. Having little in the way of a substantive, programmatic agenda, they characteristically saw their role as providing the basic housekeeping services the city needed and as distributing to clients and followers the jobs needed to perform this work. Given their size and the labor-intensive nature of their operations, schools provided one of the largest sources of patronage. Also, school-lands acquisition, school construction, and school purchasing requirements provided opportunities for ambitious politicians. It was in these areas, not the size and scope of school operation, that machine politicians took a special interest.

Second, the concept of "honest graft," to use George Washington Plunkitt's famous phrase, provided the basis for a modus vivendi between machine politicians and local business leaders. Honest graft meant giving friends and followers only those jobs and contracts that the city needed in any case. One took only the "opportunities" that arose in the course of government's usual business. Dishonest graft required public expenditure beyond the minimum needed. One way, in fact, that business leaders could be assured that graft was being contained within "honest" bounds was to keep taxes low and government operations routine. Within this framework machine politicians had less room for imaginative innovations and programs of reconstruction.

Third, machine politicians saw schools as institutions for community integration rather than as agents of social change. To the neighborhood politician, what was important about school was the place it provided for making lifelong friends, the spirit its athletic activities imparted to the local community, and the focus it gave to local social life. Few understood schools as centers for educational achievement, much less as mechanisms for society's reform. The schools' constant quest for more money, more personnel, and more varied responsibilities was regarded by the machine politicians as being driven more by organizational aggrandizement than by any substantive need. If those in city hall acquiesced, they did so more as a response to public demand than from any strong conviction of their own. Finally, it should also be remembered that in many large cities machine politicians were predominantly Catholic, whereas reformers usually were Protestant. Although Catholics came to accept public education, few zealously promoted the system's expansion, if for no other reason than its competitive relationship with parochial schools. Indeed, one of the factors that invited special attention by municipal reformers was the Protestants' belief that machine politicians starved public schools because their own children did not attend them.

Reformers not only held expansionary views of the role of public education, they also wanted to upgrade its standards, enhance the quality of instruction given, and organize its administrative structure to be more efficient. In fact, some of the most pronounced themes of the reform movement revolved around efficiency, merit, integrity, and devotion to public service. Thus, one of the central goals of reformers in education was to improve the school system's administrative structure. This meant, above all, establishing a strong, professionally oriented superintendent who was able both to shape board policy in ways consistent with professional ideals and to implement that policy. In general, reformers wanted smaller boards of education, fewer board committees, greater school-system autonomy from the city council (and municipal government in general), no staff appointees other than the superintendent reporting directly to the board, and recruitment, promotion, and salary advancement based on merit. These principles of organization, which Max Weber called a rational-legal mode of organizing activity and which at the time were being applied systematically in the private sector, were expected to give unity of direction to what had become a large, complex, sprawling institution.

These reform proposals were so widely adopted in urban education that one can hardly doubt they responded to underlying organizational imperatives. For one thing, the school system was assuming many new tasks—feeding pupils, providing medical services, creating secondary schools, initiating vocational education, and instituting extracurricular activities. Many of these new activities required a functional form of organization (with line administrators in a central office); a strong superintendent capable of managing the enterprise as a whole could hardly be avoided. Gone forever were the days when each school, directed by its own principal, could operate in virtual isolation from other system components. The need for strengthened central direction was in fact so apparent to school officials that scarcely any strong superintendent during this era could avoid being given the reform label. And if reform is interpreted only to mean strong central administration, then surely even Edwin G. Cooley can be declared a school reformer.

Reformers believed in professionalism for teachers as well as administrators, and here the reform impulse had to struggle with its own internal inconsistencies. The nub of the problem with which reformers wrestled was how to fit members of a profession—teachers—into the hierarchical administrative structure of a big-city school system. If teachers were professionals, they had to be given the autonomy to carry out their tasks in accordance with their own judgment and their own sense of mission. At the same time, if educational administration was to be rationalized, then administrators had to evaluate subordinates.

Choosing between these alternative conceptions of a reformed school system was complicated because many reform-minded teachers were women who were sympathetic to the feminist movement of the period.

They were aware that though the teaching force was overwhelmingly female, administrative posts were often reserved for men. If the public language of the day did not allow these questions to be discussed with the frankness that characterizes modern commentary on matters of gender, they could hardly have been overlooked altogether by women working in a sex-differentiated institution. In consequence, reformers could not be relied upon to give their undying loyalty to any male superintendent who wished to assert his educational authority.

In this context one understands especially well why Ella Flagg Young came to epitomize an ideal synthesis of educational reform goals. Appointed by a reform-minded board, itself primarily chosen by Chicago's first-minded mayor, Young gave coherence to the several sides of reform in a way that would not be realized again in that city until after World War II. She presided over a school system that paid teachers better salaries and reduced class sizes. She campaigned to give superintendents greater authority over the schools, asking for a well-defined, limited scope for school-board involvement. She insisted that the appointment power be lodged in her own hands and resented board interference in personnel matters. Finally, she sought to involve teachers in the policymaking process by forming school councils to deliberate on policy questions (though leaving final decisions to administrative discretion). In part because she was a woman, she was well received by the teaching staff. Only when machine politicians regained control of the board was she forced to resign.

For Young, as for most reformers, combining professionalization with administrative direction would always remain a problem. For business leaders, with their allies in the party machine, a relentless corporate model of hierarchical control overrode any such problem, as can be seen in the case of the 1915 Loeb rule controversy. The main issue this time was teacher unionization, though the questions of superintendent authority and board autonomy from city hall also entered the equation. Threats to remove teachers from office because of union affiliation were especially disturbing to reform leaders and the groups associated with them, and in this case reformers formed a solid alliance with teachers. The alliance was solidified, to be sure, by a suspicion that the political machine intended to use the new law to pack the schools with patronage workers. Even so, reformers found it possible to work with teachers on behalf of a tenure policy that would give this new profession greater independence and autonomy.

Reformers were more ambivalent a few years later when they themselves had the responsibility of giving direction to school policy. Superintendent McAndrew came to Chicago with strong support from the City Club and other reform groups. He promoted numerous organizational reforms including the platoon system and the junior high school, and he greatly extended the size and cost of school programs. He nonetheless had little time for the argument that, as professionals, teachers needed autonomy, independence, and opportunity to participate in decisions affecting school administration. When the teachers aggressively attacked McAndrew, support from reformers for "one of their own" cooled, but it never disappeared altogether. Mayor William Dever backed his superintendent of schools, even though this contributed to his own defeat in 1927.

The twin themes of urban educational reform—expansion and professionalization—were rooted in the beliefs, values, and interests of middle-class professionals who believed in science, education, expertise, and commitment to public service. The ideology was self-interested because it justified the social place of most of those committed to reform principles. Yet this self-interest was disciplined by a concomitant concern for the public interest and, in any case, was readily distinguishable from the class interests of corporate elites. Reform ideals were not simply a mask for established interests; on the contrary, these middle-class professionals found that their political agenda just as often induced them to cooperate with trade-union leaders and working-class groups.

REFORM AFTER WORLD WAR II

Once reform is appropriately defined, its locus of greatest strength is more readily identified. In this book we have shown that the diverse sources of reform came into evidence in the late nineteenth century and began to flourish in the early twentieth. The reform tide continually flowed and ebbed, and the timing of its high-water mark varied from one city to another. Further, reform was not just a concomitant of the Progressive Era. Its days did not end with the 1930s depression and Franklin Roosevelt's New Deal. Indeed, the reform legacy, as experienced by schools today, was not fully institutionalized in many American cities until after World War II. It might even be said that events described in preceding chapters were only precursors of reform, the harbingers of a political movement that would achieve its greatest success after World War II. Urban reform, especially in education, was at its zenith in the period beginning with the close of World War II and continuing into the 1960s, when the civil rights movement gave "reform" new meaning.

As has been shown elsewhere, postwar reform succeeded in almost every domain,[1] whereas early reform had been only partial. In the first place, the end of the Second World War saw the beginning of the most sustained period of educational expansion the public schools had ever enjoyed. The baby boom brought millions of new faces into the classroom; their arrival stimulated a program of great capital expansion. New parents, with higher expectations for their children, expressed horror at the conditions they observed in many American cities; they threw out the politicians they held responsible for schools that had not been modernized for two decades.

Per-pupil expenditures increased dramatically, pupil/teacher ratios fell just as rapidly, teachers were treated with a new dignity, and the percentage of the gross national product spent on the public schools more than doubled.

Second, the postwar era became, more than ever, the age of the strong superintendent. Professional administrators trained in leading university departments of education were given respect by school boards, teacher organizations, and community groups. They built schools, commandeered resources from state legislatures and also by means of aggressive tax and bond referendum campaigns, built a complex administrative infrastructure and spoke convincingly for a united educational front. These professional superintendents decisively pushed patronage politics out of the schools. Administrative and principal appointments were at the superintendent's discretion; boards were reduced to acting as a rubber stamp in personnel decisions and many other matters. School business offices were given over to professionals, who placed competitive bids whenever possible. Even in machine cities, politicians discovered that it was best to leave the schools alone when distributing their patronage. The shibboleth that schools and politics should not mix finally became a well-entrenched principle.

The teacher was given new respect as a professional. Eventually, formal wage differentials between men and women were eliminated; the same was done for blacks and whites. Teachers' salaries were raised at regular intervals, and they began to share in the postwar prosperity. At the same time, teacher organizations became more independent of administrative influence and more specifically attentive to teacher needs. With the merit system well established and tenure provisions widely adopted, teachers had a new capacity to challenge even strong professional adminsitrators. Rivalry between the National Education Association and the American Federation of Teachers encouraged both to take a more militant approach. The pressures for formal collective bargaining procedures, and even for teacher strikes, became so widespread that school boards were forced to give way.

The postwar reform in American education, though powerful and long lasting, began to lose steam in the seventies. In the wake of the civil rights movement, schools were put on the defensive, and disparate political pressures were felt by school administrators, who were challenged by the necessities of school desegregation, school decentralization, and collective bargaining. It is perhaps not an accident that, at the very time the principles of reform were being challenged in the academy by social scientists and educational historians, professional administrators (who personified reform values) were caught in intense political cross fire. Once expected to provide educational leadership, they were now only supposed to find acceptable compromises. Once thought to be the architects of school policy, they were now to be the executors of the school board, or the mayor, or some municipal finance authority. Once recruited for their credentials as educators, their political savvy and connections now seemed more important. With only a few exceptions, the day of the strong superintendent had passed.

It is a coincidence that the period of educational expansion was also replaced in the late seventies by one of caution and retreat? During this period student enrollments declined, teacher salaries dropped, expenditures as a percentage of the gross national product fell, pupil/teacher ratios stabilized, the percentage of students attending nonpublic schools crept upward, and per-pupil expenditures in public schools reached a plateau. None of these trends has proved dramatic or irreversible. A dark day has not come over American education. But the élan, energy, confidence, and self-esteem that accompany times of educational reform and expansion must constantly be renewed if American schools are to continue to enjoy the multiclass popular appeal that has historically been theirs.

Notes

CHAPTER ONE

1. Consider, for example, the claim by Michael Katz that by the late nineteenth century American schools had taken a permanent form that has not since significantly changed: "It is, and was, universal, tax-supported, free, compulsory, bureaucratic, racist, and class-biased" (Katz, 1971, xx). Colin Greer's claim is almost as bold: "The common school's mission was to maintain and transmit the values considered necessary to prevent political, social or economic upheaval" (Greer 1976). Or take the popular study *Schooling in Capitalist America*, whose authors claim that school "reforms had the intent (and most likely the effect as well) of forestalling the development of class consciousness among the working people . . . and preserving the legal and economic foundations of the society" (Bowles and Gintis 1976, 173). Consider portions of David Tyack's sensitive analysis *The One Best System*, in which he asserts that "the administrative progressives were notably successful—indeed, their success so framed the structure of urban education that the subsequent history of these schools has been in large part an unfolding of the organizational consequences of centralization" (Tyack 1974, 127).

2. Riordon 1963, 17.

3. Chambers and Burnham 1967, 277–307.

4. Cubberly 1920, passim.

5. Meyer et al. 1979, 591–613; Craig and Spear 1978, 1979.

6. Meyer et al. 1979.

7. Racine 1969, 34; Garrett 1954; Rabinowitz 1978; Turner-Jones 1982.

8. Some historiographers have contended that compulsory schooling was devised by the middle class to force workers into a structured system so that a disciplined work force could be trained (Bowles and Gintis 1976; Katz 1968). According to others, manual training, kindergartens, and evening schools were promulgated to socialize the immigrant child into middle-class values that would reduce social tensions (Greer 1976). Worker reaction is said to have ranged from sullen acceptance to outright hostility (Bowles and Gintis 1976). We found little evidence for these views in the data from Chicago, San Francisco, and Atlanta.

9. Troen 1975, 120.

10. Heidenheimer 1972, 25.

11. Kolko 1963; Wiebe 1967; Mowry 1951.

12. Evans 1929, 458.

13. Lazerson 1971.

14. Peterson and Rabe 1981 a,b, passim.

15. Tyack 1974.

16. Cronin 1973; Gordon 1937.

17. Wrigley 1982, 130.

18. Ibid.

19. Ibid., 134–35.

20. The result was a school system that provided intergenerational social mobility. Years of schooling became more important than family background as a determinant of income and occupational success. On this subject see Peterson and Karpluss 1981 and Peterson 1982.

CHAPTER TWO

1. Chicago *Tribune*, 16 June 1982, 1.

2. Ibid., 12.

3. *Education Week*, 23 June 1982, 1.

4. Chicago *Tribune*, 16 June 1982, 1.

5. Carlton 1908, 50.

6. Rantoul 1854, 134. Cited in Carlton 1908, 50–51.

7. Simpson 1831, 201. Cited in Carlton 1908, 51–52.

8. *New York Tribune*, 17 October 1850, 67; cited in Carlton 1908, 67.

9. Chicago *Record Herald*, 16 November 1905; cited in Carlton 1908, 69.

10. Carlton 1908, 69.

11. Martin 1893, 178–79. Cited in Carlton 1908, 71.

12. Carlton 1908, 71–72.

13. Ibid., 73.

14. Rabinowitz 1978, 156–57.

15. Chicago Board of Education, *Annual Report*, 1867, 81–82.

16. Ibid., 1873, 47.

17. Dolson 1964, 180.

18. San Francisco *Bulletin*, 16 July 1885.

19. Racine 1969, 48.

20. Atlanta *City Directories*, 1869–80; Ecke 1972, 49–50.

21. Racine 1969, 49–50; Ecke 1972, 49–50.

22. Urban 1977, 135; Racine 1969, 136–38.

23. Racine 1969, 136–38; also see chapter 6 of this book for a more complete discussion of political alignments and reform in Atlanta.

24. Dolson 1964, 159.

25. Ibid., 160.

26. Ibid., 166.

27. Ibid.

28. Dewey 1937, 103–4.

29. Johnston 1880, 43–44.

30. Herrick 1971, 48.

31. Carlton 1908, 84.

32. Katz 1968, 47.

33. Gompers, 21–23 May 1914, from abstract of testimony before United States Commission on Industrial Relations, New York City.

34. San Francisco *Bulletin*, 19 February 1878.

35. For example, see Atlanta *Journal of Labor*, 6 December 1907, 5.

36. Ibid., 27 May 1904.

37. Ibid., 27 May 1904, 17 June 1904, 1 July 1904, 5 May 1905, 18 August 1905, 13 July 1906, 3 August 1906.

38. Ibid., 18 May 1906, 6 December 1907.

39. San Francisco *Bulletin*, 19 February 1878.

40. Illinois State Federation of Labor, *Proceedings*, selected years.

41. Chicago *Tribune*, March 1893, 12 April 1893, 13 April 1893, 26 March 1893; *Inter Ocean*, 12 April 1893; Chicago Board of Education, *Proceedings*, 1893, 401.

42. *Knights of Labor* (Chicago), 2 October 1886, 15.

43. Ibid., 24 January 1891, 1.

44. Ibid., 17 January 1891, 8; 24 January 1891, 1.

45. *Rights of Labor* (Chicago), 24 January 1891, 1.

46. Ibid.

47. *Knights of Labor*, 4 September 1886, 1.

48. Ibid., 22 October 1887, 8.

49. Ibid.

50. *Rights of Labor*, March 1893.

51. *Voice of Labor*, 9 October 1897.

52. San Francisco *Star*, 16 December 1899.

53. Evans 1929, 258–59.

54. James 1937, passim; Evans 1929, 606.

55. Bowles and Gintis 1976, 186.

56. *Merchants Association Review* (San Francisco), September 1898.

57. Ibid.

58. Ibid., 6 March 1902.

59. Dolson 1964, 314.

60. *Merchants Association Review*, 10 March 1903.

61. San Francisco *Call*, 22 June 1881, 23 June 1881, 29 June 1881, 2 July 1881, 21 July 1881, 4 November 1881, 18 June 1882, 17 June 1882, 8 February 1883.

62. Clark 1897, 64.

63. Chicago Board of Education, *Annual Report*, 1876.

64. Clark 1897, 56; Chicago Board of Education, *Annual Report*, 1888, 29–33.

65. Herrick 1971, 77.

66. Clark 1897, 66.

67. Ibid., 61.

68. Tyack and Hansot 1982, 77.

69. Ibid.

70. Yorke 1933, 271–82.

71. San Francisco *Monitor*, 25 January 1868.

72. Swett 1872, 15.

73. Dolson 1964, 55.

74. Swett 1872, 116.

75. San Francisco *Bulletin*, 9 April 1870.

76. San Francisco *Monitor*, 1 December 1877, 20 June 1878, 7 February 1878.

77. Ibid., 7 February 1878.

78. Ibid.

79. Pierce 1957, 339, 380.

80. Hays 1974.

81. Issel 1977, 342.

82. Vare 1933, 118–19; Dorsett 1968, 41; McKitrick 1957, 505–8; Merton 1957, 71–82. All cited in Tyack 1974, 94.

83. Tyack 1974, 94.

84. Bullough 1979, 72; McDonald 1979.

85. "The Reminiscences of Christopher A. Buckley," San Francisco *Bulletin*, 27 January 1919.

86. San Francisco *Chronicle*, 24 October 1884.

87. Peterson 1981, chap. 3.

88. Erie 1975, 108.

89. Although Buckley's Democrats lost the municipal election in 1890, McDonald claims that the Republicans, under boss Martin Kelly had similar spending patterns, and he therefore considers the years 1890–92 to be years of machine-dominated fiscal expenditures.

90. McDonald 1979, 189, 193.

91. Ibid., 200–201.

92. Ibid., 202.

93. Ibid., 204–5.

CHAPTER THREE

1. Tyack 1974.

2. United States Bureau of the Census, *Population*, 1870 (Washington, D.C.: Government Printing Office).

3. Based on data in Shradar 1974, 33, 38, 53–54.

4. For a discussion of the pervasiveness of German schools in Chicago, see Townsend 1927.

5. Herrick 1971, 61.

6. Currey 1912, 297.

7. Hawley 1971, 75; San Francisco Superintendent of Public Instruction, *Annual Report*, 1871, 76, 1879, 318.

8. San Francisco Superintendent of Public Instruction, *Annual Report*, 1871, 76.

9. Ibid. 1878, 54.

10. Chicago Board of Education, *Annual Report*, 1867, 191–92.

11. San Francisco *Monitor*, 17 January 1874.

12. San Francisco, Superintendent of Public Instruction, *Annual Report*, 1875, 145–48.

13. San Francisco *Monitor*, 17 January 1874.

14. Hawley 1971, 52; also see Shradar 1974, 33, 38, 53, 54.

15. Hawley 1971, 55.

16. San Francisco *Monitor*, 26 February 1876.

17. San Francisco *Examiner*, 11 February 1878, 2.

18. San Francisco *Monitor*, 8 March 1878, 3.

19. Ibid., 16 March 1878, 78.

20. Ibid., 16 April 1878; San Francisco *Call*, 27 October 1878, 7.

21. San Francisco Superintendent of Public Instruction, *Annual Report*, 1878, 97.

22. San Francisco *Argonaut*, 13 March 1880.

23. San Francisco *Bulletin*, 21 July 1880.

24. Ibid.

25. San Francisco *Call*, 1 July 1881.

26. San Francisco Superintendent of Public Instruction, *Annual Report*, 1879, 74, 1882, 49, 1888.

27. Chicago *Tribune*, 4 January 1893.

28. Chicago Board of Education, *Proceedings*, 1892–93, 243.

29. Chicago *Tribune*, 20 January 1893, 9, 23 January 1893, 4.

30. Ibid., 7 February 1894, 4.

31. Chicago *Inter Ocean*, 22 January 1893, 7–8.

32. Chicago *Tribune*, 23 Febraury 1893, 4.

33. Ibid., 9 March 1893, 4.

34. Chicago *Inter Ocean*, 3 March 1893, 12.

35. Chicago *Inter Ocean*, 13 March 1893, 4; Chicago Board of Education, *Proceedings*, 1892–93, 243.

36. Chicago Board of Education, *Proceedings*, 1892–93, 12, 385–86; Chicago *Tribune*, 12 April 1893, 3, 13 April 1893, 12.

37. Chicago *Tribune*, 28 April 1893, 11, 18 February 1893, 12.

38. Chicago *Tribune*, 25 April 1893, 6; Chicago Board of Education, *Proceedings*, 1892–93, 424–25; Chicago *Tribune*, 12 May 1893.

39. Chicago Board of Education, *Annual Report*, 1890, 104; Chicago *Tribune*, Letter from Helen Heath, 26 February 1893, 26.

40. Chicago *Tribune*, 18 February 1893, 4, 11 January 1893, 4, 13 January 1893, 4, 12 February 1893, 29.

41. Hogan 1978a, 52–53.

42. Chicago *Inter Ocean*, 20 March 1893, 12.

43. Hogan 1978a, 56.

44. Chicago *Tribune*, 12 March 1893, 1.

45. Chicago *Inter Ocean*, 13 March 1873, 4.

46. Lazerson 1971.

47. San Francisco Superintendent of Public Instruction, *Annual Report*, 1880, 55.

48. Chicago Board of Education, *Annual Report*, 1876–77, 50–51.

49. Atlanta Board of Education, *Annual Report*, 1874, 10, 1890, 15.

50. Chicago Board of Education, *Annual Report*, 1870, 1895; United States Bureau of the Census, *Population* 1870, 1900.

51. Hawley 1971, 10.

52. Ibid.

53. Dolson 1964, 182.

54. San Francisco Superintendent of Public Instruction, *Annual Report*, 1880, 188.

55. Ibid., 1878, 95.

56. San Francisco *Call*, 7 October 1878, 2.

57. Ibid., 9 November 1880.

58. San Francisco Superintendent of Public Instruction, *Annual Report*, 1878, 79.

59. Ibid., 80.

60. Ibid., 1880, 420.

61. Cloud 1952, 293.

62. Chicago *Inter Ocean*, 3 March 1893, 12.

63. Cremin 1961, 23.

64. Ibid., 26.

65. Ibid., 31.

66. Hogan 1978a, 251.

67. Ibid., 252.

68. San Francisco *Post*, 25 October 1877.

69. Chicago Board of Education, *Annual Report*, 1877.

70. San Francisco *Bulletin*, 27 September 1876.

71. Ibid., 27 October 1877.

72. San Francisco, Board of Education, *Report of the Committee on Manual Training*, 14 March 1894, 8.

73. Ibid., 16.

74. Ibid.

75. *Truth*, 7 March 1983.

76. San Francisco *Alta*, 11 March 1873.

77. *Shop and Senate* (San Francisco), 6 December 1873.

78. *Knights of Labor* (Chicago), 4 September 1886, 1.

79. Ibid.

80. Ibid., 26 January 1889, 3.

CHAPTER FOUR

1. In order of descending size, these groups were Germans, native-born Americans with native-born parents, Irish, Swedish, Polish, Bohemians, English, Norwegians, Scottish, Canadians, Russians, colored, Italians, Danes, and French. This information is taken from the 1896 School Census, reported in *Public Schools of the City of Chicago*, 1895–96, which classified people into twenty-seven ethnic and racial groups according to the place of birth of the individual and his or her parents.

2. Hogan 1978b.

3. See Tyack 1974, 229–55.

4. Bowles and Gintis 1976, 33.

5. Katz 1971, xviii.

6. Katz 1968, part 1, chap. 1.

7. We use the term Anglo because in our quantitative analysis we were generally unable to distinguish native-born Americans of British descent from English, Scottish, and Welsh immigrants.

8. Bowles and Gintis 1976, 30.

9. However, the reverse does not hold true. A relatively equal distribution of services does not necessarily imply the presence of strong universalistic norms. If the various groups in the city had roughly equal political status, they might obtain equal treatment from the schools through the normal processes of political conflict and negotiation rather than through the intervention of bureaucratic norms. Though the likelihood of this outcome is low, it is a theoretical possibility.

10. Peterson 1976, 124.

11. Two of the schools omitted were special schools (e.g., for the deaf). The other six reported either no data or obviously erroneous data.

12. Tyack 1974, 181.

13. "The Reminiscences of Christopher A. Buckley," San Francisco *Bulletin*, 27 January 1919.

14. Tyack 1974, 97.

15. Merton 1969, 223–33.

16. Bridges 1980, passim.

17. Wolfinger 1974, 122–29.

18. Elazar 1970, passim.

19. Chicago Board of Education, *Annual Reports*, selected years.

20. San Francisco Superintendent of Public Instruction, *Annual Reports*, selected years.

21. Determination of teacher ethnicity is discussed in the appendix to this chapter.

22. The portion of the population born in Ireland was 6 percent in 1890. We are unable to determine the percentage of foreign stock because the United States census did not give information on ethnic background of native-born Americans at this time.

23. Smith 1973.

24. Dellquest 1938.

CHAPTER FIVE

1. United States Bureau of the Census, *Population*, 1880.

2. Writers' Program of the Work Projects Administration 1942, 90; Rabinowitz 1978, 155.

3. Racine 1969, 34–35.

4. Atlanta Board of Education, *Annual Reports*, 1878–1910.

5. Ibid., 1891, 17; Ecke 1972, 34–35; Racine 1969, 45–46.

6. Racine 1969, 10; Epps 1955, 11; Watts 1974, 273.

7. Bacote 1955b, 358.

8. Atlanta City Council, *Council Minutes*, 26 November 1969; Benson 1966, 28; Ecke 1972, 11.

9. Atlanta City Council, *Council Minutes*, 5 March 1971.

10. Wotton 1977, 365.

11. Atlanta *Constitution*, 23 September 1972; Atlanta City Council, *Council Minutes*, 22 September 1972, 27 November 1972, 29 September 1972, 11 October 1972.

12. Atlanta City Council, *Council Minutes*, 6 September 1975, 20 September 1975; Atlanta Board of Education, *Board Minutes*, 30 October 1975.

13. Atlanta *Constitution*, 20 July 1980, 3 August 1980, 5 October 1980; Atlanta Board of Education, *Board Minutes*, 22 January 1980, 29 April 1980, 29 June 1980, 3 September 1980, 25 August 1981; Atlanta City Council, *Council Minutes*, 4 October 1980.

14. Atlanta Board of Education, *Board Minutes*, 2 Febraury 1982.

15. Atlanta Board of Education, *Annual Report*, 1883, 10.

16. Atlanta Board of Education, *Board Minutes*, 29 November 1972, 26 December 1972, 20 April 1971; Atlanta City Council, *Council Minutes*, 13 September 1972; Atlanta *Daily Sun*, 14 September 1971, 21 September 1971, 5 October 1971; Racine 1969, 33.

17. Watts 1978, 27–28.

18. Atlanta *Constitution*, 2 December 1886.

19. Watts 1969, 196–205.

20. Atlanta *Constitution*, 20 October 1888.

21. Bacote 1955a, 335.

22. Gordon 1937, 152.

23. Atlanta City Council, *Council Minutes*, 6 January 1890.

24. Bacote 1955a, 336.

25. Atlanta Board of Education, *Board Minutes*, 24 December 1891, 28 January 1892, 25 February 1892, 28 April 1892; Racine 1969, 10.

26. Racine 1969, 41; Watts 1969, 217–18.

27. Atlanta Board of Education, *Board Minutes*, 22 August 1974.

28. Rabinowitz 1978, 172.

29. Racine 1969, 35–37; Rabinowitz 1978, 174–75.

30. T. Chase to M. E. Strieby, 28 August 1978; Thornberry 1977, 122.

31. Atlanta Board of Education, *Board Minutes*, 2 October 1977, 9 October 1977; Thornberry 1977, 110–12.

32. Racine 1969, 35–37; Rabinowitz 1978, 174–75.

33. Gordon 1937, 9.

34. Atlanta *Independent*, 10 September 1904.

35. Unidentified newspaper clipping found in Atlanta Girls' High School Scrapbook, 1908, Atlanta Public School System Archives.

36. Atlanta *Independent*, 9 October 1909, 29 January 1910; Atlanta *Constitution*, 27 January 1910.

37. Atlanta Board of Education, *Board Minutes*, 26 November 1913.

38. Ibid., 4 August 1914.

39. White 1948, 29.

40. Ibid., 31.

41. Ibid., 32.

42. Ibid., 33.

43. Atlanta *Constitution*, 9 January 1920; Atlanta *Independent*, 3 February 1921.

44. Ecke 1972, 196.

45. Racine 1969, 253; Ecke 1972, 214, 237–38; Newman 1978, 158–59.

46. Newman 1978, 243–44; Racine 1969, 257–58.

47. Ecke 1972, 69–70; Racine 1969, 116.

48. United States Bureau of the Census, *Population*, 1870, 91; United States Bureau of the Census, *Population*, 1880, 416, 447.

49. San Francisco, *Municipal Reports*, 1870, 275; San Francisco Superintendent of Public Instruction, *Annual Report*, 1880, 300.

50. San Francisco Superintendent of Public Instruction, *Annual Report*, 1864–65, 31.

51. Beasley 1919, 181.

52. Lortie 1973, 53, n. 57.

53. Beasley 1919, 173.

54. Wollenberg 1976, 18, 20; Lortie 1973, 14.

55. Saxton 1971, 7.

56. Chang 1936, 263.

57. San Francisco Superintendent of Public Instruction, *Annual Report*, 1869, 43.

58. Saxton 1971, 17.

59. The number of Chinese children who attended private schools was more than four times the number attending public schools. In 1980, for example, 372 Chinese pupils attended private schools and 473 did not attend schools at all. When we consider that the Chinese traditionally did not believe in educating girls, the percentage of children takes on greater significance. In the 1890 school census, girls constituted almost 48 percent of the total number of Chinese children. If we assume that the greater number of these girls were not being educated, it appears that a large percentage of boys attended schools of some sort.

Although exact figures are not available, Chinn's estimate of attendance in private language schools indicates that the great majority of Chinese boys in private schools attended Chinese-language schools; San Francisco Superintendent of Public Instruction, *Annual Report*, 1890, 24–25; Chinn 1969, 68.

60. Saxton 1971, 106.

61. Chang 1936, 229–30.

62. San Francisco Superintendent of Public Instruction, *Annual Report*, 1865, 32, 1869, 43.

63. Chang 1936, 297; Wollenberg 1976, 33.

64. Hawley 1971, passim, discusses Pelton's unique view of education.

65. Chang 1936, 294–96.

66. Wollenberg 1976, 37.

67. Nee and Nee 1972, 43, 53.

68. San Francisco *Call*, 8 July 1882, 5 August 1882.

69. Chang 1936, 306.

70. Thompson 1931, 72.

71. Wollenberg 1976, 40–43.

72. Thompson 1931, 76.

73. San Francisco Superintendent of Public Instruction, *Annual Report*, 1890, 24–25.

74. San Francisco *Call*, 19 June 1902.

75. Wollenberg 1976, 44.

76. Kennan 1907, 247.

77. Thompson 1931, 143.

78. Kennan 1907, 247.

79. United States Senate 1906, 4.

80. Wollenberg 1976, 53.

81. Thompson 1931, 50.

82. Ibid., 127.

83. Kennan 1907, 247.

84. Ibid., 249.

85. Thompson 1931, 160.

86. United States Bureau of the Census, *Population*, 1900.

87. Herrick 1971, 53.

88. Spear 1967, 44.

89. Ibid., 44–45

90. Ibid., 45

91. Ibid.

92. Katznelson 1976, 86; United States Bureau of the Census, *Population*, 1930, vol. 3, part 1, p. 363.

93. Drake and Cayton 1945, 174.

94. Homel 1972, 120.

95. Ibid.

96. Ibid., 110–11.

97. Gosnell 1935, 280.

98. Homel 1974, 48–49.

99. Ibid., 77.

100. Homel 1972, 81–82.

101. Levit 1947, 37–38

102. Homel 1972, 113.

103. Ibid.

104. Ibid., 128.

105. Ibid., 118.

106. Ibid., 116.

CHAPTER SIX

1. Atlanta *Journal*, 28 May 1897; Atlanta *Constitution*, 29 May 1897.

2. Atlanta *Constitution*, 29 May 1897.

3. Atlanta *Constitution*, 30 May 1897.

4. Atlanta *Journal*, 31 May 1897; Atlanta *Constitution*, 1 June 1897.

5. A classic statement of the class-conflict model together with a valuable summary of the literature can be found in Banfield and Wilson 1963. Other important contributions include Burnham 1970, Holli 1969, Hayes 1972, Merton 1957, Hawley 1973, Hofstadter 1955, Mowry 1951, Hays 1964, Lineberry and Fowler 1967, Shefter 1977, Kolko 1963, Chambers and Burnham 1967, and Wiebe 1962, 1967. A critique of the class-conflict model and some compelling negative evidence are provided in Wolfinger and Field 1966.

6 Cooper 1896, 1934, 853–54; Martin 1902, 645–46; Southern Historical Association 1895, 1:750.

7. Grantham 1958, 25–26, 29–31; Urban 1978, 4–7; Southern Historical Association 1895, 937; Cooper 1934, 44–46.

8. Atlanta Board of Education, *Annual Report*, 1898, 82–104. A full list of the new rules governing the public school system is presented in the 1898 school board report. Ecke 1972, 55–56, provides a summary of the most important changes made by the new board.

9. Atlanta Board of Education, *Annual Report*, 1898, 14.

10. Ibid., 1900, 21.

11. Watts 1978, 71–72, 74–76, 160–64, 1974, 282–85.

12. Ibid., 71–72, 74–76, 160–64.

13. This consensus was maintained on very much the same terms into the middle of the twentieth century. See Key 1949, chap. 1, esp. 5–9, for a discussion.

14. Atlanta *Journal*, 1 March 1897.

15. Ibid., 11 August 1896.

16. Ibid., 2 and 19 February 1897. See also Watts 1973, 176–82; Jenkins 1974, 4–5; and especially Bolden 1978, 11–27, for an authoritative discussion of the factional split and its salience in Atlanta politics.

17. Atlanta *Journal*, 3 February 1897.

18. Ibid., 8–12 August 1896.

19. On the 1897 city council, for example, all five of the English partisans were mentioned in contemporary honorary biographies, while only one of the ten Brotherton representatives was mentioned.

20. Grantham 1958, 31–35, 131–55; Bolden 1978, 64–65, 268–73.

21. Atlanta *Constitution*, 29 August 1896.

22. Southern Historical Associaiton 1895, 937; Grantham 1958, 26–27. Bolden 1978, 15 provides evidence of another tie between Smith and Collier.

23. For Grant, see Martin 1902, 655, 657; Southern Historical Association 1895, 1:793–95; and Cooper 1934, 858–59. For Bleckley, see Southern Historical Association 1895, 1:715–18. For Rawson, see Martin 1902, 693–93. For Inman, see Southern Historical Association 1895, 1:833–34, and Cooper 1934, 846–48. For English, see Southern Historical Association 1895, 1:767–69; and Cooper 1934, 852–53.

24. Martin 1902, 633–37; Cooper 1934, 837–39; Woodward 1971, 13–14.

25. Strickland 1980, 4.

26. Racine 1969, 11–12.

27. Atlanta City Council, *Council Minutes*, 19 April 1894.

28. Racine 1969, 81–91.

29. Strickland 1980, 11–13.

30. Atlanta *Journal*, 19 April 1897.

31. Ibid.

32. Ibid., 5 April 1897.

33. Ibid., 28 May 1897.

34. Ibid., 22 April 1897.

35. Atlanta City Council, *Council Minutes*, 29 May 1897. Among the three was former president W. S. Thomson, the sole member of the old board to be reappointed by the mayor.

36. Atlanta *Constitution*, 1 June 1897; Atlanta *Journal*, 30 May 1897; Georgia State Legislature, *Legislative Report*, 10 December 1897.

37. Information on the occupations and addresses of board members was obtained from the annual editions of the Atlanta *City Directory*, 1872–1918.

38. Atlanta *Constitution*, 29 May 1897.

39. Atlanta *Journal*, 28 May 1897.

40. Atlanta *Constitution*, 30 May 1897.

41. Atlanta Board of Education, *Board Minutes*, 15 February 1897.

42. Atlanta Board of Education, *Annual Report*, 1897, 12.

43. Atlanta *Journal*, 28 January 1897.

44. Ibid., 1 February 1897.

45. Atlanta Board of Education, *Board Minutes* 15 February 1897; Atlanta Board of Education, *Annual Report*, 1899, 22.

46. Atlanta Board of Education, *Annual Report*, 1898, 14.

47. Atlanta *Journal*, 6 February 1897.

48. Ibid., 28 January 1897.

49. Moreover, Atlanta school reforms in the 1910s and 1920s brought about major increases in per-pupil expenditures.

50. In biology it is possible to argue that the "survival of the fittest" ensures the emergence of beneficial properties, but only an extreme social Darwinist would argue that competition among organizational structures is so intense that random change can in a short period yield functional structural innovations.

CHAPTER SEVEN

1. Merriam 1929, 22.

2. Bright 1930, 69–70.

3. See Counts 1928 and Herrick 1971 for discussion of Thompson's relations with the schools.

4. Wendt and Kogan 1953, 81.

5. Bright 1930, 73–78; Wendt and Kogan 1953, 126–33.

6. Bright 1930, 84.

7. Chicago *Tribune*, 17 July 1915; Reid 1968, 167–68.

8. Chicago *Tribune*, 2 September 1915, 1; Dodge 1941, 83–84; Counts 1928, 53–54.

9. National Education Association, *NEA Proceedings* 54 (1916): 352–54; Chicago *Tribune*, 6 July 1916, 15; 14 July 1916, 8.

10. Robert Buck Papers, Chicago Historical Society, file 2, flier dated 27 June 1916, with a list of the teachers dropped and grades they had received; Chicago Teachers' Federation, CTF Files, box 45, contains *The Day Book* 5 (28 June 1915), with an article, "School Board Hits Teachers' Union—68 Fired"; see also Chicago *Tribune*, 28 June 1916.

11. Chicago *Tribune*, 27 June 1916, 17; *Chamberlin's* 159 (July 1916): 26.

12. Presidents' Papers, Special Collections, Regenstein Library, University of Chicago, box 14, folder 23, letter from Scholz to Judson, 23 March 1917; Kelly 1938, 2–21; Reid 1968, 185.

13. *American School* 2 (July 1916): 196; *New Republic*, 15 July 1916, 267; Chicago Teachers' Federation, CTF Files, Chicago Historical Society, box 45, stenographic report of AFT mass meeting in New York City, 6 July 1916, 45.

14. Chicago Teachers' Federation, CTF Files, Chicago Historical Society, box 45, stenographic report of a mass meeting, 17 July 1916; see also the Chicago *Tribune*, 18 June 1916, part 2, 1, and 4 July 1916, 15. The PEA met in early July and called for putting merit into teacher selection and for the board to reconsider their action. A statement was signed by Mary McDowell (University of Chicago Settlement), Mrs. Henry Kuh, Mrs. Raymond Robins, Grace Abbott, Mrs. William Hefferan (Women's City Club), Bernard Flexner, Allen Pond (City Club), Carl Thompson, George Mead,

Charles Judd (the latter two professors at the University of Chicago), Victor Olander (Illinois State Federation of Labor), and E. O. Brom.

15. Chicago Board of Education, *Proceedings*, 26 May 1915, 1152–53; 3 June 1915, 1191–93; 16 June 1915, 1238–44; 23 June 1915, 1259–62.

16. Chicago Teachers' Federation, CTF Files, Chicago Historical Society, box 43. *CTF Salary Bulletin*, 22 May 1915, quotes Board of Education Committee on Efficiency and Economy, report no. 27330. See also Chicago City Council, *Council Proceedings* 21 (June 1915): 992, 996.

17. Chicago *Tribune*, 7 July 1916, 1; Chicago *Daily News*, 7 July 1916, 3.

18. Herrick 1971, 132.

19. Robert Buck Papers, Chicago Historical Society, file 3, letters from Buck to Mead and Buck to Judd; also invitations to and responses from the experts.

20. Chicago Teachers' Federation, CTF Files, Chicago Historical Society, box 45, letter from Albertine Raven to Haley reporting on results of interview with board member Clemensen, 29 July 1916.

21. Chicago *Tribune*, 15 July 1916, 1.

22. Committee on Schools, Fire, Police and Civil Service of the City Council, 9 December 1917, 2–8.

23. Chicago City Council, *Council Proceedings*, 19 January 1917, 2904, 2929–30; Chicago Teachers' Federation, CTF Files, Chicago Historical Society, box 46, pamphlet 681, copies of two bills approved by city council; *Illinois House Journal*, 21 February 1917, 225.

24. Chicago *Daily News*, 15 June 1916, 7.

25. Chicago *Tribune*, 10 February 1917, 6; 18 February 1917, 10; 20 February 1917, 9; Chicago Teachers' Federation, CTF Files, Chicago Historical Society, box 46, stenographic report of a mass meeting against the Haley-Buck bill.

26. Chicago Teachers' Federation CTF Files, Chicago Historical Society, box 46, copy of Supreme Court decision, 19 April 1917; Counts 1928, 54–55; Chicago *Daily News*, 19 April 1917, 1; Chicago *Tribune*, 20 April 1917, 15.

27. Chicago *Tribune*, 9 February 1917, 3.

28. Chicago Teachers' Federation, CTF Files, Chicago Historical Society, box 46, stenographic report of a mass meeting against the Haley-Buck bill, 23 February 1917; *Chicago Tribune*, 24 February 1917, 8.

29. Chicago Teachers' Federation, CTF Files, Chicago Historical Society, box 46, stenographic report of mass meeting against Haley-Buck bill, 23 February 1917.

30. Chicago *Daily News*, 12 February 1917; Chicago *Tribune*, 3 February 1917, 15; 26 February 1917, 9.

31. Chicago *Tribune*, 20 February 1917, 9; Presidents' Papers, Special Collections, Regenstein Library, University of Chicago, box 14, folder 23, letter from Scholz to Judson, 3 March 1917; Reid 1968, 185.

32. Chicago *Tribune*, 25 February 1917, 11; Chicago *Daily News*, 26 February 1917, 8.

33. Chicago *Tribune*, 24 February 1917, 8; 25 February 1917, 11; 26 February 1917, 8.

34. *Illinois House Journal*, 16 May 1917, H.B. 416, 971.

35. Chicago *Daily News*, 16 March 1917, 6; Chicago *Tribune* 23 March 1917, 13; 24 March 1917, 10.

36. Chicago *Daily News*, 4 April 1917, 1.

37. Chicago Teachers' Federation, CTF Files, Chicago Historical Society, box 46, extracts from Senate debate, 5 April 1917.

38. Presidents' Papers, Special Collections, Regenstein Library, University of Chicago, box 54, folder 4, letter from Pond to Judson, 18 April 1917.

39. Chicago Board of Education, *Proceedings*, selected years; *Lakeside Annual Directory of the City of Chicago*, selected years (Chicago: R. R. Donnelley).

CHAPTER EIGHT

1. Callahan 1962; Tyack 1974; Tyack and Hansot 1982.

2. Tyack 1974.

3. Cremin 1961, viii.

4. Tyack 1974, passim; but see, for example, 132 and 167; Bowles and Gintis 1976, 189; Tyack and Hansot 1982, section 11, for example.

5. Ecke 1972, 450.

6. Herrick 1970, 131–90; Counts 1928, passim; Salisbury 1970; Wrigley 1982, chap. 5.

7. The Otis Law is discussed in chapter 7.

8. *Chicago School Finances*, (Chicago Bureau of Efficiency, 1915–25, 1927), 77–79.

9. Chicago Board of Education, *Annual Report*, 1925–26, 75.

10. Herrick 1971, 179–80. We discuss this fiscal crisis and its political consequences in chapter 9.

11. Ecke 1972, 85–105.

12. Ibid.

13. Ibid., 118.

14. Illinois State Federation of Labor, *Proceedings of the Thirty-second Annual Convention*, 1914, 52.

15. Sola 1973, 142–52.

16. Herrick 1971, 119.

17. Dewey 1913, 374.

18. See chapter 3 for a further discussion of this point.

19. Chicago Board of Education, *Annual Report*, 1924, 12.

20. Dolson 1964, 448.

21. Ibid., 456.

22. Ibid., 520.

23. Ibid., 528–29.

24. San Francisco *Examiner*, 3 December 1932.

25. Ibid.

26. Chicago Board of Education, *Annual Report*, 1913, 123.

27. Young 1900, 55. Cited in Donatelli 1971, 195.

28. Chicago *Inter Ocean*, 20 December 1912. Cited in Smith 1979, 187.

29. Wiebe 1967, 117.

30. Ibid., 117–18.

31. Tyack 1974, 62.

32. Rice 1893, 200–202. Cited in Donatelli 1971, 48.

33. Chicago *Tribune*, 3 December 1906, 9, col. 1; cited in Smith 1979, 136–37.

34. Smith 1979, 137.

35. Herrick 1971, 111.

36. Ecke 1972, 119.

37. Ibid., 122.

38 Chicago Board of Education, *Annual Report*, 1913, 123; cited in Donatelli 1971, 398.

39. Cited in Counts 1928, 125.
40. Chicago Board of Education, *Annual Report*, 1924.
41. Chicago *Tribune*, June 1924; cited in Herrick 1971, 149.
42. Counts 1928, 177.
43. Herrick 1971, 148.

CHAPTER NINE

1. Drake 1940, 165.
2. United States Bureau of the Census, *Occupations*, 1930, 23.
3. Thurner 1966, 248.
4. Ibid., 254.
5. Herrick 1971, 217.
6. London 1968, 86–87.
7. Simpson 1930, 120–58.
8. Herrick 1971, 187.
9. The Chicago *Herald and Examiner*, 20 April 1933, 11, contains a report of the county treasurer that shows a total of $206,014,892 owed.
10. Comptroller, City of Chicago 1930, 14.
11. Ibid., 14.
12. Gottfried 1962, 248.
13. Sargent 1933, 161.
14. Ibid., 80.
15. London 1968, 106.
16. Herrick 1971, 209–10; Hazlett 1968, 46–47.
17. Chicago *Tribune*, 14 August 1933, 8; cited in Hazlett 1968.
18. Herrick 1971, 190.
19. *Margaret Haley's Bulletin*, 31 December 1927; cited in Herrick 1971, 135.
20. *Federation News*, 22 December 1928, 2.
21. Ibid., 19 January 1929, 4.
22. Landwermeyer 1978, 125.
23. Hazlett 1968, 48.
24. Chicago *Herald and Examiner*, 17 July 1933, 1, 4.
25. *Federation News*, 29 July 1933, 1, 4 (Chicago Historical Society).
26. Herrick 1971, 165.
27. Ibid., 165.
28. Chicago Teachers Union, *CTU News Bulletin*, 25 February 1939; cited in Hazlett 1968, 136.
29. *Federation News*, 29 July 1933, 5.
30. Ibid., 18.
31. Peterson 1976, 21.
32. Hazlett 1968, 67.
33. Peterson 1976, 21.
34. Cited in Levit 1947, 27.
35. Chicago Citizens' Schools Committee, *Chicago Schools*, vol. 10 (Chicago: Citizens' Schools Committee, 1935).
36. Levit 1947, 44.
37. Peterson 1976, 21.
38. Charter amendment no. 37, 1918, 16–22.
39. Mowry 1951, 147–50.
40. San Francisco *Examiner*, 6 October 1932.
41. San Francisco Superintendent of Public Instruction, *Annual Report*, 1936.

42. Dolson 1964, 546, n. 14.
43. San Francisco Superintendent of Public Instruction, *Annual Report*, 1935.
44. Dolson 1964, 89.
45. San Francisco *Examiner*, 10 June 1906.
46. *American Teacher*, May 1931, 1.
47. Dolson 1964, 502.
48. Citizens' Committee for the study of Teachers' Salaries 1929, 1.
49. Ibid., 91.
50. San Francisco *Labor Clarion*, 4 March 1932.
51. San Francisco *Examiner*, 6 May 1936.
52. Quoted in Racine 1969, 207.
53. Racine 1969, 299–300.
54. Urban 1978, 12–13; Deaton 1969, 104.
55. Sutton 1931, 27–29.
56. Ecke 1972, 118–19.
57. Racine 1969, 169.
58. Tyack 1976, 233.

CHAPTER TEN
1. Peterson 1983.

References

Allen, I., Jr., with Hemphill, P. 1971. *Mayor: Notes on the sixties*. New York: Simon and Schuster.

Allswang, J. M. 1971. *A house for all peoples: Ethnic politics in Chicago, 1890–1936*. Lexington: University Press of Kentucky.

American School 2, no. 7 (July 1916).

Bacote, C. 1955a. The Negro in Atlanta politics. *Phylon* 16:333–50.

———. 1955b. William Finch, Negro councilman and political activities in Atlanta during early Reconstruction. *Journal of Negro History* 40:341–64.

Banfield, E. C., and Wilson, J. Q. 1963. *City politics*. Cambridge: Harvard University Press.

Bean, W. 1967. *Boss Ruef's San Francisco: The story of the Union Labor party, big business, and the Grant prosecution*. Berkeley: University of California Press.

Beasley, D. L. 1919. *The Negro trail blazers of California*. Los Angeles.

Benson, A. 1966. Race relations in Atlanta as seen in a critical analysis of the City Council proceedings and other related works, 1865–1877. Master's thesis, Atlanta University.

Bolden, W. 1978. The political structure of charter revision movements in Atlanta during the Progressive Era. Doctoral dissertation, Emory University.

Bowles, S., and Gintis, H. 1976. *Schooling in capitalist America: Educational reform and the contradictions of economic life*. New York: Basic Books.

Bridges, A. B. 1980. A city in the republic: New York and the origins of machine politics. Doctoral dissertation, University of Chicago.

Bright, J. 1930. *Hizzoner Big Bill Thompson*. New York: Jonathan Cape and Harrison Smith.

Bullough, W. A. 1979. *The blind boss and his city: Christopher Augustine Buckley and nineteenth-century San Francisco*. Berkeley: University of California Press.

Burnham, W. D. 1970. *Critical elections and the mainsprings of American politics*. New York: Norton.

Callahan, R. E. 1962. *Education and the cult of efficiency*. Chicago: University of Chicago Press.

Carlton, F. T. 1908. *Economic influences upon educational progress in the United States, 1820–1850*. Madison: University of Wisconsin; reprinted 1965, New York: Teachers College Press.

Chambers, W. N., and Burnham, W. D. 1967. *The American party system*. New York: Oxford University Press.

Chang, F. Y. 1936. A study of the movement to segregate Chinese pupils in the San Francisco public schools up to 1885. Doctoral dissertation, Stanford University.

Charter amendment no. 37. 1918. In *Proposed charter amendments to be submitted November 5, 1918*, 16–22. San Francisco: Board of Election Commissioners.

Chinn, T. W. 1969. *A history of the Chinese in California: A syllabus.* San Francisco: Chinese Historical Society of America.

Citizens' Committee for the Study of Teachers' Salaries. 1929. Salary schedules for San Francisco public schools. San Francisco Board of Education Archives.

Clark, H. 1897. *The public schools of Chicago: A soiological survey.* Chicago: Univesity of Chicago Press.

Cloud, R. W. 1952. *Education in California: Leaders, organizations, and the accomplishments of the first hundred years.* Stanford, Calif.: Stanford University Press.

Collins, C. W. 1976. Schoolmen, schoolma'ams and school boards: The struggle for power in urban school systems in the Progressive era. Doctoral dissertation, Graduate School of Education, Harvard University.

Committee on Schools, Fire, Police and Civil Service of the City Council of Chicago. 1917. *Recommendations for the reorganizaton of the public school system of the city of Chicago.* Chicago: Chicago Historical Society.

Commonwealth Club of California. 1917. Schools of San Francisco. *Transactions* 13:436–75.

Comptroller, City of Chicago. 1930. *Seventy-fourth annual report.* Chicago: Department of Finance.

Cooper, W. 1896. *Official catalogue of the Cotton States and International Exposition and South, illustrated.* Atlanta, Ga.: Illustrator Press.

———. 1934. *Official history of Fulton County.* Atlanta, Ga.: Walter W. Brown.

Counts, G. S. 1928. *School and society in Chicago.* New York: Harcourt, Brace.

Craig, J. E., and Spear, N. 1978. The diffusion of schooling in nineteenth-century Europe: Toward a model. Paper presented at the annual meeting of the Social Science History Association, Columbus. Ohio.

———. 1979. Marginality, integration, and educational expansion: The case of nineteenth-century Europe. Paper presented at the Conference of Europeanists, Washington, D.C.

Cremin, L. A. 1961. *The transformation of the school: Progressivism in American education, 1876–1957.* New York: Vintage Books.

Cronin, J. M. 1973. *The control of urban schools.* New York: Free Press.

Cubberley, E. P. 1920. *The history of education.* Boston: Houghton Mifflin.

Currey, J. S. 1912. *Chicago: Its history and its builders, vol. 1.* Chicago: S. J. Clarke.

David, S. M., and Peterson, P. E., eds. 1976. *Urban politics and public policy: The city in crisis.* 2d ed. New York: Praeger.

Deaton, T. M. 1969. Atlanta during the Progressive Era. Doctoral dissertation, University of Georgia.

Dellquest, A. 1938. *These names of ours.* New York: Thomas Y. Crowell.

Dewey, H. E. 1937. The development of public school administration in Chicago. Doctoral dissertation, University of Chicago.

Dewey, J. 1913. An undemocratic proposal. *Vocational Education* 2:374–77.

Dodge, C. C. 1941. *Reminiscences of a school master.* Chicago: Ralph Fletcher Seymour.

Dolson, L. S., Jr., 1964. The administration of the San Francisco public schools, 1847–1957. Doctoral dissertation, University of California, Berkeley.

Donatelli, R. V. 1971. The contributions of Ella Flagg Young to the educational enterprise. Doctoral dissertation, Department of Education, University of Chicago.

Dorsett, L. W. 1968. *The Pendergast machine.* New York: Oxford University Press.

Drake, S. 1940. *Churches and voluntary associations in the Chicago Negro community*. Chicago: Work Projects Administration, District 3.

Drake, S., and Cayton, H. B. 1945. *Black metropolis*. New York: Harcourt and Brace.

Ecke, M. W. 1972. *From Ivy Street to Kennedy Center: Centennial history of the Atlanta public school system*. Atlanta: Board of Education.

Elazar, D. J. 1970. *Cities of the prairie: The metropolitan frontier and American politics*. New York: Basic Books.

Epps, E. G. 1955. The participation of the Negro in the municipal politics of the city of Atlanta, 1867–1908. Master's thesis, Atlanta University.

Erie, S. P. 1975. The development of class and ethnic politics in San Francisco, 1870–1910: A critique of the pluralist interpretation. Doctoral dissertation, University of California at Los Angeles.

Evans, M. G. 1929. A history of organized labor in Georgia. Doctoral dissertation, University of Chicago.

Garrett, F. 1954. *Atlanta and environs*. Athens: University of Georgia Press.

Gordon, A. 1937. *The Georgia Negro*. Ann Arbor: Edwards Press.

Gosnell, H. F. 1935. *Negro politicians*. Chicago: University of Chicago Press.

Gottfried, A. 1962. *Boss Cermak of Chicago*. Seattle: University of Washington Press.

Grady, H. W. 1890. *The New South*. New York: R. Bonner's Sons.

Grantham, D. W. 1958. *Hoke Smith and the politics of the New South*. Baton Rouge: Louisiana State University Press.

Greenstone, J. D., and Peterson, P. E. 1973. *Race and authority in urban politics*. New York: Russell Sage.

Greer, C. 1976. *The great school legend*. New York: Penguin Books.

Hawley, M. M. 1971. Schools for social order: Public education as an aspect of San Francisco's urbanization and industrialization process. Master's thesis, San Francisco State College.

Hawley, W. D. 1973. *Nonpartisan elections and the case for party politics*. New York: John Wiley.

Hayes, E. C. 1972. *Power structure and urban policy: Who rules Oakland?* New York: McGraw-Hill.

Hays, S. P. 1964. The politics of reform in municipal government in the Progressive Era. *Pacific Northwest Quarterly* 55:157–69.

———. 1974. The changing political structure of the city in industrial America. *Journal of Urban History* 1:6–38.

Hazlett, J. S. 1968. Crisis in school government. Doctoral dissertation, University of Chicago.

Heidenheimer, A. J. 1972. The politics of public education, health, and welfare in the U.S. and Western Europe: How growth and reform potentials have differed. Paper presented at the American Political Science Association Meetings, Washington, D. C.

Herrick, M. J. 1971. *The Chicago schools: A social and political history*. Beverly Hills, Calif.: Sage Publications.

Heyns, B. 1978. Schooling in capitalist America: A review essay. *American Journal of Sociology* 83:999–1006.

Hofstadter, R. 1955. *The age of reform*. New York: Alfred Knopf.

Hogan, David. 1978a. Capitalism and schooling: The political economy of public education in Chicago, 1880–1930. Doctoral dissertation, University of Illinois at Champaign-Urbana.

———. 1978b. Education and the making of the Chicago working class, 1880–1930. *History of Education Quarterly* 18:227–70.

Holli, M. G. 1969. *Reform in Detroit*. New York: Oxford University Press.

Homel, M. W. 1972. Negroes in the Chicago public schools, 1910–1941. Doctoral dissertation, University of Chicago.

Huntington, S. 1968. *Political order in changing societies.* New Haven: Yale University Press.

Issel, W. 1977. Class and ethnic conflict in San Francisco political history: The reform charter of 1898. *Labor History* 18:341–59.

James, L. H. 1937. The politics of organized labor in relation to Negro workers in Atlanta, 1869–1937. Master's thesis, Atlanta University.

Jenkins, H. 1974. *Forty years on the force.* Atlanta: Emory University Institute for Research on Social Change.

Johnston, S. 1880. *Historical sketches of the public school system of Chicago: The Twenty-fifth annual report of the Board of Education.* Chicago: Clark and Edwards.

Katz, M. B. 1968. *The irony of early school reform: Educational Innovation in mid-nineteenth century Massachusetts.* Boston: Beacon Press.

———. 1971. *Class, bureaucracy and schools: The illusion of educational change in America.* New York: Praeger.

———. 1979. An apology for American education history. *Harvard Educational Review* 49:236–66.

Katznelson, I. 1976. *Black men, white cities.* Chicago: University of Chicago Press.

Kelly, A. H. 1938. History of Illinois Manufacturers Association. Doctoral dissertation, University of Chicago.

Kennan, G. 1907. The Japanese in the San Francisco schools. *Outlook* 86, no. 5 (1 June): 246–52.

Key, V. O. 1949. *Southern politics.* New York: Random House.

Kolko, G. 1963. *The triumph of conservatism: A reinterpretation of American history, 1900–1916.* New York: Free Press.

Landwermeyer, F. M. 1978. Teacher unionism Chicago style. Doctoral dissertation, University of Chicago.

Lazerson, M. 1971. *Origins of the urban school: Public education in Massachusetts, 1870–1915.* Cambridge: Harvard University Press.

Levit, M. 1947. The Chicago Citizens' Schools Committee. Master's thesis, University of Chicago.

Levitt, E. 1936. The activities of local teacher organizations in Chicago since 1929. Master's thesis, University of Chicago.

Lineberry, R., and Fowler, E. P. 1967. Reformism and public policies in American cities. *American Political Science Review* 61:701–16.

London, S. D. 1968. Business and the Chicago public school system, 1890–1966. Doctoral dissertation, University of Chicago.

Lortie, F. N., Jr. 1973. San Francisco's black community, 1870–1890: Dilemmas in the struggle for equality. Master's thesis, San Francisco State University.

McDonald, T. J. 1979. Urban development, political power and municipal expenditures in San Francisco, 1860–1910: A quantitative investigation of historical theory. Doctoral dissertation, Stanford University.

McKitrick, E. L. 1957. The study of corruption. *Political Science Quarterly* 72:502–14.

Martin, G. H. 1893. *Evolution of the Massachusetts public school system.* Boston.

Martin, T. H. 1902. *Atlanta and its buiders.* Atlanta: Century Memorial.

Merriam, C. E. 1929. *Chicago: A more intimate view of urban politics.* New York: Macmillan.

Merton, R. K. 1957. *Social theory and social structure.* New York: Free Press.

———. 1969. The latent functions of the machine. In *Urban government: A reader in administration and politics,* ed. E. C. Banfield. New York: Free Press.

Meyer, J. W.; Tyack, D.; Nagel, J.; and Gordon, A. 1979. Public education as nation-building in America: Enrollments and bureaucratization in the American states, 1870–1930. *American Journal of Sociology* 85:591–613.

Mowry, G. E. 1951. *The Californora Progressives*. Berkeley, California: University of California Press.

Nee, V. G., and Nee, B. 1971. *Longtime Californ': A documentary study of an American Chinatown*. New York: Pantheon Books.

Newman, J. W. 1978. A history of the Atlanta Public School Teachers Association, Local 89 of the American Federation of Teachers, 1919–1956. Doctoral dissertation, Georgia State University.

Peterson, P. E. 1976. *School politics, Chicago style*. Chicago: University of Chicago Press.

———. 1981. *City limits*. Chicago: University of Chicago Press.

———. 1982. Effects of credentials, connections, and competence on income. In *The social sciences: Their nature and uses*, ed. William R. Kruskal. Chicago: University of Chicago Press.

———. 1983. *Federal policy and American education*. New York: Twentieth Century Fund.

Peterson, P. E., and Karpluss, S. S. 1981. Schooling in democratic America: The effects of class background, education and ability on income. In *Research in public policy analysis and management* ed. J. P. Crecine, 2: 195–210. Greenwich, Conn.: JAI Press.

Peterson, P. E., and Rabe, B. G. 1981a. Career training or education for life: Dilemmas in the development of Chicago vocational education. Paper prepared for the Vocational Education Study Group in the Educational Policy and Organization section of the National Institute of Education, Washington, D.C.

———. 1981b. Urban vocational education: Managing the transition from school to work. Paper prepared for the Vocational Education Study Group, National Institute of Education, Washington, D.C.

Pierce, B. L. 1957. *A history of Chicago*. Vol. 3: *The rise of a modern city*. New York: Alfred A. Knopf.

Rabinowitz, H. N. 1978. *Race relations in the urban South, 1865–1890*. New York: Oxford University Press.

Racine, P. N. 1969. Atlanta schools: A history of the public school system, 1869–1955. Doctoral dissertation, Emory University.

Rakove, M. 1975. *Don't make no waves, don't back no losers: An insider's analysis of the Daley machine*. Bloomington: Indiana University Press.

Rantoul, R., Jr. 1854. *Memoirs*. Boston.

Ravitch, D. 1978. *The revisionists revised: A critique of the radical attack on the schools*. New York: Basic Books.

Reid, R. L. 1968. The professionalization of public school teachers, 1895–1920. Doctoral dissertation, Northwestern University.

Reller, T. L. 1935. *The development of the City Superintendency of Schools*. Philadelphia: Author.

Rice, J. M. 1893. The public schools of Chicago and St. Paul. *Forum* 15:200–215.

Riordon, W. L. 1963. *Plunkitt of Tammany Hall*. New York: E. P. Dutton.

Salisbury, R. H. 1970. Schools and politics in the big city. In *The politics of education at the local, state, and federal levels*, ed. M. W. Kirst, pp. 17–32. Berkeley, Calif.: McCutchan.

Sanders, J. W. 1970. The education of Chicago Catholics. Doctoral dissertation, Department of Education, University of Chicago.

Sargent, F. W. 1933. Taxpayer takes charge. *Saturday Evening Post*, 14 January.

Saxton, A. 1971. *The indispensable enemy: Labor and the anti-Chinese movement in California*. Berkeley: University of California Press.

Shefter, M. 1977. New York City's financial crisis: The politics of inflation and retrenchment. *Public Interest* 48:98–127.

Shradar, V. 1974. Ethnic politics, religion, and the public schools of San Francisco, 1849–1933. Doctoral dissertation, Stanford University.

Simpson, H. D. 1929. *The tax situation in Illinois*. Chicago: University of Chicago Press.

————. 1930. *Tax racket and tax reform in Chicago*. Measha, Wis.: Collegiate Press.

Simpson, S. A. 1831. *A manual of workingmen*. Philadelphia.

Smith, E. 1973. *New dictionary of family names*. New York: Harper and Row.

Smith, J. K. 1979. *Ella Flagg Young: Portrait of a leader*. Ames, Iowa: Educational Studies Press.

Sola, P. A. 1972. Plutocrats, pedagogues and plebes: Business influences on vocational education and extracurricular activities in the Chicago high schools. Doctoral dissertation, Department of Education and History, University of Illinois at Urbana-Champaign.

Southern Historical Assocation. 1895. *Memoirs of Georgia*. Atlanta: Southern Historical Association.

Spear, A. H. 1967. *Black Chicago: The making of a Negro ghetto, 1890–1920*. Chicago: University of Chicago Press.

Strickland, C. 1980. The rise of public schooling in the Gilded Age and the attitude of parents: The case of Atlanta, 1872–1897. Mimeographed. Atlanta, Ga.: Emory University.

Sutton, W. 1931. Ten years of progress. Atlanta Board of Education Historical Archives.

Swett, J. 1872. *History of the public school system in California*. Berkeley: University of California, Bancroft Library Archives.

Thompson, R. H. 1931. Events leading to the order to segregate Japanese pupils in San Francisco public schools. Doctoral dissertation, Stanford University.

Thornberry, J. J. 1977. The development of black Atlanta, 1865–1885. Doctoral dissertation, University of Maryland.

Thurner, A. W. 1966. The impact of ethnic groups on the Democratic party in Chicago, 1920–1928. Doctoral dissertation, University of Chicago.

Townsend, A. 1927. The Germans of Chicago. Doctoral dissertation, University of Chicago.

Troen, S. K. 1975. *The public and the schools: Shaping the St. Louis system, 1838–1920*. Columbia: University of Missouri Press.

Turner-Jones, M. 1982. A political analysis of black educational history: Atlanta, 1865–1943. Doctoral dissertation, University of Chicago.

Tyack, D. 1974. *The one best system: A history of American education*. Cambridge: Harvard University Press.

————. 1976. Needed: The reform of a reform. In *Urban politics and public policy: The city in crisis*, 2d ed., ed. S. M. David and P. E. Peterson. New York: Praeger.

Tyack, D., and Hansot, E. 1982. *Managers of virtue: Public school leadership in America, 1820–1980*. New York: Basic Books.

United States Senate. 1906. *Japanese in the city of San Francisco, California: From the president of the United States, transmitting the final report of Secretary Metcalf*. S. Doc. 147, 59th Cong., 2d sess.

Urban, W. J. 1977. Progressive education in the urban South. In *The age of urban reform*, ed. M. H. Ebner and E. M. Tobin. Port Washington, N.Y.: Kennikat Press.

———. 1978. Hoke Smith and the politics of vocational education. Paper presented to the annual meetings of the History of Education Society, Chicago.

Vare, W. S. 1933. *My forty years in politics*. Philadelphia: Roland Swain.

Watts, E. J. 1969. Characteristics of candidates in city politics: Atlanta, 1865–1903. Doctoral dissertation, Emory University.

———. 1973. The police in Atlanta, 1890–1905. *Journal of Southern History* 39:165–82.

———. 1974. Black political progress in Atlanta, 1868–1895. *Journal of Negro History* 59:268–86.

———. 1978. *The social bases of city politics*. Westport, Conn.: Greenwood Press.

Wendt, L., and Kogan, H. 1953. *Bill Bill of Chicago*. New York: Bobbs-Merrill.

White, Walter, 1948. *A man called White: The autobiography of Walter White*. New York: Random House.

Wiebe, R. H. 1962. *Businessmen and reform: A study of the Progressive movement*. Cambridge: Harvard University Press.

———. 1967. *The search for order*. New York: Hill and Wang.

Withcombe, E. G. 1977. *The Oxford dictionary of English Christian names*. 3d ed. Oxford: Clarendon Press.

Wolfinger, R. E. 1974. *The politics of progress*. Englewood Cliffs, N.J.: Prentice-Hall.

Wolfinger, R. E., and Field, J. O. 1966. Political ethos and the structure of city government. *American Political Science Review* 60:306–26.

Wollenberg, Charles, 1976. *All deliberate speed: Segregation and exclusion in California schools, 1855–1975*. Berkeley: University of California Press.

Woodward, C. V. 1951. *Origins of the New South, 1877–1913*. Baton Rouge: Louisiana State University Press.

———. 1974. *The strange career of Jim Crow*. New York: Oxford University Press.

Wotton, G. H., Jr. 1973. New city of the South, Atlanta 1843–1873. Doctoral dissertation, Johns Hopkins University.

Wrigley, J. 1982. *Class politics and public schools: Chicago, 1900–1950*. New Brunswick, N.J.: Rutgers University Press.

Writers' Program of the Work Projects Administration. 1942. *Atlanta: A city of the modern South*. New York: Smith and Durrell.

Yorke, P. C. 1933. *Educational lectures*. San Francisco: Textbook Publishing Company.

Young, E. F. 1900. *Isolation in the schools*. Chicago: University of Chicago Press.

Ziegler, H. N.; Jennings, M. K.; and Peak, W. 1974. *Governing American schools*. North Scituate, Mass.: Duxbury Press.

Bibliographical Note

Primary research materials were consulted in all three cities. Data sources included annual reports and board minutes of the Atlanta Board of Education, council minutes of the Atlanta City Council, Atlanta City directories at the Southern Historical Association in Atlanta, and items from the Atlanta Public School archives. At the Chicago Board of Education, annual reports and proceedings of the board, school censuses, and *Reports of the Elementary Teachers' General Council* were examined. Other archives used were those of the Citizens' Schools Committee; the Chicago Historical

Society, which contains the Robert Buck Papers, files of the Chicago Teachers' Federation, and city directories and maps; the Newberry Library, which includes the Carter H. Harrison Papers; the University of Chicago's Regenstein Library Special Collections; and the Illinois State Federation of Labor, including reports of annual conventions and the *Weekly News Letter*. San Francisco collections consulted include the archives of the board of education, the Bancroft Library on the Berkeley campus of the University of California, and the San Francisco Historical Society.

Newspapers, journals, and directories examined include: Atlanta—*Constitution, Daily Sun, Independent, Journal, Journal of Labor;* Chicago—*Chronicle, Daily News, Herald and Examiner, Inter-Ocean, Record Herald, Tribune, Lakeside Directory of Chicago;* San Francisco—*Alta, Argonaut, Bulletin, Call, Examiner, Monitor, Post, Star, Shop and Senate.* Other publications used include the *Christian Science Monitor, Illinois Guardian, Illinois House Journal, Knights of Labor, Labor Enquirer,* Merchants Association *Review* of Chicago, and San Francisco *Rights of Labor, New Republic,* and *Voice of Labor.*

Index